THE 7 SECRET KEYS TO STARTUP SUCCESS

WHAT YOU NEED TO KNOW TO WIN

DAVID J. MUCHOW

**Foreword by
US Senator Byron Dorgan (ret.)**

Skyhorse Publishing

Skyhorse Publishing books may be purchased in bulk at special discounts for sales promotion, corporate gifts, fund-raising, or educational purposes. Special editions can also be created to specifications. For details, contact the Special Sales Department, Skyhorse Publishing, 307 West 36th Street, 11th Floor, New York, NY 10018 or info@skyhorsepublishing.com.

Skyhorse® and Skyhorse Publishing® are registered trademarks of Skyhorse Publishing, Inc.®, a Delaware corporation.

Visit our website at www.skyhorsepublishing.com.

10 9 8 7 6 5 4 3 2 1

Library of Congress Cataloging-in-Publication Data is available on file.

Cover design by Kai Texel
Cover image: Getty Images

Print ISBN: 978-1-5107-7064-5
Ebook ISBN: 978-1-5107-7065-2

Printed in the United States of America

To Marilee, my amazing wife, and my rock for over fifty great years. A wonderful friend, mother, and grandmother. Simply the best!

CONTENTS

ACKNOWLEDGMENTS

This book was a team effort. Thanks to my clients over the years who have given me the experiences that have inspired the business, legal, and other stories in the book; Georgetown University's Walsh School of Foreign Service, especially Dean Hellman, Rosie O'Neil, Ted Moran, and Rodney Ludema, who gave me the opportunity to teach Law, Business, and Entrepreneurship there, and the amazing students who make it so fulfilling; my expert literary agent and kind advisor, Nancy Cushing-Jones, who was so helpful in finding the great publishing team at Skyhorse Publishing— Caroline Russomanno, my editor there, whose brilliant insights and attention to detail have been so helpful; and Tony Lyons and Mark Gompertz at Skyhorse who supported this book; US Senator Byron Dorgan (ret.) for taking the time to write the Foreword; Carol Stevens, whose enjoyable fiction classes and comments were so helpful; Carole Sargent, PhD, director, Office of Scholarly Publications, Georgetown University, who guided me with my book proposal; Mike Masucci, film producer, with great story structure skills; Maureen Hirsch of Clydes Restaurant Group for pictures of The TOMBS Restaurant (and just for the record, the CIA never hired waiters at The TOMBS—at least as far as I know)! And Dennis Welch, president of Articulate PR and Communications, for his insights on publicity campaigns; Roland McAndrews, Partner, Bookoff McAndrews for patent advice; Lynn Jordan, Partner, Kelly

IP, for trademark advice; and Elizabeth Jia of Arc Moon for her design work.

To my wife Marilee, who patiently put up with me while I was writing; our son Scott Muchow, a great sounding board and source for ideas who always encouraged me; our daughter Heather Schwager; grandchildren Zoe and Zadie Schwager, who helped with graphics and proofreading; and our granddaughter, Lily Catherine, who inspires our extended family with her endless energy and joy. To all of you, thanks!

FOREWORD

Much of the economic success the United States enjoys has come from the innovative work of entrepreneurs from Henry Ford to Bill Gates. And our continued success will come from the new and exciting entrepreneurs and innovative companies that will keep us competitive in this rapidly changing world.

Serving as a US senator, I had the opportunity to know many men and women who dreamed of starting their own business. I watched some succeed and build large, profitable businesses, and saw some fail. And I wondered, *what was the difference?* It seemed to me it was having the knowledge you needed to build the business. That is exactly what this book is about.

I also understood the connection between private sector businesses risking their capital to create jobs, building products, and providing services and the public sector establishing the rules to help guide those businesses. I know the public and private sectors must work as partners to continue building the American economic engine and our standard of living. Businesses also need help understanding the tools they need to succeed.

This book provides those tools. While most business executives have expertise in some areas, it takes much more to grow a successful company. They need to create a team, understand marketing, hire personnel, and raise capital—all while re-engineering their product. And they face a barrage of basic questions such as:

- How to divide equity among partners?
- How to compensate workers; and
- How to raise capital within the SEC's rules?

That's where this book comes in. This is not your uncle's or aunt's business book. *The 7 Secret Keys to Startup Success* makes a unique contribution. It breaks the mold by providing more of the essential, practical, legal, and business information that growing businesses need to succeed.

It covers the basics like incorporating and raising money. Then it shows you step-by-step what, when, and how to do each task. It's like having a seasoned lawyer and business consultant by your side all the way from concept to commercialization and beyond.

As many as eight-out-of-ten new companies fail in the first year. So it's amazing that so little attention has been paid to *why* companies fail. David Muchow has worked with hundreds of startups and other companies over decades and unlocked the major reasons for these failures. These include mistakes that CEOs don't even know they're making, like giving away too much equity and not putting agreements in writing. So, this book also tells you what *not* to do as well as what *to do*. In short, it helps you to avoid what David calls "Startup Suicide."

It also contains new, useful information you won't get in business school, law school, or anywhere else; and is packed with charts, model legal forms, and other information, such as how to calculate rate of return and reduce legal fees.

At the policy level, it discusses the need for a national dialogue to better support new businesses. It's a call to action so they can go from a concept to commercialization in months, not years.

The 7 Secret Keys to Startup Success covers more ground than other books because the author has worked in every area of business development, from the shop floor to being an inventor, a serial CEO, attorney, and teaching law, business, and entrepreneurship at Georgetown University.

Finally, business books should be fun to read. So, at the end of each chapter there are fictional stories inspired by actual cases, illustrating the principles in the chapter. These involve the adventures of Professor Scooter Magee, a business expert who travels around fixing failing companies.

I enjoyed this trailblazing book that's packed with the critical business and legal information you need to succeed—and is lots of fun as well!

—US Senator Byron Dorgan (ret.)

Sen. Byron Dorgan (ret.), served in the US House and Senate for three decades. He is a New York Times *bestselling author of five books, has been a visiting professor at Georgetown University, and is a senior policy advisor at a premier Washington, DC law firm.*

PREFACE

When I was a law student at Georgetown, my favorite professor was Sam Dash who taught criminal law. He had a mastery of the subject matter and had lived it as the district attorney in Philadelphia and senate chief Watergate counsel in President Nixon's impeachment hearings. His exciting stories vividly illustrated legal principles and kept us riveted. When teaching Law, Business, and Entrepreneurship at Georgetown, I found the same thing. Students were eager to learn but they particularly liked the stories about the characters and cases I'd encountered over decades of law practice and business.

The result is a new kind of startup book. The one book you need to succeed that's also fun to read!

- **It has more of what you really need to know to succeed.** Most startup books cover the same topics—build a team, create a business plan, etc. *The 7 Secret Keys to Startup Success* covers those basic topics and guides you step-by-step through the startup process. But it breaks the mold by providing so much more.
- **Practical advice in more key startup areas.** It gives you more of the practical keys to success in every area—from marketing and finance to protecting your intellectual property, cryptocurrency, and managing startup chaos.

- **Legal and business advice.** It provides legal as well as business tips, tricks, and advice to keep you from violating the many complex laws in hiring, fundraising, and other areas. You'll gain practical advice from my years as a corporate lawyer and federal prosecutor.
- **Prevents "Startup Suicide™."** Most startups fail in the first year. This book shows you not just *what to do*, but also *what not to do* so you can to avoid the big mistakes that lead to Startup Suicide.
- **Information you can't get anywhere else.** You'll gain real-life legal and business insights and advice not available anywhere else, from my working with hundreds of startups and major companies for over thirty years.
- **Charts, model forms, and more.** *The 7 Secret Keys to Startup Success* is packed with charts, tables, and model forms to get you up and running faster.
- **The first startup book that's fun to read.** It's filled with interesting legal cases and business lessons involving figures like Ivanka Trump, Oprah, and others that illustrate key things you need to know. Then, after each chapter there is a fun short story, inspired by real cases, which drives home *The 7 Secret Keys to Startup Success.*
- **Building a national entrepreneurship eco-system (NESS) to support entrepreneurs.** Finally, with a call to action, we discuss how to create a new national support system for entrepreneurs that can help them go from a concept to commercialization in ninety days.

Your feedback is always welcome! Contact me
at info@davidmuchowauthor.com.

ABOUT THE AUTHOR

David J. Muchow is managing partner, Muchowlaw. He is a thirty-year business expert, serial entrepreneur, corporate lawyer, and inventor who has advised hundreds of businesses from startup to exit. Dave is an adjunct professor of Law, Business, and Entrepreneurship at the Walsh School of Foreign Service, Georgetown University. He serves on various tech, energy, and non-profit boards, has helped turn ideas into publicly traded companies, and was a founder and officer of a one billion dollar publicly traded mutual fund. Earlier, he served on Capitol Hill, and with the National Security Council staff, the Office of Management and Budget, and as a prosecutor and special assistant to the assistant attorney general, U.S. Department of Justice, where he received the US Attorney General's Special Achievement Award and was chairman of the Federal Advisory Committee on False Identification. He has served with various law firms, been a lobbyist and foreign agent, general counsel and director of international programs for the American Gas Association, and was a founder and CEO of SkyBuilt Power, which built the world's first rapidly deployable solar/wind power stations for the CIA and military; and an associate producer with Fab Films for the PBS film, *When My Times Comes*. Dave is a frequent speaker and consultant on law, business, and entrepreneurship, and author/co-editor of numerous publications including the seven-volume treatise, *Energy Law and Transactions*, *Regulation of the Gas Industry*, and *The*

Energy Handbook. He attended Georgetown University, (BSFS '66), Cornell Law, and Georgetown University Law Center (JD '71). Dave and his wife Marilee live in Arlington, Virginia, where they enjoy spending time with their children Heather and Scott and three grandchildren, Zoe, Zadie, and Lily.

LIST OF CHARACTERS

Finally, a startup book that's fun to read! Business books should be fun to read as well as instructive. At the end of each chapter, there are fun examples/stories, inspired by real events, which demonstrate the principles in each chapter using the adventures of Professor Scooter Magee, the Startup Expert.

Scooter helps startups prevent "Startup Suicide" and achieve success while fighting the CIA and others. Think: Professor Indiana Jones in Raiders of the Lost Ark *meets* Bar Rescue *or* Silicon Valley! *Enjoy Scooter's adventures and his practical startup lessons!*

Scooter Magee and Family

Scooter Magee. Professor at Georgetown University, the "Startup Expert"

Megan Magee. Scooter's wife

Zoe, Zadie, and Lily. Their grandchildren

Sammy. Scooter and Megan's dog

The Montevideos

Sr. Vincent Montevideo. Chairman, Zapata, SA

Scarlett Montevideo. Vincent's daughter and fashion heiress

CIA

Chuck "Bulldog" McCatchum. Chief, Threat Analysis Directorate

Johnson. Bulldog's assistant.

Souk Kaep. Technician, Siam Reap, Cambodia Station

Chan. Kaep's Assistant

Dr. Heinrich Johansson. Chief Scientist, Project Tailgate

Derek Martin. Lab Researcher, Project Tailgate

Jason Kingston. Agent

Sarah. Experimental dog

Frank Early. Night Detail Officer, Project Tailgate

FBI

Jackson Tapper. Division Chief, Washington Field Office

JW McKinney. Special Agent, Washington Field Office

Other Clients

Fred Delaney. Air conditioner inventor

Natalya, Toni, and Karen Fusser. Feuding sisters who own restaurant

Baraz Azad. COVID PPE entrepreneur

Susan Glover. COO, Aeris Gloves

Sally Martin. Salmonella poisoning victim

Others

Kelly. Server at Cowboy Cafe

Jorani. Woman selling birds at Angkor Wat

Cold Fingers (CF) Gelato. Russian mob figure and spy camera client

Crunch Hym. Cold Finger's partner

John Martin. In salmonella lawsuit

Caroline. Woman at the Animal Welfare League

Bud Lawrence. Scooter's former boss

Jacob Abner. Cryptocurrency founder

Sally Ann McKay. Scooter's high school friend

Bobby Joe. Toni's boyfriend

Boris "Nuts" Spassky. Cold Finger's creditor

Kathy Burt. Scooter's friend

Jacob Spassky. Boris Spassky's son

H. Bosley Jenkins III. Investor on Queen Mary 2

Chapter 1

PLAN FOR SUCCESS

If you don't know where you are going, you'll end up someplace else.

—Yogi Berra

THE 7 SECRET KEYS TO STARTUP SUCCESS

The 7 Secret Keys to Startup Success are the seven key areas of operation in which startups must make smarter decisions to avoid failure and achieve success. They are:

- Plan For Success
- Manage Your Startup's Risks
- Lock Up Your Intellectual Property
- Be Smarter About Personnel Management
- How to Shake the Money Tree ... Legally
- The Smarter Roadmap to Marketing and Sales
- Use "Management Zen" to Reduce Startup Chaos

Each of these keys is a chapter in this book. Each chapter then details the specific steps to be taken and not taken. Other keys could be added but based on my experience in working with hundreds of startups and larger companies over many years these are the most important ones for startups.

I've seen many startup successes and failures. Unfortunately, many of the lessons aren't taught in B-schools, found in books, or used. That's why I call them "secret" keys. Nevertheless, they're critically important. They include things you may only learn by making costly mistakes or when it's already too late, like how to save money on legal fees, how to raise money without violating SEC rules, protecting your intellectual property, and how to fire your partners without getting sued.

PREVENTING "STARTUP SUICIDE"

For startups, knowing what *not to do*—the dangerous mistakes that startups often make—can be as important as knowing what *to do*. Think about learning to ski in the winter. The first things an instructor tells you are things *not to do*: "Don't fall forward, and don't put your skis pointing downhill or you'll go there." Startups with no prior experience are easy prey for big mistakes that lead to "Startup Suicide™." Most startups fail. Sometimes the founders never understand what really happened. But they gave away too much equity, failed to get insurance, didn't write down their oral agreements, and stumbled into a downward cycle of failure—sometimes topped off with a devastating lawsuit. This book shows how to avoid these common mistakes and increase your odds of success.

THE PRACTICAL BUSINESS AND LEGAL THINGS YOU NEED TO KNOW TO WIN

Think of this book as your expert business consultant and lawyer to guide you step-by-step on the road to success. While it has the basics found in other startup books, such as how to raise money and prepare a business plan, we won't spend much time on the well-plowed ground of other books. Rather, the focus is on the many critical, practical things you need to know to survive and succeed that you won't find anywhere else.

Many business books deal with general information on management or "motivation." That's fine, but I've never had a client ask about motivation. Entrepreneurs are some of the most highly motivated people on the planet. Rather, they ask me about practical things like, "Should I incorporate in Delaware? How can I cut my legal fees and when do I need a non-disclosure agreement?"

FINALLY, A STARTUP BOOK THAT'S FUN TO READ!

Let's face it, many business books are boring—they read like encyclopedias. Startups are innovative—so startup books should be innovative, too, and not just useful but also fun to read. So there are interesting cases and stories throughout the book. Then at the end of each chapter there's a fun example and story to illustrate the lessons in the chapter. The stories are inspired by real cases and revolve around Professor Scooter Magee, the "Startup Expert." Scooter travels around in his old Austin Healey and fixes broken startups. Along the way he fights off the CIA and deals with a wide variety of characters and inventors. Think Harrison Ford in *Raiders of the Lost Ark* meets *Silicon Valley* or *Bar Rescue*. You can skip the stories if you want but try a few.

Important Legal Caveats: While this book discusses some general legal and financial principals, it can't provide legal or financial advice to you. The appendices contain parts of contracts and other documents, but don't use those as-is. The laws and facts are different in each jurisdiction. So, on any legal and financial matters, be sure to seek advice from your attorney and financial advisor. Finally, any relationship between real people and events is purely coincidental.

YOUR BASIC STARTUP PLAN: STEP-BY-STEP

Building a startup is like running through the jungle in the dark. You could end up as someone's dinner. You need to be very careful or you'll be committing "Startup Suicide."

The other day I was reviewing a contract for a client that had some very dangerous language buried in a boring heading called "Section 44, Assignment Clause." An assignment is a transfer of the rights and benefits in a contract from one party to another. But this language wasn't even assignment language. It made the founder personally liable for everything under the contract, including all of the founder's personal assets: "Assignment ... The Parties signing as officers of entities also agree that by their signatures, they shall also

bind themselves <u>personally</u> to the terms set forth in this Agreement."
(emphasis added)

In addition to having a lawyer review your contracts, try to avoid
being personally liable in any business matter unless you're doing
something like getting a bank loan. Banks often require personal
guarantees for startup loans. I once talked with a US senator whose
family owned a string of banks and even his own banks required
him to personally guarantee his loans. Except in the case of loans, if
it's a commercial deal, just the company and not you should assume
liability. So, as you create your new venture, be careful!

Most startups begin with an idea. Maybe you've seen something
that doesn't work and you have a better idea. Or someone asks you to
join their startup. But there are lots of challenging steps to get from
an idea to commercialization. Before you know it, you'll be drinking
from a firehose with everything coming at you at once—legal problems, partner issues, vendor agreements, raising money, marketing
problems with your product or service, and more. So, you'll really
need a plan to stay focused. Otherwise, you'll be held hostage by
fighting the crisis of the moment and never reach your goals.

You can think of the major steps in a company's life in three
stages:

- Stage 1 is "Beachhead." This is where you organize the
  company and personnel and take steps to protect it, like
  hiring a lawyer to draft non-disclosure, non-compete
  agreements. and locking up your intellectual property.
- Stage 2 is "Operations." This includes managing and
  growing the company.
- Stage 3 is "Exit," where you cash out.

While many of the 7 Secret Keys apply to any stage in a business,
because this is a startup book, it's focused on the startup stage, Stage
1, Beachhead. This first chapter will give you a high-level overview
of the startup process. Then, the following chapters will go deeper
into many of the most critical areas discussed. The steps listed below
can be done in a different order or in parallel, but make sure you at
least consider doing all of them.

Illustration 1

BASIC STARTUP STEPS, 0-60

✓   Develop a Plan.

✓   Get a Partner With Money.

✓   Build a Balanced Core Team.

✓   Form a Business Entity.

✓ Use Non-Disclosure (NDA) and Non-Compete Agreements.

✓ Protect Your Intellectual property (IP).

✓ Get Personnel Documents In Place.

✓ Choose The Best Way To Compensate Employees.

✓ Create a Board Of Directors, Board of Advisors.

✓ Extensive Market Research – Define What "It" Is.

✓ Design a Minimum Viable Product, Field Test it.

Note: These are the Earliest Startup Steps Before Marketing and Sales. Many steps can be done in parallel or different order.

WHAT IS YOUR BUSINESS?

Peter Drucker, the renowned business expert, has said that there are just two questions to ask regarding business success. First, "What business will you be in?" and "How's business?"[1] Sometimes start-ups only think about building and selling their product or service—I'll often use the term "product" to include "service" as well. But there is a whole spectrum of things you could do with your product, from just licensing the use of it by others to sales and maintenance.

And maybe it's not a product at all, just a leased service or a Software as a Service (SaaS) in which software is licensed on a subscription basis and hosted from a central server.

Select Your Slice of the Pie

If your invention is patentable and has some real market value—a patent lawyer and others can help you determine that—you could simply license the intellectual property, such as a patent or copyright from your invention and hand off everything else to others, such as the manufacturing, marketing, distribution, sales, etc. If that worked, you could collect a royalty and sit on your yacht. This would save a lot of headaches. Do you really want to worry about running a factory and Occupational Safety and Health Administration (OSHA) regulations? You could also finance the sale of the products and make money from the financing fees, or you could consider offering a maintenance agreement to provide another source of income. This is the frosting on the sales cake. Here's how maintenance plans work. You create a spread sheet and drop in the labor and parts costs and the failure rates for the equipment. Then you price the maintenance plan so that—given a typical failure rate of the product—you've still got enough money to cover it, plus a 25–50 percent profit on it. You can even get an insurance policy behind that to protect yourself from a big failure. Maintenance plans can be an excellent source of income.

Exit Strategy

What do you want to do and by when? Would you like to grow the company and raise its value? Do you like running a company? Or would you like to get sales up and running, add value, and then cash out with a greater profit after some time, say, three-to-five years?

So, think about these different options, which will help focus on the best options for you as you take the following first startup steps.

FIND PARTNERS FOR EARLY FUNDING

Let's get real. As James Hunt, managing partner of the MITA Group, a private equity fund, once told me, "The number one reason companies fail is that they run out of money." Sure, that's obvious, so obvious that it's often overlooked. But it's also very true. So, your first job is to make sure that never happens. Running a business is a bumpy ride. A partner or other source of money like a big line of credit or high net worth investors provides the shock absorbers you need to survive the ride. Even Thomas Edison, one of the world's most successful investors, continuously had to raise money for his many projects. There are an unlimited number of ways to run out of money, which we'll discuss, but it comes down to always having enough money to stay in business. One solution that's obvious but frequently overlooked is to get one or more partners or investors as soon as possible who have enough money to support you when your cash flow hasn't started or is inadequate.

I learned this lesson in 2005. I was a founder and CEO of Sky-Built Power, a startup company that produced the first rapidly deployable solar and wind power systems for the military and intelligence community. These plug-and-play units in freight containers provided power with no fuel and minimal maintenance to remote areas for the Iraq war effort and Homeland Security. In-Q-Tel, the CIA's venture capital firm, provided SkyBuilt with critical financial support and our first sales. In-Q-Tel's mission is to identify and support startups with transformational technologies that can be used by the military and intelligence agencies. The name came from "intel" for intelligence and "Q" because CIA Director George Tenet liked "Q," the crusty quartermaster and research director in the early James Bond movies.

Building these cutting-edge systems required hundreds of thousands of dollars to solve complex engineering challenges. Fortunately, my good friends and SkyBuilt board members, Bill Buck, Ken Schweers, S. Kinnie Smith, and Bob Hahne, were kind enough to invest and lend money essential to launching the company and maintaining cash flow, while Scott Sklar provided expertise on solar systems. We never could have gotten off the ground and kept going without their critical financial and other support. Make sure you focus on having enough financial backing to keep going. One common metric is to raise enough funding to last twelve to eighteen months.

Then you'll be freer to concentrate on developing the product and getting to profitability.

SELECT AN EXPERIENCED LAWYER TO AVOID RAZOR BLADES IN THE SOUP

Be sure to get a lawyer right away. Your lawyer will help you with typical startup matters, including creating the company and putting personnel agreements in place. Having a good lawyer right off the bat will help you avoid big mistakes that can kill your company. Your lawyer should be able to use experience to see the razor blades in the soup that can cripple a startup. Look for a lawyer who's experienced in startups as well as a broad range of business matters. When hiring a lawyer, consider using smaller or mid-size firms. Bigger firms frequently have higher overheads. Most of the startup work is routine, so you don't need the highest paid, specialized attorneys to do it. Your lawyer should review all contracts until they become routine, to protect you from making bad deals. Contract language can be very tricky and often just a few words you don't understand can leave you with a costly mistake or a deal that's too hard to get out of if it goes bad.

> TIP: NEVER SIGN A CONTRACT WITHOUT HAVING A LAWYER LOOK AT IT, UNLESS IT'S FAMILIAR AND YOU FULLY UNDERTAND IT. CONTRACTS ARE LIKE WARS: EASY TO GET INTO AND HARD TO ESCAPE.

BUILD A SOLID CORE TEAM
Be Humble, Ask for Help, and Listen

Understand that you need help. As the startup's CEO, you're probably good at some things, even amazingly good. But that doesn't mean you are good at all things. And the job of CEO is like drinking out of a firehose. You'll need to work on more than one thing at a time while maintaining a reasonable balance in managing all parts of the company, from product development to marketing, legal, fundraising, and personnel. If you don't put a well-qualified team together to help, you'll be overwhelmed and unable to focus on the bigger issues that are more important and strategic.

Every entrepreneur usually has a strong suit that's also a weakness. For example, software entrepreneur gurus just can't stop trying to improve their software. There's always one more feature to add and some code to tweak. It's the fun part for them. We all like to spend more time on the things we enjoy doing and understand. To make it worse, entrepreneurs tend to be creative folks, so for them, creative activities are a lot more fun than the routine, boring tasks like paperwork, legal contracts, and petty personnel issues. But you can't let any of those balls drop or the company will go down with them. This goes double for personnel matters. One of the biggest reasons that startups fail in the first year is personnel issues. People need attention. They want to feel like a part of the company; and when they don't they quit, and you not only have to spend time and money getting someone else, but sometimes they get so mad that they find a lawyer and sue you. It's extremely difficult to raise money from investors when you're a defendant in a lawsuit (See chapter 4 for more personnel tips).

How do you keep on top of all the things your company needs at once? I'll get back to that later (See chapter 7 for some answers to this problem).

No Sycophants

Another big reason to create a solid, core team is to keep you balanced and allow you to thrash out options and ideas before running off in the wrong direction. Pick your core team carefully. A startup can be all consuming and you may be spending more time with your team than with your significant others. You don't want any sycophants. Get talented people dedicated to the company who will feel comfortable arguing with you. Their ideas can help you get to a better result.

Who Should Be on Your Core Team?

The core team must be people that you trust and have the skills and experience you need, perhaps five people or so. In a typical startup you might have the sparkplug—the CEO, who has produced the ideas for the company—a technical expert like a chief technology officer (CTO), a chief financial officer (CFO) or treasurer, and a marketing person. Other duties like developing software and building a web page can be outsourced, which will save overhead.

SELECT THE RIGHT BUSINESS ENTITY AND STATE FOR REGISTRATION

Having a company in place rather than doing everything personally in your name makes you look more professional and ready to do business. It also provides liability protection. In case there's a lawsuit or claim against the company, you want the company, not you personally, to absorb the liability. If things get really bad, the company—instead of you—can file for bankruptcy.

Company Formation Steps

Here's a high-level view of the basic company formation steps. They will vary by state and local rules. In creating a company, your attorney will walk you through the different types of entities, like a sole proprietorship, partnership, limited liability company (LLC), a corporation (called a Corp. or C Corp. or simply a corporation), S corporation (S corp), and benefit corporation, and whether the company should be "for profit" or "non-profit" (also called "not-for-profit"). Each of these entities has its pros and cons, including different tax impacts on you and any other equity owners in the company and on the company itself.

In What State Should I Form My Company?

You should discuss with your lawyer in which state your entity should be registered. States vary in their efficiency, registration fees, tax policies, shareholder protections, and privacy provisions. For example, Delaware is a popular state for startups. It offers flexibility in structuring your company. Only one person needs to be a director and officers don't need to be residents. Directors' names don't need to be required on formation documents, and there's no state income tax. Its Court of Chancery has expertise in the most complex corporate legal matters. Because over half of the Fortune 500 companies are registered there, it has additional prestige. However, other states have many of those features. For example, Nevada, Florida, Wyoming, South Dakota, and others have no state income tax.

However, if you register in any state but aren't a resident, then you need a third party in that state to act as your "resident agent" to receive service of process in case of a lawsuit or to handle any other legal matters for your company in that state. That registered agent service costs money. And you'll also need to be registered in the state in which you are actually running the business. That means that you have to pay twice and need to comply with both states' reporting requirements. Because of this, I often recommend incorporating in the state in which you live and do business to keep things simple and inexpensive. You can always register in a different state later. For example, some major investors might want to have you registered in Delaware or another state where they're located.

Types of Business Entities

Here are just a few of the more popular business entities and some key features for you to consider.

Sole Proprietorship

A sole proprietorship is what you have when you're engaged in business but haven't formed a separate legal entity. It's the default position. The advantage is that you don't need to do as much to start your business and you could get a trade name. It might be a fit for a very low risk business that you want to explore. The downside is that your personal and business matters are totally intermingled. If your business is sued, you're personally liable as well! Your business liabilities become your personal liabilities. It also appears to potential investors and customers that you're engaged in something more like a hobby rather than a "real" business. So, they are hesitant to invest in or provide business loans to sole proprietorships.

Partnerships

A partnership is a simple business form for two or more people. There are various kinds.

General Partnership (GP)

A general partnership can be formed in most states simply by signing a partnership agreement. You do not even need to register as a business entity with the state. Profits, losses, and liabilities flow directly through to the owners' personal income for tax purposes. Each partner can bind the partnership unless otherwise specified in the partnership agreement. That leaves the door open for potential liability.

Limited Partnership (LP)

LPs often have one general partner who has unlimited liability and controls the business, while the other partner(s) have limited liability. The limited liability partners may have various degrees of control over the company as described in a partnership agreement. Profits and losses flow through to the partners' personal income tax, and the general partner pays self-employment taxes.[2]

Limited Liability Partnership (LLP)

LLPs are like general partnerships (GPs) but provide limited liability to all the partners; and absent unusual situations, partners are not responsible for the actions of other partners.[3]

Limited Liability Company (LLC)

Often, startups choose an LLC as their first entity. All the income and expenses from an LLC flow directly through to the equity holders and their personal income tax returns. Because startups often lose money at first, those losses can reduce your taxable income. The entity itself is a "pass through entity" for income and expense purposes and is not separately taxed.

Another advantage of LLCs is that they can be less expensive to form and simpler to operate and maintain. For example, there typically is a flat state annual registration fee of fifty to a hundred dollars from the state in which you operate the LLC, regardless of how many members there are. With a corporation, however, fees tend to be higher and are frequently based on the number of shares, which can make your annual registration fees much more expensive. For example, in Virginia, an LLC's annual registration fee is fifty dollars, but for a corporation with 270,000 or more authorized shares (even if the shares were just "authorized" and not "issued" yet), it would be $1,700.[4]

In LLCs, the equity holders are called "members" and the equity share is called a "membership interest." This contrasts with corporations where the equity holders are called "shareholders" or "stockholders." In practice, however, people often refer to members of LLCs as stockholders or shareholders as well.

C Corp

A C corp is also very popular. It is a separate legal entity from its owners and can be taxed, have its own profits and losses, and be separately legally liable. It is more expensive to set up and requires more record keeping and reporting than LLCs.

One advantage is that C corps can have "qualified stock option plans" with "incentive stock options." This provides more favorable tax treatment for the recipients because the profits they make when the options are exercised are taxed at the capital gains rate which typically is lower than the ordinary income tax rate. Because LLCs don't have "stock," just "membership interests," they can't have stock options. LLCs can, however, issue equity in the form of membership interests to employees and officers and others as an incentive or provide "warrants," which operate in a similar manner to stock options.

On the minus side with a C corp, there is double taxation. First, the corporation is taxed on its earnings. Then, if it distributes its earnings in the form of dividends to shareholders, those earnings become taxable income to the shareholders. In order to "go public" and be listed on a public stock exchange, you must be a C corp.

As with other entities, if you sell your shares after holding them for at least a year, the difference between the acquisition price (called the "basis") and the sale price creates a "capital gain" (if the sale price is higher than your acquisition price) or a "capital loss" for tax purposes (if the shares are sold for less than the basis or acquisition price). If they are sold in less than a year, the gain or loss is treated as "ordinary income."

S-Corp

An S-Corp or S Corporation is not a different legal structure; rather it's an Internal Revenue Service (IRS) tax election that allows more favorable tax treatment for an entity. For example, a single-member LLC is taxed by the IRS as a sole proprietorship by default. This means that the LLC pays a Federal Insurance Contributions Act (FICA) self-employment tax on all income one earns from the business, plus personal income tax based on your personal tax rate. Like a corporation, an S corp has a separate life so if a stockholder leaves the company the S corp continues in existence.

On the other hand, if the LLC files with the IRS and receives S-Corp tax treatment, it can reduce taxes. Here's how that could work. You can pay yourself a salary which has to be "reasonable compensation," similar to what a typical employee would make for your job. Then you would only pay one-half of the usual payroll tax amount, plus a Federal Unemployment Tax Act (FUTA) unemployment tax and personal income taxes on your salary. The business would pay the other one-half of the payroll taxes which can be written off as a tax deduction. Profits would not be subject to payroll taxes.[5] Another advantage is that an S-Corp can have stock options.

The downside is that the IRS places restrictions on S-Corps. For example, you will need to pay yourself a paycheck, deduct payroll taxes, and file quarterly estimated returns. Also, to qualify for S corporation status, the corporation must meet the following requirements:

- Be a domestic corporation;
- Have only certain types of shareholders (They may be individuals, certain trusts, and estates but may not be partnerships, corporations, or non-resident alien shareholders);
- Have no more than one hundred shareholders;
- Have only one class of stock; and
- Not be an ineligible corporation (i.e., certain financial institutions, insurance companies, and domestic international sales corporations).

So, if you're not going to have income for some time, the additional steps to create an S Corp might not be worth it because there won't be any tax savings. You can always convert to an S Corp in the future. Tax laws change, so be sure to consult your tax advisor before selecting an entity and its tax treatment.

Benefit Corporation (B corp)

A benefit corporation, also called a "public benefit corporation" or "B corp," is a for-profit entity that requires the company to have a positive impact on society, workers, the community, and the environment in addition to its usual business activities. Startups might choose to create a benefit corporation because it fits with their corporate goals to provide societal benefits. In some states, a C corporation may change to a benefit corporation just by changing its bylaws, while in others it may have to file with the state to change its name. In a benefit corporation, directors must consider the public benefits in addition to profits and the company publishes annual benefit reports. These reports typically have twelve or so third-party standards to be followed to satisfy state reporting standards, but third-party certification of compliance to those standards is not required.[6]

Close Corporation

A close corporation (or "closely held corporation") is a less formal corporation, used by a small group of shareholders, usually not more than thirty-five. It can be run by the members without a board of directors and without an annual meeting, but it cannot be publicly traded. The shareholders are treated like a general partnership, but if they run the company they keep their limited liability and assume the fiduciary duties of a fiduciary and may be held liable for violation of those duties.[7]

Nonprofit Corporation

A nonprofit corporation is a corporation that has received a tax exemption from the IRS. Nonprofits must perform work that benefits society such as educational, religious, literary, charity, scientific, or trade association work. Their rules of operation are set by the IRS and are more restrictive than those of for-profit corporations.

For example, a nonprofit's lobbying activities may be restricted; they can't distribute profits to members or to political campaigns.

Cooperative

A cooperative ("co-op" or "coop") is "an autonomous association of persons united voluntarily to meet their common economic, social, and cultural needs and aspirations through a jointly-owned enterprise."[8] Cooperatives are owned by their members, with each member having one vote (unrelated to the value of their holdings) when electing the board of directors. Cooperatives are commonly used in New York City for residential housing, and nationally by electric and gas utility companies, including "rural electric cooperatives."

GET YOUR COMPANY'S PAPERWORK IN ORDER
Pick a Name

To form a legal entity, the first step is to pick a name. You're not naming your first born, so don't go crazy figuring out a name. You can always change it later, although this will take more time and expense the longer you wait to do so because more documents will need changing. And, you'll lose the brand name identity you might have created.

Your products can have different names. For example, your company could be named IBC Corp, but you could name your products anything else.

When you've picked a name, you can do an online search at the appropriate office in your state where you're going to register the company and make sure you're not infringing on someone else's name. The state's registration office might be called the Department of State (New York) or the State Corporation Commission (in Virginia). To be more certain that the name isn't infringing on another name, you can have a more extensive trademark search done by a trademark agent. These are usually non-lawyers specifically trained in such searches. They might charge hundreds of dollars for that.

Tax ID Number

You'll need to get a Tax ID number or "Employee Identification Number" (EIN or FEIN) from the IRS. You will need it when you open a bank account, file your tax return, and for other transactions. You can simply go online to IRS.gov and search for "EIN." It only takes a few minutes. This Federal EIN is used for state tax filings as well.

Bylaws and Operating Agreement

Remember to adopt in writing the basic rules under which the company must operate. They're called bylaws for a corporation and an operating agreement for LLCs. When you enter into agreements with other parties and raise money from investors, they often will want to see them. Not having them or having inferior ones are a signal to others that you don't know how to run your own railroad.

They include such things as:

- the address of the company;
- procedures for annual and special meetings;
- elections and voting requirements;
- quorum requirements;
- creating the board of directors and its procedures;
- election and duties of officers;
- stockholder's rights; and
- indemnification of officers by the company.

Although you can get form bylaws documents from the internet for under fifty dollars, they usually provide very thin coverage for the many situations in which a company can find itself. I think of those three-to-to-five-page documents like wearing summer clothes in the arctic—they're clothes, but sometimes they don't give you adequate protection. So have a lawyer draft them up for you. Lawyers can be expensive but fixing problems from inferior corporate documents can be even more expensive. For an outline of a bylaws document and some typical terms, see Appendix 1.

Authorizing Resolutions

Adopt organizational resolutions, which appoint officers, authorize the opening of financial accounts, appoint a law firm and/or accounting firm, issue equity, and approve all prior actions of the founders, etc. Sometimes these resolutions are called "organizational actions in writing in lieu of a meeting," or something similar. They are the written versions of the resolutions that the company would normally adopt if it held an in-person organizational meeting. Or you can hold an in-person meeting and orally pass the resolutions instead. But then they should be written, signed by an officer, and placed in the minutes of the company. See an example of an organizational action in writing at Appendix 2.

Get a Business License
These are usually not expensive. The state or local governments want to know what kind of a business you have and whether there will be any zoning (how many parking spaces, etc.) or other issues regarding the business.

Zoning
Get a zoning permit, if required by local authorities. This is sometimes included in the business license filing.

Tax Filing
Register with federal, state, and/or local tax authorities.

Open Financial Accounts
Once you have done some of these basics, you can open a checking or other financial accounts. Banks typically require that you bring in your state-issued certificate of incorporation (and some will confirm that online with the issuing state office), bylaws, and resolutions appointing a treasurer.

Create a Legally Compliant Webpage
When you're setting up a webpage, there are a number of things you should consider, including a separate webpage tab for legal notices. Some of these are required and some are optional.

Terms and Conditions

Terms and Conditions are optional and include your company's requirements for use of the website. They provide information on protecting your intellectual property rights to the information on the site, detail prohibited uses of the site, provide consents for the site to use information that the user provides, describe payments of fees, and limit your company's liability while using the site.

Cookies Policy

Cookies are text files that a hosting company places on the user's computer to collect information, provide communication with the user, offer focused advertising, and other services. A cookies policy is not generally required except in special situations, such as if your site engages with European Union (EU) users (see the General Data Protection Regulation section next). A cookies policy discloses what cookies are used, who provides them, how the site places and uses them, and how preferences for them can be changed by the user.

Privacy Policy

A privacy policy describes the company's practices for collecting, using, protecting, and disclosing "personal information" that the user provides to the site, and a policy regarding their use is required by the Federal Trade Commission and state privacy laws. "Personal information" includes an e-mail address, physical address, phone numbers and names, and biometric or other personal identifiers.

General Data Protection Regulation (GDPR)

This is an EU regulation that governs the protection of data and privacy on the web in the European Union and European Economic Area (EEA).[9] You need a website policy regarding these matters when data is transferred in or out of those jurisdictions, such as when a user in the European Union uses a website in the United States.

California Privacy Rights Act

This California law[10] imposes privacy protections on certain companies doing business in California. If your business is located in

California or has substantial transactions there (as defined in the Act) you must include language on your site to comply with the required consumer rights imposed by the Act.

Other Requirements

Other privacy regulations are being added from time to time as well, so be sure to have your attorney check for those on a regular basis.

Other Steps

Set up your letterhead, get business cards if you wish, and you're in business.

USE NON-DISCLOSURE (NDA) AND NON-COMPETE AGREEMENTS

The business world can be a dangerous jungle. People steal ideas and products all the time. Someone once took marketing materials off my website and put it on theirs so that they could sell my products. So, how can you protect your ideas from being stolen but still talk about them to those you need to, like investors and potential customers?

One answer is a non-disclosure agreement or NDA. That requires the parties who sign it not to disclose any confidential or proprietary information about the existence of the NDA, your business dealings, and the products and services being discussed. There are exceptions to non-disclosure agreements, such as instances where the information is already publicly available, cases in which you need to disclose information to your agents or advisors to perform duties for the business, or if a court requires disclosure.

Some investors and others won't sign NDAs. They'll tell you that they don't want to remember what's confidential and what's not and from whom. If they have negotiating power in the transaction, you may have to go along with that. A good NDA also has other provisions such as language preventing the recipient from competing against you (a "non-compete") and a provision that prevents one party from circumventing the other on a deal ("non-circumvention" provision) such as bypassing the agent to take control of the deal. Sometimes they're referred to as "a non-compete, non-disclosure Agreement" (NCNDA). A good NCNDA should have all these provisions: an NDA and non-compete and non-circumvention language. For an example, see Appendix 3.

Another way to protect your proprietary information and data is simply not to disclose them. When raising investment capital or getting a customer, you have to tell the other party something. But you can start by telling *what* your product or service does, but not the all-important secret sauce of *how* it does it. Once you get into more serious discussions, you can reveal more information as required and under an NCNDA. That leads us into how to protect your intellectual property.

PROTECT YOUR INTELLECTUAL PROPERTY

TIP: DON'T BLOG ABOUT YOUR SECRET SAUCE OR YOU MIGHT NOT BE ABLE TO GET A PATENT ON IT!

You may develop valuable intellectual property that you'll want to protect.

Intellectual property includes: "...creations of the mind, such as inventions; literary and artistic works; designs; and symbols, names and images used in commerce."[11]

It can include customer lists, software, trade secrets, patents, inventions, franchises, patents, copyrights, and trademarks. It's sometimes distinguished from other more tangible property such as "real property" (real estate) and "personal property" such as computers or desks.

There are various ways to protect your intellectual property. You could keep the information secret. That creates a trade secret, which is any proprietary, commercially valuable information or data kept secret by not telling anyone (or only disclosing it under the protection of an NDA). You also can file for a copyright, patent, or a trademark. (See chapter 3 for a full discussion of each of these.)

Startups sometimes make a big mistake by publicly disclosing their invention before they patent it. Once it's out in the public, you may not be able to get a patent, even if you're the one that invented it and made it public. This is because you can only get a patent from the U.S. Patent and Trademark office (US PTO) for what is novel (meaning new), non-obvious, and useful. So, (subject to certain exemptions, such as if you file for a patent within one year of any disclosure[12]) if the invention is already public, such as if you blog about it before you file for a patent, it's not "novel" anymore because it's in the public domain and you may be denied a patent.

CREATE PERSONNEL AND OFFERING DOCUMENTS

> **TIP: YOU'RE VIRTUALLY "MARRIED" TO YOUR STARTUP PARTNERS SO BE SURE TO GET A "PRENUPTIAL" PARTNERS AGREEMENT!**

Get Personnel Documents in Place

While the proof is elusive, most startups probably fail in the first year. One of the major reasons is that the partners don't get along. You might end up spending more time with your startup partners than your significant others. You're "married" to them, so you need the business version of a prenuptial agreement. To protect each other and your company, you should have a written agreement with every employee or independent contractor working for the company. This should spell out how the person is compensated, what their duties are, how their engagement with the company can be terminated, what happens if they get equity and then leave the company, etc. (See chapter 4 for more partnership information). One of my clients started a company without any personnel documents in place. Then his partner wanted to leave. A one-year battle followed with lawyers and accountants over how much money that partner was due from past business income and his oral claim of a 30 percent equity stake. We finally got a settlement, but this expensive mess was totally avoidable. Don't let this happen to you.

Have Your Offering Documents Drafted by a Lawyer

Once you start raising money, you'll need to prepare documents that describe the terms of your offering, such as how many shares of equity are being offered and for what price. You may want to limit who can invest to sophisticated investors with plenty of net worth, called "accredited investors."[13] This makes it harder for such investors to claim that you lost their money because they already would have signed a document saying that they are sophisticated investors and understand that they could lose all their money by investing in your new venture.

This is a very dangerous area legally and you should have a lawyer advise you on how to proceed. For example, the U.S. Securities and Exchange Commission (SEC) has rules that govern how you must "issue an offering" and raise money. If you fail to follow those rules, you can be subject to civil and even criminal penalties. In addition, each state has laws (also called "Blue Sky Laws") that regulate how funds can be raised (making "offerings") in their states. For example, you might think that if your uncle in California invests $20,000 in your new company that it's just a "friends and family" investment so you don't have to do anything to comply with federal or state security regulations. But unless there's an exemption, most states require you to register and pay a fee before or shortly after making an equity offering. So, check with your lawyer before raising funds (See chapter 5 for further details).

HIRE AN ACCOUNTANT AND MINIMIZE TAX SUPRISES
Setting Up the Books and Records of the Company
You should engage an accountant early in the startup process. Accountants can help you track your income and expenses and provide valuable financial advice. You also don't want to clutter your desk with random receipts and expenses. Your accountant can help you set up a good bookkeeping system to track all of this. Quick Books is one easy-to-use software program to do that. Once you understand how to use Quick Books or another software accounting program, you can input the information yourself, link it to your bank account, easily print checks, and save money on accountants. When you file your income taxes, the information your accountant needs will already be well organized and ready to input into your company's tax return. That can save you and your accountant time and money.

Your accountant can also help you save money by properly classifying various types of expenditures. Some can be "expensed" like rent or wages, allowing you to deduct those costs annually for tax purposes. Other expenditures may be "capital expenses," such as expenses for computers, office furniture, and software. Those typically are depreciated for tax purposes over time based on their useful life which results in lower annual tax savings.

Prepare a Business Plan

Your team, lawyer, and accountant can help you prepare a business plan. That's a document, usually ten to twenty pages, which describes your company, product, management, marketing plan, and financial matters. There's a lot of work in putting a good business plan together, but it is worth it because it forces you to think about what you're doing in some detail. A key part of the plan is a pro-forma profit and loss statement (P&L). This is a spreadsheet detailing three-to-five years of income, expenses, and profit or losses. It shows investors how the company will be performing, and you can use it to manage the company as well (see Chapter 5). Sure, it starts being out of date the minute you produce it because your business is always changing, but it is the best guide you have for the company's financial plans and will help you track your financial results.

> **TIP: KEEP THE PAR VALUE OF YOUR COMPANY LOW TO REDUCE TAXES.**

Minimizing Taxes

Accountants are also helpful with legal tax avoidance strategies. One tricky area is when you get equity in your company. You need to get good accounting advice early on before accepting any equity to minimize its tax impact.

For example, suppose that you start a company. It has one million shares of equity "authorized." "Authorized" means the maximum number of shares that the company has approved to be issued to shareholders or holds in reserve ("treasury stock"). Once shares are issued to investors, they're called "issued shares."

Now, suppose that you plan to issue yourself a total of four hundred thousand shares of stock in two batches ("tranches") of two hundred thousand shares each. The company sets the share price for the first tranche at ten cents per share. The value of those shares will become taxable income to you when they are issued. Two hundred thousand shares multiplied by ten cents per share equals $20,000 of taxable income to you even if the company doesn't have any income to offset that tax. So, you need to be careful about how many shares you get and what price you set for them. That's why you often see a start-up's share price set low, such as at $0.001 per share. That stated price is called "par" value or "nominal value," which is usually unrelated to the current market value of the company. At $0.001 per share, the taxable income would only be $200 ($0.001 multiplied by $200,000).

Now, suppose that the company does great and shares are now worth a hundred dollars each. You give yourself the second tranche of two hundred thousand more shares. Now you'll be taxed on two million dollars of income (one hundred dollars per share multiplied by two hundred thousand shares). Ouch! But an accountant or tax lawyer can structure this so that you can prepay taxes on the value of the stock when the first tranche was granted, not when the later tranches are received. This is done by filing an "83(b) election" with the U.S. Treasury Department. *But that must be filed within thirty days of when the first stock issuance was granted.*[14]

> **TIP: TO AVOID GETTING SUED, BE SURE TO NOTIFY EMPLOYEES ABOUT THEIR 83(b) ELECTION OPTION BEFORE GRANTING THEM SHARES.**

Of course, if the shares go down in value at the time of the second tranche, then you would have overpaid your taxes on the front end. This shows how useful an accountant can be and how important it is to engage one right away and not make a costly mistake by waiting too long.

To avoid a situation in which an employee gets a tax bill from receiving the company's equity and then argues that the company should have disclosed that, your employee handbook and any employment agreement should contain language disclosing this possibility; and the employee should acknowledge that the employee will consult with an accountant or attorney on the tax implications prior to receiving the equity.

SELECT THE BEST WAYS TO COMPENSATE EMPLOYEES
Salaries
Usually, startups don't have much money for salaries. But there are other forms of compensation that may be helpful. These include paying someone on a commission based on the sales they close, or compensation can be in shares of equity in the company such as by offering stock or stock options.

Stock Options
An "employee stock option" is a right for the employee to purchase a certain number of shares in the company at a certain price (the "exercise price") for a certain period in the future under certain conditions. For example, the company might give you an option to purchase a thousand shares of its stock at a discounted price at any time over the next five years whenever the company hits a defined goal, such as one million dollars in sales. The company also benefits because it is not giving away any equity yet and may never have to, unless the event that triggers the option occurs.

Independent Contractors vs. Employees
Often, it makes sense for companies to use "independent contractors" rather than "employees." This reduces the company's overhead expenses for employee benefits like health insurance and 401(k) savings plan contributions. Independent contractors must pay their own federal payroll taxes under the Federal Insurance Contributions Act ("FICA"). That's 15.3 percent of gross wages. The employer pays nothing. On the other hand, if the worker is an "employee," the company must pay one-half of the 15.3 percent or 7.65 percent, and the employee pays the same amount. There are restrictions, however, on the use of independent contractors, such as when they are working full time or otherwise acting more like employees, so be sure to

check with your lawyer on using them to avoid violating the Fair Labor Standards Act, enforced by the U.S. Department of Labor (see Chapter 4 for details).[15]

CREATE A BOARD OF DIRECTORS/BOARD OF ADVISORS

As a startup, you want your company to look professional and to demonstrate to others that you have a team that can do the job. You also want and need advisors to second guess you, help you reach the best decisions, and open the doors to potential customers or suppliers. Too often, CEOs keep charging ahead in the wrong direction unless they have a good team of advisors or a board to keep them on track and give them a dose of reality. Startup CEOs are dogged and often have trouble seeing their own failings. A board provides a good reality check and moral support. Of course, some board members can also drive you crazy but generally having a board is very useful.

A board of directors sets policy for the company, while the management runs the company and executes the board's policies. Sometimes boards try to run the company and control the officers, so you will want to pick your board members carefully. They should be supportive, but not intrusive.

Composition of the Board

Think about creating a board of five to seven persons. It should be an odd number to avoid a tie in voting. You might want to have an experienced lawyer, marketing person, CFO, or accountant and one or more officers, typically the president and CEO. The other seats should be for people who can help you grow the business and open doors to your target markets. For example, when I ran a military contracting company, I invited a retired three-star Air Force general, John Fairfield, and a former assistant secretary of the Army, Mario Fiori, to be on the board. They were very helpful in finding marketing opportunities and dealing with the complex military procurement process.

Sometimes when selling to big companies or the government, the person or business unit that wants your products doesn't have the authorization or money to buy them. I remember one time when I was talking on the phone with a colonel in Iraq at a forward operating base. I could hear the gunfire in the background. He wanted to buy our solar/wind power stations and get rid of diesel power because it was too hard and dangerous to resupply the fuel. The Army found that for every twenty-four fuel convoys in Iraq one soldier was killed with improvised explosive devices (IEDs) on the road. But the colonel didn't have any authority to get the funds. Only the Pentagon did. So, we had to work with both the colonel who wanted the product and the Pentagon folks with authority to free up the money. Having board members who know how to do that definitely helps.

Compensation

Board members of a startup don't expect to be paid. Once the company starts making money, you could compensate directors by giving them stock options based on their attendance at board meetings. For example, if you decide that attending a board meeting remotely is worth $300 of their time and attending in person is worth $500 per meeting plus travel expenses, then you could give them stock options equaling those values for every meeting they attend. Later, when the company is making enough money, you could pay them in cash.

Fiduciary Duty of Directors

Under state law, members of a board of directors have a legal, fiduciary duty to the company and to the shareholders. This includes the duties of utmost good faith, honesty, loyalty to the company, and the duty to exercise due care in the management of corporate affairs. As a result, some people may not want to join your board unless you have directors' and officers' liability insurance (D&O insurance) to protect them from potential lawsuits. You usually can get that for less than $2,000 per year and it also protects you, officers, and other designated persons in the company.

Board of Advisors

You could also create a board of advisors. This typically is an informal arrangement. CEOs use them for informal advice and to help open doors to grow the company. Having well-known advisors on your letterhead or in your marketing materials can enhance the image of the company. And they usually don't have a legal or fiduciary duty to the company or shareholders. They also don't expect to get paid when you're still a startup.

DO EXTENSIVE MARKET RESEARCH–DEFINE WHAT "IT" IS

At the beginning, all you have is a bunch of assumptions, just hypotheses, about your new product (or service or both) and who the customer is. You need to figure out both of those to be successful.

> **TIP: NEVER SIGN A CONTRACT UNLESS YOU CAN REASONABLY GET OUT OF IT!**

Regarding what your product should be, don't start signing expensive design or prototyping contracts too early in the process because your idea will change repeatedly in the early stages. Never sign a contract that doesn't allow you to get out with minimal cost. This is where having a good lawyer when you're starting up can be very useful.

Regarding the customer, for your product to be commercially successful, someone needs to write a check to buy it. But they won't buy it unless they want it, and you don't know yet what they want and how much they'd be willing to pay. Sometimes even the customer doesn't know what it wants. Steve Jobs didn't worry about that when he created the iPhone because it was so innovative. Customers loved it when they saw it even though they never had seen one before or wanted one. But you're not Steve Jobs. So, you need to do your best to find out what the customer wants.

Customer Discovery

You should talk with a hundred or so potential target customers and find out what they want. Yes, a hundred. You'll learn a lot. Your idea and its features and price point will become more realistic. The product may even change from a product to a service such as leasing the product, downloading it on a subscription basis, or leasing it rather than selling it.

Prepare for the Discovery Conversation

Make a list of the questions you need answered before talking with the market research targets. Typically, these are potential customers. For example, if your product is a portable heater, does the customer want lower initial costs for the unit, lower operating costs, a quieter unit, more efficiency, or is the customer happy with what he/she has? How is it going to be used? Is it for constant use or intermittent use? How big are the rooms in which it might be used? Is the market residential, commercial, or military, as well as civilian, domestic, or international? You get the idea.

Mostly Listen

When you meet with potential customers during market discovery, mostly listen; don't talk too much. You're not in selling mode. This is market research. Find out what you don't know and haven't thought of yet. You're trying to get inside the customer's head and understand his/her needs so you can meet them. You might say something like this:

- "I have this idea, but I need your help."
- "Would this be of interest to you?"
- "Does it solve a problem you have?"
- "If not, what is your problem and what would meet your needs?"
- "If I built what we're discussing, would you be interested in buying it?"
- "At what price or terms?"
- "What if I financed this and paid for it up front at no cost to you? You'd save money on day one compared to your electricity bill now. Then you'd just pay me a monthly fee."

What Is the Competition?

Your product needs to be cheaper, faster, better, or in some way superior to make folks want to buy it compared to other, similar products. Often the competition is something as simple as the customer doesn't want the hassle of changing suppliers or learning about something new. Think about how reluctant a customer might be to switch bundled services (TV, cell phone, etc.) from one internet provider to another just to save a few dollars. What is your secret sauce? What's your value added? Is it enough to get buyers to buy? Find out what they pay now. Talk about how much they could save. What would it take for them to switch to your product?

DESIGN A SIMPLE PROTOTYPE, A MINIMUM VIABLE PRODUCT (MVP), AND FIELD TEST IT.

Suppose you have an idea for a new widget. First, build a workable product. Forget the bells and whistles. Make it out of cardboard if necessary. Get it out in the field and get operating data. If it's a heater, for instance, get real time data from a data logger (operating times, weather conditions, time of day, wind speed, solar radiation, etc.) and get customer feedback. Eric Ries, in his classic book *The Lean Startup*,[16] describes this minimum viable product (MVP) process in detail. Your goal is to learn what product or service the customer wants. Focus on learning, not perfection. You need to learn as fast as possible before your money runs out. Making mistakes with a design or two is okay and can even be valuable because your customer will tell you whether you have the right design or features before you spend too much time and money going the wrong way. Once you get the results of the field test, you can adjust the prototype design to improve it. Then build the next iteration and repeat the process, as necessary.

When I was developing solar/wind power stations for the CIA, it took many working prototypes and hundreds of changes to get a reliable product. Sometimes we'd make one change that would require many more to keep all the systems in balance. Even after you start selling your product you'll need to keep adding value to it to stay ahead of the evolving competition. Find ways to continually value engineer it to make it faster, stronger, more efficient, less expensive, more reliable ... whatever. Build, learn, and revise. Don't stop.

Thomas Edison provided a classic example of how much effort it can take to develop a reliable commercial product. As an inventor, Edison made a thousand unsuccessful attempts at inventing the light bulb. When a reporter asked, "How did it feel to fail a thousand times?" Edison replied, "I didn't fail a thousand times. The light bulb was an invention with a thousand steps." Edison, who created more than a thousand inventions and was one of the pioneers of General Electric, succeeded despite being severely hearing impaired and being told by teachers that he was "too stupid to learn anything." Ironically, he was fired from his first two jobs for being "non-productive."[17] More recently, James Dyson, the inventor of the Dual Cyclone vacuum cleaner and Pure Cool purifying fan, worked for four years and developed 5,127 prototypes while perfecting his vacuum cleaner.[18]

So be realistic. Developing a safe, cost effective, reliable product can take a lot of time and money. Don't rush the process or you risk a failed product and commercial rejection when you launch it.

There's a lot more to consider. For example, how do you market the product and/or service? Through reps that take orders, distributors who warehouse the products, direct sales door-to-door, to manufacturers of tiny houses, or on the internet, etc.? See chapter 6 for further details on those issues.

Business books should be fun to read as well as instructive. So, at the end of each chapter are fun examples/stories, inspired by real events, which demonstrate the principles in each chapter using the adventures of Professor Scooter Magee, the Startup Expert.

Scooter helps startups prevent Startup Suicide and achieve success while fighting the CIA and others. Think Professor Indiana Jones in Raiders of the Lost Ark *meets* Bar Rescue *or* Silicon Valley! *So, read on and enjoy Scooter's adventures and his practical startup legal and business lessons!*

Examples of the Failure to Plan: Fire, Ready, Aim at the Cowboy Café

In this chapter we meet Professor Scooter Magee, startup expert, who helps an inventor save money and demonstrates the value of a good business plan.

It was true. The Forbes *cover story said it. CNN and Fox News even agreed. Georgetown Professor Scooter Magee was a genius in fixing broken startups, turning innovative ideas into fortunes, and making companies millions. He was the "Startup Expert." Until he wasn't. Until something or someone turned his life upside down. Was it the CIA? Scooter had to figure things out and fast. Everything was closing in. Being roadkill was not an option.*

It started off as a good day for Scooter Magee. A day to enjoy. Good for him. But all too soon he would be careening down a slippery slope into hell. And he wouldn't have a clue who or what caused it.

For Scooter, nothing was as much fun as being an entrepreneur. It was a constant roller coaster ride. Success or failure was always just a phone call away. That's why he traveled around in his classic 1962 Austin Healey 3000 convertible helping startups get back on track. After thirty years as a startup lawyer, consultant, and professor, he'd pretty much seen it all. All the stupid things that he and hundreds of other startups had done. His passion was to prevent "Startup Suicides."

One Saturday morning, his friend Fred Delaney, amateur-class tinkerer, called Scooter. Fred was excited and wanted to meet right away for lunch. Scooter figured he'd better show up—Fred was a walking hand grenade who was as likely to blow up his own business as succeed. And Scooter was happy to get out of the house.

Around noon Scooter pulled off Langston Highway into the parking lot next to the tattoo parlor at the Cowboy Café—the last authentic dive bar in Arlington, Virginia. You knew that right away when you opened the door. There was a stuffed head of a steer with big horns sticking out of the wall, with the rest of its lop-sided body painted in awful, faded colors behind it. The air conditioner had been dripping on it for years. And there were signs all over the place, like "Hippies Use Side Doors" and "Beer Speaks. People Mumble." Over the kitchen was another sign, "Many People Have Eaten in This Kitchen and Gone on to Lead Normal, Healthy Lives."[19]

There was an old, dark, sticky atmosphere about the place. But for Scooter, it all added up to a comfortable feeling. *Thank God they'd never improved the place*, Scooter thought. *Like they say, "There are many arguments for doing it but no good reasons."* He'd been going there for years—it was authentic. When you're older, authenticity means a lot.

Scooter walked in the door. Kelly, the young server who had just cut her first country song on TikTok, walked toward him, pushing her long, brown hair behind her ear. "The usual?" That wasn't an ask; it was a confirmation. Whenever Kelly saw him coming in, she quickly poured a Diet Coke and placed his usual order with the cook for a chopped steak, medium-rare, buried in grilled onions and gravy. Scooter didn't experiment with sure things. He had good taste for bad food.

Fred was sitting in the back corner at Scooter's favorite booth, waiting to talk with him and trying to unstick his long-sleeved shirt from a brown glob of dried ketchup. Fred looked rumpled as usual in his wrinkled plaid shirt. He blended in well with the faded picture of three old cowboys on the wall behind him. He could have strutted right out of that picture. Five Miles was with him. Fred had named his dog "Five Miles" so he could say he walked five miles every day. Scooter loved dogs and Five Miles was easy to love. He was a spotted hound dog of questionable parentage with sad but knowing eyes. He didn't just lie on the floor; he turned around a couple of times and then flattened himself, spread eagle, like syrup on a pancake. Five Miles looked up at Scooter with those sad eyes, and when the food arrived Scooter placed a little chopped steak on a spoon, topped it with an onion and some gravy and slipped it to the hound, who gulped it up and then happily pancaked himself asleep.

Soon, Five Miles was snoring, but Fred was very much awake and excited. "Scooter," he said, "I need you to help me raise $300,000.

And quick! More folks are moving to trailers to retire. But the twenty bucks per month for electricity for heating and cooling is killing people on their retirement budgets. I've invented a four-phase air conditioner that goes on the roof and cuts the electric bill to zero!"

"How does it work?" Scooter asked.

"Well, that's still a secret but it captures energy from the electromagnetic fields all around us. us You don't need an electric compressor, which uses most of the electricity in an air conditioner. I've made a prototype that works; and listen to this! I've just signed a contract with a manufacturer to build a thousand units for only $300,000. We'll sell them for $500 each, make $500,000, and clear a profit of $200,000! Can you get me the $300,000? I need it by next Tuesday."

Scooter struggled for words. This was a mistake on so many levels that Scooter didn't know where to start, except he knew the more immediate problem was how to help Fred without hurting his feelings. Fred didn't know it yet, but he was committing "Startup Suicide." This was a classic "Fire, Ready, Aim" mistake. He was building the product first, based on nothing more than assumptions, without really knowing what the product should be, who the customer was, and what the competition was. Even worse, he was blowing $300,000 on one design that was almost certainly the wrong one.

"Please stop!" Scooter said. "Look, the concept could be technically interesting. But you're about to blow $300,000! See if you can get out of the contract."

"Why?" asked Fred, somewhat shocked.

"Lots of reasons. Let me explain. You need a business plan. As Yogi Berra said, 'If you don't know where you're going, you'll end up somewhere else.'"

For the next fifteen minutes, Scooter gave Fred a quick lesson on planning ahead and how to structure his startup's rollout to Ready, Aim, Fire. Instead, poor Fred had "Fired" without being ready or taking aim. The discussion was wide-ranging and included everything from the importance of market research to knowing what the customer wants, to rigorous field testing, safety, certification requirements, and more. All of which needed to be done before mass production.

When they were finishing lunch, Scooter said, "Look, I just dumped a lot of information on you. I'll send you a summary of what we just discussed. In the meantime, just find a way to get out of that contract before it explodes on you and you commit Startup Suicide. One of the biggest challenges for any startup is to minimize the chaos and stay focused on the big picture."

"Thanks for your time, Scooter," said Fred, as they walked out the door. Five miles woke up and looked at Scooter.

"Good dog!" Scooter said as he patted him. Scooter had no idea what his love of dogs was going to do to him in a few days. As for Fred, he looked as beaten down as a rented mule in a hailstorm, but at some level he knew Scooter was right.

Scooter went home and let himself enjoy the moment. He'd saved another lost startup soul. He was at the top of his game.

"I've come a long way from those days as a poor kid," he thought. Last month's article in *Forbes* was the cherry on top. *Forbes* dubbed him the "Startup Expert." He thought things were looking good. But he was wrong. Very wrong.

When Scooter got home, he had a call waiting for him on his voice mail. It sounded like the caller's name was "Fingers" or something. He called back.

11:00 hours, July 4
Threat Analysis Directorate
SCIF 403x, CIA Headquarters, Langley, VA

Chuck "Bulldog" McCatchum, directorate chief, was barking as usual. "Everyone sit down and shut up. You too, Jenkins. Raul, that means you! Forget it's the Fourth of July and listen up. We've got our own fireworks show right here." He threw a picture up on the screen. "We just got this picture inside a jail from our Warsaw link. It was taken by a Cambodian spy locked up in an interrogation facility there. High quality, 2800 xprs and flawless pixels. The problem is he was in solitary confinement, naked, had been strip searched, and locked up for a week. So how was he still able to send a picture to his handlers? If this is a super camera with transmission capabilities, we've got to figure it out and fast, or nothing will ever be secret. In the meantime, get the word out to your contacts at the NSA and FBI to pick up any unusual intel chatter about cameras. We need leads, guys. Don't just sit there. Get out of here and get on it!"

One Week Later, 09:00 hours, July 11
Angkor Wat, Cambodia

Souk Kaep was tired of this. It was the third time this week the CIA's miniature spy camera-microphone had failed at Angkor Wat. It could have been anything—rats, bats, birds, or rain. He guessed rain. That's what you get when you hide a KW-23 super-sensitive camera in a strangler tree trunk during rainy season.

He parked on the west side of the four-hundred-acre Angkor Wat site, the largest temple complex in the world, with over one thousand buildings. It was only 09:00 but already 33 Celsius. Steam from last night's rain was rising off the broken pavement. He walked over the weathered stone bridge across the three-mile-long moat around the temple and dodged the puddles and scurrying rats on the gravel path to the massive four pillar building. There he merged with a noisy Italian tour group to avoid notice (while noticing the cute blonde tour guide in the miniskirt) and climbed the ancient steps to the first level. Souk stopped in the entrance hallway overlooking one of the big courtyards. There it was: the 100-foot strangler fig tree with giant roots crawling up the crumbling sandstone wall. It had totally swallowed the host tree and was holding up the crumbling ancient wall. That was good. There hadn't been any serious wall maintenance there since the year 1150, when Suryavarman II of the Khmer Empire built it.

He waited for the group of noisy tourists to pass. Then he took what looked like a smart phone out of his pocket, pressed three buttons, and watched the meter. Nothing. He shinnied up the tree a meter or two, scaping his leg on the bark, to a fork in the branches, pulled out the old camera, and popped in a new one. Souk called Chan at the safe house on his encoded cell phone.

"Chan, I just put in a new camera, are you getting the data?"

"Give me a minute; I'm in the middle of a soccer game! Can you call back; the score's tied!"

"Look, Chan, look, this is important, are you getting the data?"

"Not yet. Oh … here it comes. Yeah, looks good, I see you. What'd you do to your pants?"

"I ripped them climbing the stupid tree. Next time you're doing this."

"Hey, stop complaining. Switch places? Sure. I'm double-locked in this stinky old place with no windows and a squeaking fan for twelve hours a day and you're running around outside scoping out the cute blondes."

The new camera started taking 180-degree panoramic pictures and listening to conversations up to thirty meters away. Every four hours it would batch-send the data to the safe house in Siem Reap, six kilometers away, to be recorded and analyzed.

For centuries, Angkor Wat has been a place of intrigue and deals, most recently drug deals, where people from around the world could meet and do what they wanted without being noticed in the crowds of tourists. As Somerset Maugham would have said, it was a "sunny place for shady people," and one of the thousand places around the world the CIA was constantly watching.

More dark clouds were forming as Souk hurried from the temple to avoid the coming rain. Food and souvenir vendors were hustling tourists into their tents on both sides of the path to his car. He stopped to see an old woman in a torn shawl under the drooping tent. He needed to buy a bird in a cage for a Buddhist "merit release."

"Hi Jorani, it's that time again," said Souk, smiling. He looked at the many bird cages hanging from the top of the tent. "I'll take that one over there," he said, pointing to a black metal cage with a small brown bird hopping around in it.

She handed him the cage, they chatted for a while, she took his money, and said "Au Kun" or *thank you*. The bird bounced around as he hurried to his car and got there just as the rain began.

Following ancient Buddhist merit customs, Souk and his family would mentally put the weight of all their cares on that unsuspecting little bird, open the cage door, and let it go. It was just a small prayer offering—one of 500,000 caged birds released every year in

Cambodia—but it meant a lot to his family spiritually. To the bird, not so much. Ninety percent of released birds soon died. But it was easier using birds than crabs, fish, or ants.

When he got to the safe house, Chan was already scanning last week's downloads.

"Haven't found anything yet," he mumbled as he sipped a cup of cold coffee then threw the rest away.

CIA's instructions were clear. Immediately report any intel with unusual talk with the word "camera." Chan looked at the scanner just as it beeped. There already were 350 hits for the word "camera."

"Ugh."

For the next two hours Souk and Chan focused on different Boolean word searches, "Camera and this," "camera and that." Nothing. Finally, Souk searched for "camera and money." It beeped! Luckily, there was only one recording. He put on his earphones and listened to it. Maybe there was something to hear but there was too much static and background noise to know. For the next half hour, he tried different software filters to reduce the noise and tease out the words.

Finally, he heard the key phrases before the static kicked in too loud again. "Wow!" Souk excitedly opened the secure link to Langley, uploaded the results, and hit "send." He leaned back in his chair as a slow grin came across his face. *This was pretty good timing*, he thought to himself. *My one-year employment contract is up for renewal next month. Amazing luck!* He looked at the bird that had stopped bouncing around and was watching him intently. "Thanks, buddy, I think I'll keep you a little longer. Have some more birdseed!"

14:15 hours, July 10
CIA's Threat Analysis Directorate
Langley, Virginia

"Bulldog, our man in Siem Reap just messaged in. Got a hit at Angkor Wat. Listen to this." Johnson pushed play.

"Look, Cold Fingers, you want this camera? Then give me [static] and the full 250,000 now. No more bargaining or I'll walk. Plenty of other folks want it."

"Okay, okay…" a second voice responded. Then there was static and the sound of rain. The recording ended with a final burst of static.

"Johnson, get tech on the line and tell them we need better mics in the field. This is ridiculous! The guys that build these are dumber than a downhill cabbage!"

"Okay, Boss, will do, but who pays two fifty for a camera? I think we've got something here. I ran a voice scan analysis. There's a high probability it's Cold Fingers Gelato, formerly a Cambodian hit man for the Khmer Rouge and now an international mercenary. He was Last seen in DC. NSA picked him up yesterday in Cambodia making a call to some guy's cell phone at Georgetown University, a Professor Magee. They're talking about lunch at The TOMBS."

"Ok, Johnson, get the US Attorney's office to put a tap on Magee's cell phone. Let's see what's going on and get your team ready at The TOMBS. Check out this Magee character to see what's up with him and if he's got any mob connections. Yea, maybe we've finally got something to work with!"

Chapter 2

MANAGE YOUR STARTUP'S RISKS

If you treat risk management as a part-time job, you might soon find yourself looking for one.

—Deloitte white paper[1]

Business is risky. Even risk management is risky. I went to find a good risk management quote on the internet but downloaded a virus instead! Risk management is one of those things that startups don't usually think about. But they should. There are all kinds of risks to startups and businesses. They can be strategic, operational, financial, and more. They can be subtle or obvious, harmless or fatal. But you need to be able to identify, assess, mitigate, and monitor them. How you handle those risks could be more important than anything else you do in running the company. That's why risk management is one of *The 7 Secret Keys to Startup Success*.

BIG RISKS IN SHEEP'S CLOTHING

Sometimes a big risk looks like a little one. Here's an example. One day I got an e-mail out of the blue from a lawyer. He was screaming that one of my startup clients (I'll call him "Joe") had "glued" a marketing flyer on his windshield. He called my client names that I won't repeat. He said he would post horrible things about the company on Joe's website and threatened to sue. I looked the lawyer up and he was a litigator from an Ivy League law school with a major law firm.

I e-mailed Joe, "Call me right away and don't do anything until we talk." The first mitigation step in risk management is "don't make things worse."

Joe's a nice guy and I figured that he would want to call the lawyer right away and apologize, even though the lawyer was a pure ego-driven jerk and my client hadn't glued anything to his windshield. The flyer had just gotten wet and stuck to the windshield.

The risk here is that the lawyer could be a walking nitroglycerine distributor, ready to explode for any reason. Some lawyers, unfortunately, will sue over anything and everything. I've even been sued by people I had never known. To a hammer, everything is a nail, and to some clients and lawyers, every person is a lottery ticket disguised as a lawsuit. Joe was raising money from investors and if he had gotten sued, that would have killed his fundraising and his startup.

So, What's the Best Way to Handle a Risk Like This?

1. First, Joe could apologize. But if Joe called up the lawyer and said one wrong thing, the company might get sued. Joe could be sued personally as well. I've been in suits where lawyers even sued spouses of the defendants just to get more leverage in the case. Clients don't have as much experience as lawyers in these matters and Joe might just accidentally say something to make things worse and trigger a suit.
2. Or Joe could do nothing. He could assume it's a lawyer who had a bad day and wanted to throw his weight around. So why not just do nothing and let the lawyer cool off? But then the lawyer would get away with it which seems unjust.

> **TIP: SOMETIMES LETTING THINGS MARINATE IS THE BEST ANSWER TO A CRISIS.**

When there's a crisis, it's human nature that our first reaction is fight or flight. Sometimes, however, the best thing you can do is nothing.

Just let it marinate, let folks calm down, and then more calmly assess the situation and your options.

In this case, I told Joe that he should do nothing and just let the lawyer calm down. I wanted to retaliate myself, because the lawyer was violating the bar ethics rules about using inappropriate language, and I was mad that he was treating Joe this way. That would make me feel good, but it wouldn't be in the client's best interest because it might start a lawsuit and lead to months of proceedings with the bar. And lawsuits can take years. As one lawyer once told me, "I never suggest a lawsuit unless it's about money and lots of it." In this case, there weren't even any monetary damages. And lawsuits are like wars: easy to get into and hard to get out of. I told Joe that if he felt he just had to do something, he should let me handle it very carefully. That would put down a marker and show the lawyer that Joe had legal representation to defend the company and countersue if necessary.

As the CEO of this startup, you're used to thinking that the company is your baby and you can do anything you want with it. But once you're a company, it's not your part-time hobby anymore. And it isn't just about you. You must think about the impact of whatever you do on your employees, customers, and investors. Sometimes marination is salvation!

WHAT IS RISK MANAGEMENT?

Dealing with these kinds of problems is risk management. Let's look at a few basic risk management concepts that can be useful for startups.

Risk management is the "identification, evaluation, and prioritization of risks"[2] followed by steps to minimize, monitor, and control bad events.

Risks can come from anywhere, internally and externally. And they span every area of operations from design, production, legal, financial, accidents, to government relations, marketing, and natural disasters.

Risk management is far too big a subject to cover in detail here. Here we'll focus on a couple of the most common risks for startups and how to avoid them.

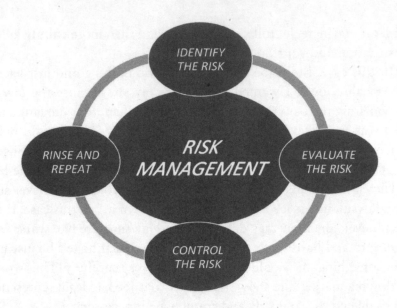

IDENTIFY THE RISK

Some risks are obvious, like getting a threatening letter from a law-yer or having an employee sue you. But don't just look at your current risks. Brainstorm with your team about what risks the company may have in the future. This will take some time but it's worth it. In the process, you might find ways to improve your products or services as well. Of course, no matter how well you do this there are the "black swan" events that you'll probably miss, like the sudden worldwide impact of COVID-19 beginning in 2020. Ultimately, the answer may be a bigger line of credit to survive those unexpected long periods of reduced income.

EVALUATE THE RISK

Even with the obvious risks, ask yourself, "Why did this happen?" Try to get to the root cause to avoid it happening again. When evaluating the risk, think about how likely is it, over what period of time, and how great is the potential impact on the company? Then focus on the risks that score highest in these categories.

CONTROL THE RISK

What can you do to mitigate or eliminate the risk?

Find the Cause, Prevent the Real Risk

First, think about the root cause—the real cause that may be hidden. If a product failed, is it because of bad materials, assembly, failure of communication, or some bad training six months ago? Dig deep. Keep peeling the onion. Ask five questions in a row to get deeper. Often the real cause isn't obvious.

The Best Way to Limit Risk Is to Prevent It

Get your employees to help you spot risks before any harm is done. You could create anonymous risk reporting by your employees and reward those who uncover and mitigate risks.

Revise the Product or Service to Reduce the Risk

If it's a product that is likely to fail and produce damages or injuries, how can you reduce those risks? If you can't figure that out, understand that certain products or markets just may be too risky for your business. You can't swim up a waterfall. Get out before you dig a bigger hole.

> **TIP: YES, YOU NEED INSURANCE!**

Get Insurance

You always should have insurance to protect you and your company from liability from lawsuits. It typically only costs a few thousand dollars but it lets you sleep at night. Once you get insurance, adding higher coverage amounts such as via an umbrella insurance policy can be much less expensive per thousand dollars of coverage than the base coverage. Here are three kinds of insurance you might consider. Your broker can shop for the best deals.

General Liability Insurance

Usually, the first type of insurance policy that companies buy is a "broad form" (meaning broad coverage) general liability insurance policy. This insures your company against personal injury claims, fire, flood, and other damage. It can come in many varieties and extra coverages (riders) may include protection against theft of intellectual property, cyberattacks, and employment discrimination claims. It also can include coverage for false and misleading statements (libel and slander) and claims against employees as well as attorney's fees, interest charges, and defense costs.

Directors and Officers Insurance (D&O Insurance)

This policy protects directors and officers, committee chairs, and other specifically named officials from liability. In the simplest terms, if you are acting on behalf of the company and do something or fail to do something (errors and omissions or E&O) that leads to liability, you're covered by the insurance if you're doing it in good faith, not for your personal benefit, and it is not an intentional wrongful act.

Special Insurance Lines

If you're in a particular line of business with unique risks, such as flying airplanes, operating on the water, or selling food, a typical general liability policy might not be sufficient. You may need a rider or a special line of insurance. Be sure to check with your insurance agent or broker whenever you enter a new line of business to be sure you're covered.

Make sure that you read and understand everything in the policy, particularly the exclusions from coverage. Some policies have so many exclusions they look like non-insurance policies. I ran into a situation a while ago when my client was subpoenaed to produce documents in a lawsuit. But an exclusion stated that because the client wasn't named as a defendant, the insurance policy didn't provide any coverage for the expenses involved in complying with the subpoena which required many days of document research.

Pass off the Risk to Another Party

Another way to reduce risk is to pass it off contractually. For example, if you have a distributor selling your product you could try to pass the risks off to it. The distributor who accepts the risk would then be agreeing to "indemnify" your company—which means pay for any claims. Then, if the distributor were to make exaggerated or false claims to increase sales or the product fails, resulting in a claim against both of you, the distributor would be on the hook for damages, not your company.

Contracts can also provide for limitations on liability such as not exceeding specified dollar amounts or exempting certain types of claims. For example, one party may agree to indemnify the other for all claims up to one million dollars except in the case of intentional wrongful actions or gross negligence. Another common example is:

> In no event shall either party be liable to the other party for any incidental, consequential, indirect, special, or punitive damages (including, but not limited to, lost profits, business interruption, loss of business information or other pecuniary loss) regardless of whether such liability is based on breach of contract, tort (including negligence), strict liability, breach of warranties, failure of essential purpose or otherwise and even if the party has been advised of the possibility of such damages.

You also can consider sharing risks. For example, in construction contracts, parties with different trades (construction or maintenance services) often join in a joint venture to make a unified bid on a major project. They can use a joint venture agreement that shares the risks of performance and liability. More complex projects may have a risk officer who can focus on risks and help reduce or avoid them.

Risk Retention
If the risk is small and the remedy is great, you can simply retain the risk, accept any loss, and pay for it either out of earnings or with insurance. All risks not avoided are "retained" (the "retention").

Own the Risk
You can accept the risk and budget for it. Or turn it into a new profit center. When I was building power stations, we offered a maintenance and insurance option for customers which guaranteed replacement of failed parts. We prepared detailed spreadsheets that identified each component and system that was likely to fail,

over what time period, and what the cost would be in materials and labor to fix it. Then we priced the maintenance and insurance high enough so that even in a bad-case scenario we could still make a profit.

Isolate the Risk in a Separate Company

You also can limit risk by creating a separate entity to handle a particular product line or service. For example, in the residential real estate rental business, it's common practice to put each rental property in a separate company. Then, if there's a big claim against one company for a slip and fall or other tenant injury, it won't affect the assets or credit of your other businesses.

This approach is common in "project financing." Usually when a company defaults on a loan or has other liability, claimants have a claim to all the shareholders' assets and cash flow. This is called "recourse financing." In contrast, with project financing, a separate, limited liability "special purpose vehicle" (SPV) is created for the project. Then, if the SPV defaults on a loan or incurs other liability, the only recourse by the claimants is against the SPV's assets, not against the partners who invested in it and own it. This is called "non-recourse financing."

Put Your Personal Assets in Trusts and Other Vehicles

If your business gets sued, you may be personally sued as well. Often, you can get out of being personally liable unless you were directly involved in the acts creating liability or your assets and the business assets were comingled. But if you can't escape liability, then the plaintiff may get a judgment against you and your personal assets. This could destroy your life's savings. To help prevent this, you should consult with an asset protection attorney. There are many options to reduce this liability. These are very fact specific depending on your situation and the particular state statutes involved. But some of these options include:

Transfer Your Assets
Put your business assets in another's name, such as your spouse or partner.

Use LLCs and Trusts

Create LLCs or other entities for your assets and then place those entities in a trust. Once the assets are in the trust you're no longer the legal owner of the assets. But you still could retain control over them as if you owned them. Then the assets could be out of reach from bankruptcy or a creditor; note that this varies a lot with state law. Also, if a lawyer looks for your assets and sees that you don't have any, the odds of being sued can be substantially reduced.

Put Assets in Life Insurance

You could put some of your assets in life insurance. Creditors are mostly interested in current cash, so waiting for the death benefit after someone dies is usually not an attractive option for them. Depending on the state law involved, the insurance proceeds paid to beneficiaries might be protected from creditors or bankruptcy.

Put Assets Offshore

There are more sophisticated remedies as well, such as putting your assets in special purpose offshore entities. Countries like the Cayman Islands, Nevis, Cyprus, and Switzerland are popular choices for asset protection, privacy, and minimizing or avoiding taxes. This would make it even more difficult and expensive for a plaintiff to proceed against you.

Continually Learn About the Risks

Educate yourself about the risks in your line of business. What kind of lawsuits are being brought and by whom? Check with your attorney and/or join a trade association and find out what the key risks are and how others are dealing with them.

MONITOR, RINSE, AND REPEAT

Schedule a time to go over the steps in this risk reduction process on a regular basis. This is not a one-time exercise.

SOME OF THE MOST COMMON STARTUP MISTAKES: "PIERCING THE CORPORATE VEIL" AND MORE

Now let's look at some of the most common mistakes that startups make that can lead to Startup Suicide.

TIP: WATCH WHAT YOU SAY; IT COULD CREATE A BINDING CONTRACT!

Failure to Get Things in Writing

If it's important, put it in writing and be specific to prevent mis-understandings. When agreements aren't reduced to writing, it creates misunderstandings. Misunderstandings lead to hurt feelings and anger—the rocket fuel that drives lawsuits.

Let's look at a typical startup CEO talking with Janet, his employee:

> **Janet:** Hey, I've been working for almost a year now on this startup and haven't been paid. I'm responsible for 30 percent of the total time it's taken to build this startup. I realize that the company's still trying to raise money but when can you pay me?
> **CEO:** Janet, don't worry, I'll take good care of you.

Two years later, the company's making lots of money. Janet finds a lawyer and sues the company for 30 percent of the current total value and income of the company. Her argument is that she's entitled to 30 percent of the company's equity and income because she created 30 percent of it and there was an implied-in-fact oral contract based on the CEO's promise to "take good care" of her. An implied-in-fact contract is not a written contract. It is a contract that a court of law implies. But it's just as binding as a written contract. The elements of an implied-in-fact contract are:

- mutuality of intent regarding an offer and acceptance of the offer;
- consideration—something given in exchange for a promise (In this case the consideration was the continued performance by Janet in relying on the CEO's promise, sometimes called "detrimental reliance");
- lack of ambiguity in the terms; and
- authority to make the offer, which the CEO clearly had.[3]

The CEO's casual statement and Janet's reliance on it could tie the company up in knots for years defending the case and pending litigation would scare many investors away—or give clever ones an excuse to invest at a lower valuation.

This easily could have been avoided. First, the CEO shouldn't have made such a statement. Second, the CEO should have had a written employment agreement with Janet that clearly described her compensation or lack of it. Without something in writing, it's just her word against the CEO's. And juries tend to go for the underdog. Third, the company's employee handbook should include language that voids all employment agreements that are not in writing.

Failure to Execute the Basic Organizational Documents

Lots of startups don't have all the necessary organizational documents. They file online to create the entity, think they're done, and launch into business. Then, when they try to enter a contract or raise money, they aren't even authorized to sign a contract because they never appointed any authorized officers and they don't have a business license. Under some circumstances, this could allow another party to challenge and even void any contracts.

Here are some typical basic documents that an entity should have:

A Certificate of Incorporation

The "certificate of incorporation" is the state-issued document that creates a corporation. The comparable document for an LLC is called a "certificate of organization" or something similar depending on the jurisdiction. This is the state-issued document that creates the legal entity. You can file online for that with the state office that creates businesses.

Bylaws (for a Corporation) or an "Operating Agreement" for an LLC

These are the basic organizational rules governing the operation of the entity. They describe how the entity operates, who the shareholders are, and how to issue shares. It protects the company and officers by limiting liability and includes other high-level corporate matters. See Appendix 1 for an example of an abridged bylaws document.

Organization Action in Writing or "Writing in Lieu of the Organizational Meeting"
This document provides the resolutions that are approved at the organizational meeting of the company, such as the appointment of officers and/or members of a board of directors, setting the fiscal year, issuing shares of "stock" for a corporation (or "Membership Units" if it's an LLC), creating committees, etc. Like other documents, it can be signed by the organizers without having an in-person meeting. See Appendix 2 for an example.

Business License
This is the state, county, or local license to operate the business. It usually costs a hundred dollars or so annually. Some jurisdictions don't require a license until the company exceeds some annual amount of gross revenues.

Zoning Permit
This is issued by the local government. It tells the government what kind of a business you will have, such as a consulting or manufacturing business and the number of parking spaces required. Sometimes the zoning permit is issued as a part of the business license process.

Registration with the State Tax Office
This is a simple process that you can usually do online and there's no charge (except for the taxes you'll have to pay later!).

IRS Federal Employee Identification Number (EIN or FEIN)
You will need to get a tax ID number from the IRS for your new entity. You can do this online at irs.gov or on the phone with the IRS.

Setting Up a Separate Company Bank Account and Records
You need to keep the new entity's books and records separate from your personal or any other accounts. Have an accountant help with this if necessary to get it done correctly.

Piercing the Corporate Veil
When talking with clients for the first time, I'll ask them if they have an operating agreement or bylaws and have appointed officers in writing. If they haven't done these things, then they might not have the authority to sign contracts, and the contracts or other documents could be voided. In addition, if the company doesn't have separate books and records from the founder(s) then it looks as if the founder(s) are acting personally and not in their company capacity. This can lead to "piercing the corporate veil." This is a court's action that sets aside the entity's limited liability protections. The result is that officers and directors are now personally liable for the company's actions and debts, etc. Courts are reluctant to pierce the corporate veil unless there is misconduct, such as an intermingling of personal and company assets when persons use a company for personal purposes or fraudulent transactions.

Not Using a Lawyer
Yes, lawyers can be expensive. But mistakes can be much more expensive. You should run major decisions and contracts by an attorney until you feel comfortable that you understand the way to do things without incurring undue risk. It's much easier not to scramble an egg than it is to unscramble it.

One of the most common causes of lawsuits is misunderstandings. Those can be minimized by reducing agreements to a well-written contract drafted by an attorney and signed by all parties. Non-lawyers draft contracts all the time, but this usually results in gaps in how they're worded that can lead to misunderstandings or other problems. Doing this the right way helps prevent parties from believing different things about the same deal which can lead to arguments and litigation.

You should also get a good financial adviser—not just a book-keeper—so that you can make good financial plans and decisions, legally minimize taxes, etc.

Failure to Raise Enough Money on Time

Raising money is very difficult. Understandably, lenders and inves-tors want to minimize their risk. They'd love to see quarter after quarter of increasing profitability before investing in the company. But you don't have any of that when you start up. You need to allow lots of time—many months—to raise the necessary first round of funds. And if possible, it would be great to raise enough money to carry the company through twelve to eighteen months of operating expenses ("the burn rate"). That way you can focus on growing the business and help avoid sleepless nights of worrying about running out of money. See more on this in chapter 5.

Failure to Get and Act on Advice

Sure, you're a hot shot entrepreneur, probably good at doing some things, maybe even excellent. But don't let that go to your head. You probably don't know enough about many aspects of running a busi-ness. These include legal, finance, marketing, PR, sales, compliance, personnel, management, etc. Take an honest look at your knowl-edge and judgment gaps and build a team to fill those gaps. Then be humble, learn to listen to them, and ask for help.

Examples of Risks: Cold Fingers Gelato at The TOMBS

Every startup faces risks. Scooter shows how to use time and other strategies to mitigate risks ... even extreme risks.

Meanwhile
Playa Vik Hotel, Mansa Beach, José Ignacio, Uruguay

Señor Vincent Montevideo, the imposing chairman of Zapata, the largest fashion empire in South America, was lounging on a couch around the rectangular fire pit at the Playa Vik Hotel on Mansa beach in the chic Uruguayan village of José Ignacio. The crowds had gone. He was enjoying the quiet with his second Cohiba Siglo VI, rated at 93 points by *Cigar Aficionado*. He ran his fingers through his thick black and grey hair and slowly savored the woody notes and the hint of vanilla. It was smooth all the way down to his knuckles. The smoke was spiraling up. He wondered which way the fickle winds would blow the smoke—and him.

It was magic hour and the golden sunlight was flickering over the top of the gentle waves. He took in the panoramic view of the coast that looked even better after an hour of margaritas. The Vik was in a class by itself—the titanium walls, the huge, sculpted bronze door (a modern interpretation of Ghiberti's Doors at Florence's Baptistery), and the Patagonian ebony floors that flowed from inside to the terraces on the beach.

That was all good. But the tax thing wasn't. Especially since his only daughter Scarlett was involved. "Taxes are government-created cancer," he mumbled "They spread their insatiable tentacles until they strangle all the healthy cells in a business."

Scarlett was president of Zapata S.A. Brazil, Zapata's biggest South American division. She had been doing a great job. A natural at business. Vincent smiled with pride as he remembered how, when she was only two, she just couldn't sit still. If there was a fence or rock, she'd run to climb it and she was still climbing. Sure, she had every advantage being born to his family, but she would have made it without that. With her business sense and charm, profits had been going up over 20 percent each year. She was a hard driving CEO.

But one thing he had learned about her management style: You could tell her what to do, but never tell her how to do it. That was her territory and you better not invade it or it would backfire and there'd be hell to pay.

But then a pandemic hit, sales crashed, and Zapata desperately needed more money. Vincent got a $100-million investment from Asian investors. Scarlett signed all the papers. Sure, the 20 percent interest rate was too high, but there was no choice. His lawyer told him the deal was tax free because it was based in Cyprus. But his lawyer was wrong, messed up the paperwork, and the tax authorities placed a $30-million lien on Scarlett's division, parent Zapata, and personally on Scarlett and Vincent. Their stock plummeted from $125 to sixteen US dollars.

Then it somehow got even worse. It turned out the money was hot money from an organized crime ring. Scarlett and Vincent were both under criminal investigation. Scarlett had panicked and fled to the United States and Vincent hadn't heard from her for weeks. That wasn't like her. Vincent was ashamed of what had happened and what he had done to Scarlett. He needed to fix this. Whatever it took.

Now it was getting dark. The waiter took away the pitcher and his empty glass. The cigar had turned to ashes. Vincent looked out into the ocean. The waves were cresting higher now. The ocean had swallowed the sun and all the beauty was gone.

***

The planes flying down the Potomac to Reagan were loud and low as Scarlett paced the floor in her penthouse suite at the Enclave Residences in Georgetown. From her terrace she could see Key Bridge to the West and the Kennedy Center and Washington Monument to the East. But she wasn't looking at any of that. She was checking her watch. Her Christian Dior Grand Bal, mother of pearl, 211 diamond watch. Despite all that, it also told time. About as well as a Timex. They'd be here in five minutes. *When are those Xanex extended-release pills going to kick in?*

The doorbell rang. Scarlett took a deep breath and reluctantly opened it. "Ms. Montevideo, I'm Special Agent JW McKinney, FBI. We talked yesterday. This is Jason Kingston, CIA." They showed her their badges.

"Can ... can I get... you something to drink?"

Kingston scanned the rooms for electronic devices, then, while out of Scarlett's sight, he took pictures of her medicine cabinet and bedroom drawers and closets.

"No, thanks, we just came from the coffee shop downstairs. Thanks for seeing us. Could you please turn off that cell phone? Thanks. Now, if it's okay with you, why don't we just get to it?"

"Oh ... okay."

"We know everything. You're in a heap of trouble."

"I don't know what you're talking about. If you have anything to say, you can say it to my lawyer." *If only I had one in the US,* she thought to herself.

"We don't need to say much. Just look at FBI Exhibits 1 through 10." He handed her a thick file labeled *Secret, Scarlett Montevideo, Criminal Investigation.* Kingston continued. "Exhibit 1 is the Uruguay tax fraud matter. That alone could mean twenty years for you and your father. Exhibit 2 is the conspiracy to launder Asian money and Exhibits 3-10 are other potential charges the prosecutors would probably add. You get the picture. And believe me, you and your father really don't want to see the inside of a Uruguayan jail."

Scarlett didn't say anything. She just looked down and hoped they didn't see her left leg trembling under her skirt.

"But we're here because we can make all this go away. We figure you didn't intend to do anything wrong—mostly you were in the wrong place at the wrong time. Here's the deal. The FBI wants your cooperation on the Cambodian espionage investigation I mentioned on the phone. We think there's a lot more there. And the CIA can use your international business contacts. But mostly, the CIA needs you to help on some special projects from time to time."

"What do you mean 'special projects?'"

"Mostly observing. Talking to people to gain information. Nothing dangerous. Just some occasional help. We'll train you for two weeks at the Farm, the CIA's facility in Southern Virginia. If you fully cooperate with the FBI and work with us for two years, we'll make all the legal troubles go away for you and your father. On the other hand, if you don't agree or work with us or drop out, then well ... you know what happens."

"Slow down. How do I know that Uruguay would even agree to drop the charges?"

"Ever since the extradition agreement between the United States and Uruguay in '73, we've been doing these kinds of deals. We help them; they help us."

"If I helped, when would it start?"

"The day after tomorrow. Just a little assignment."

Her eyes widened. She swallowed. "The day after tomorrow?"

"Yes."

"You'll put this in writing, right?"

"Yes. We'll get it signed by the general counsel's office at the FBI and CIA, and you can talk with their offices tomorrow to confirm it. We'll get you confirmation from Uruguay as well. And the US will block Uruguay from extraditing you there until all charges are dropped."

"If I decide to do this, what's the 'little assignment' you mentioned?"

"Just a nice little lunch, you'll see."

Then, they left.

The Next Day

It was 2:30 a.m. Scooter slid out of bed, put on his jeans, a polo shirt, and his Dockers with the nylon rawhide laces that came untied three times a day. Those laces drove him crazy. What is nylon doing in rawhide laces anyway? It's like putting pantyhose on the Marlboro Man. Georgia Tech once did a research report on why shoelaces always came untied and found that it was the long loose ends that flapped around. *I hope no one paid too much for that study*, Scooter thought. Made sense though. Loose ends need attention, with shoes and anything else in life.

He padded down the stairs to his basement workshop. There were the usual tools, and the most important thing: a big box filled with what looked like random junk. There was scrap wood, Styrofoam, batteries, and some random hardware that Zoe, Zadie, and Lily, his granddaughters, used to build fun stuff with Poppy. His small tool bag was already packed. He grabbed it, left his house on N. 52 St., Arlington, Virginia, and got in the Healey. Scooter pulled the choke out one notch and listened to the low rumble of the muffler and resonator, heard the car cough and gurgle until the water temperature gauge on the far-left side of the dashboard crept up. He pushed the choke back in and the engine started purring.

Two miles later he was at the Virginia side of Chain Bridge. He could hear the Potomac River splashing below though he couldn't see it in the fog. He pulled into a dirt parking lot at the West entrance to the bridge and killed the engine. During the day, local fishermen filled up the small lot with their pickups. They usually fished with a random branch jammed into a coke bottle so they could wind the line around the bottle. Old school. Now, no one was around. Through the fog he could barely see the traffic light where the end of the bridge met Canal Road. He got out and walked quickly down there. Scooter hid a penny-sized electronic device under the railing near the traffic light. Next, he measured the width of the inbound lanes on the bridge and Canal Road, and found the frequency of the wireless signal controlling the traffic light. He hurried back to the car and lowered the convertible roof. Scooter turned on some switches on the tall black box strapped to the passenger seat. He adjusted the modified lasers on the box to focus outward at the required angles, locked them in place, and dialed the traffic light's frequency into the black box. All the lights on the box now glowed a steady green. He flicked a final switch and watched the traffic light at the end of the bridge change from red and lock onto green. All was ready.

Scooter looked for any cars. There weren't any. He slowly drove from the parking lot onto the bridge. Still no traffic.

It was a "go!" He took a long, deep breath then floored the car until it hit exactly 100 mph. Scooter raced to the end of the bridge, spun the wheel ninety degrees hard right, did a beautiful, controlled right-turn skid onto Canal Road in a cloud of smoke and burning rubber, then accelerated again when the Healey had settled perfectly straight, right smack in the middle of the inbound lane.

"Nailed it!" he yelled. A quarter of a mile later he downshifted hard, hit the brakes, and heard the car backfire in celebration. Scooter breathed again. After another mile he made a leisurely U-turn and drove home. *This data is going to be really useful*, he thought, smiling. In fact, it would turn out to be far more useful than he imagined.

As he pulled into his driveway, his stopwatch said 19.07 minutes; one minute less than he had planned. Scooter lived for precision, whether he was driving or writing a legal brief. To him, chaos was an unacceptable personal failure. He loved to race the Healy at Summit Point raceway in West Virginia but hated to lose. On the track, you needed guts, but the professional racers knew that winning was really about the many little things, the physics, the things you *can* measure. What was the best entry angle on each turn? When do you hit the brakes to unweight the rear wheels so the car skids around to the best angle with the right balance to accelerate on the next straightaway? Where do you put your thumb on the wheel so you don't break it in a panic turn? He was going to practice, again and again until he reached perfection.

It was late, but before going to bed Scooter went to his computer and researched the name Cold Fingers. If this guy was "the" Cold Fingers he was reading about, the one with the Cambodian mob connections, this wasn't good. *Whoa, this is the guy who wants to meet for lunch? Maybe I should cancel. On the other hand, if I do, I might make it worse. Guess I should at least see what's up.* Scooter did some more research and finally went back to bed.

***

The next morning, while Scooter was having breakfast, his wife Megan came by. They had been separated for a few weeks now, and she was living nearby at her mother's house.

"Morning Megan."

"Morning," Megan said, more softly than usual. "I'm just coming by to pick up some clothes."

"Okay. Something wrong?"

"Not sure. Mom has been sounding funny lately. She's never like that. I think something's wrong."

"What do you think it is?"

"I don't know but she didn't sound so good. I hope she's not sick or something. She and Dad have been acting a little funny with each other. Like a little distant."

"Distant?"

"They haven't been acting the way they usually do with each other."

"I hope everything's okay," Scooter said, as he cut up three strawberries and put his favorite Trader Joe's thick-sliced raisin toast in the toaster.

Chirp! Screeeeeech!

They turned to the window and saw a squirrel being thrown a good ten feet from the bird feeder onto the big leaves of the Oak Leaf Hydrangea.

"Got Charlie again!" Scooter yelled. The dark grey squirrel slid off a foot-wide leaf, knocked off a few flowers on the way, got back up on his feet, shook himself a couple of times to get the rest of the flowers off his fur, gave a long stare at Scooter, and bounded away.

"That's three flying squirrels this week!" Scooter said proudly. Megan scowled.

"It's okay, they're not hurt. I once saw a squirrel get electrocuted at the top of an electric pole, fall to the ground, and walk away just fine. Remember, that's why I planted that hydrangea with the big leaves where it is. It's their trampoline."

"That squirrel needs a good lawyer," replied Megan.

"Need me to help with anything?" Scooter asked.

"Nope."

"Okay, bye then. I'll be in the office for a while, and then some guy wants to meet me at The TOMBS for lunch in Georgetown. Something about help with starting a new camera company."

"Okay."

Scooter got up and tucked in his shirt. His belt was becoming more essential after eating a quarter pint of Ben & Jerry's butterscotch ice cream every night for years. His socks didn't match but Scooter didn't care. He wandered around the kitchen. The house was quiet. His old refrigerator used to hum. Like the heartbeat of the house. But the heartbeat was gone. The house was empty. The only sound was the icemaker in the new refrigerator ... randomly dropping a few ice cubes.

Scooter went downstairs to his office, sat at his desk, and tried to focus on work. But work didn't work. He got up and walked around his office. Walking helped him think sometimes. But he couldn't stop thinking about what had happened with him and Megan two weeks ago when she left home.

"We need some time," she had said, looking down and holding back tears as she put some things in her car.

"Okay," he'd said, lamely, putting her suitcases in the trunk. "Let's ... let's ...ah ... keep talking."

Then she pulled herself together, got in her car without looking back, and drove away. He couldn't see her wipe her eyes. He watched the car all the way down the street until it disappeared around the corner. He still stood there. It really hurt. Scooter didn't want her to go but tried to believe she was right about a separation. They both needed to step back and figure out what had gone wrong with their twenty-year marriage. The perfect one.

The one that began in Florida at Winter Haven High School's Senior Ball. Megan was his high school sweetheart. Around midnight, for the last dance, the mirror ball was off and the lights were lowered in the gym. It started like any other dance. But then the band, other dancers, and everything around them seemed to be melting away into a soft and beautiful place where they were alone together. He stroked her hair and felt her silk blouse and her soft neck. She put her arm around his neck and melted into him. He stepped on her toe and she laughed. They danced closer and closer, slower and slower until their dance became a passionate embrace. He kissed her and missed a little. She did so much better. Then they both succeeded. The music finally stopped. Time stopped. But they didn't. Their bodies merged. They became one. They had fallen in love.

Yet, things hadn't been right between them for a while. Maybe it was the slow accumulation of little things, combined with a few bigger ones. Like the time two weeks ago when they yelled at each other over something seemingly small that had gotten blown way out of proportion. He didn't even remember what it was about. He liked to block out unpleasant memories.

I guess that says something about me, he realized.

What he did remember was how it stung and scared both of them. Marriages need basic maintenance just to keep the flame alive, and much more work to keep it bright.

Maybe those "little" things were the problem, he thought. *The signals I missed, she missed. Did I listen enough? The times I missed our kids' sports practices. Didn't give her something she needed from me? Megan wasn't perfect either. The things she did and didn't do, especially ... we need to discuss those. But I don't want to think about those now. Both of us had drifted apart on our own currents and diverged too far. I was too focused on my law practice and traveling more. She was busy with her endless travel for client meetings. At some point those things out-ranked our time with each other.*

Maybe this is like barnacles on a boat. They start out so small— less than a millimeter. What damage could they do? But then they build piles of rock-hard colonies that slow the boat down and cause fouling that chokes off the air intakes to the engine. Their marriage was fouling. Boats need maintenance to clean off the barnacles. Marriages need maintenance too. Accountants call it "deferred maintenance." That's appropriate. Everyone wants to defer maintenance. It isn't fun. You want to avoid it as long as possible because it's work. *Even worse, the work could reveal more damage that needs fixing. Sometimes we'd be upset about something, not want to discuss it, and just retreat to our corners. But that creates more barnacles. Then they just grow and grow.*

Scooter found himself walking around in circles as he talked to himself. *I don't understand what happened,* he thought. *But I need to figure this out. Correction, we need to figure this out. We need to fix some stuff, and I'm still mad about some things, but I can't ... just can't ... lose Megan!*

Around 11:30 he headed to The TOMBS in Georgetown. At the end of Chain Bridge, he turned right onto Canal Road (smiling as he made that turn a lot slower than last time) zipped east into Georgetown, took a left onto 33rd Street and passed the window at Georgetown Cupcakes. The window was advertising a journey through bliss: a "Chocolate Ganache Valrhona chocolate cupcake with a thin layer of Callebaut chocolate ganache icing topped with a pink fondant flower." He thought about stopping but was running a little late.

He turned left onto Prospect Street and parked near the 1789 Restaurant, an upscale restaurant with an elegant Tudor-style interior. As he walked to the restaurant, he didn't notice the two women across the street looking at him.

"Look, it's Harrison Ford!"

"No, no, that's not Harrison Ford. He just looks like him. That's Professor Magee; I had him last year for business law."

"Sure looks like him..."

He walked past the famous Exorcist Stairs. Those steep, black stairs dropped some three stories from Prospect Street to Canal Road that followed the Potomac River below. They received Hollywood fame from the 1973 film *The Exorcist*, often called the "Scariest Movie of All Time." It was so scary that theatres even posted warning signs on their doors. In the movie's climax, Jesuit Father Karras, chased by the Devil, threw himself down those stairs in an act of self-sacrifice. Those stairs made Scooter feel uneasy whenever he saw them; yet they somehow beckoned him. *The Exorcist* was just a movie. But it was more chilling because it was based on a real exorcism in 1949. Scooter believed that Evil is everywhere, getting ready to show itself. It seemed to hover over the stairs like an invisible cloud, and Scooter could sense it, even smell it. Next to the stairs were the gargoyles on the Old Trolly Car Barn. They hovered over the stairs like guardian devils.

Scooter crossed the street, passed the 1789, and went down The TOMBS Restaurant's steep, dark stairs with blue and grey walls. *Nothing like this place*, he thought. The Union blue and Confederate grey of Georgetown University symbolized the coming together of the country at the Jesuit college after the Civil War. He could already smell the hamburgers and fries as he forced opened the stuck, blue metal door at the bottom of the stairwell and turned left. Inside was the big oval bar, bustling with students and faculty. To the right were old English style booths and tables. World War I posters shared space on the brick walls with blue and grey crew oars. The University was founded in 1789, and the place looked like it had been around even before George Washington spoke to the first graduating class on the nearby steps of the Georgian-style Old North Building.

"Hi, professor," said the assistant manager, one of his former students. "Your guest is at your favorite table."

"Thanks, Sonia, hope you're doing well." He smiled at her and made his way over to his usual corner table.

"Are you Scooter?" asked a thirtyish, stocky guy with black hair showing from under a Mets cap who peered up from the table. He looked like a young Marlon Brando with short sleeves rolled up and a gold chain around his neck. No cigarette pack showing, though. And Brando never had a playboy bunny tattoo.

"That's me," Scooter replied. "Do you go by Cold Fingers?"

"Cold Fingers or CF; Cold Fingers Gelato."

"Why Cold Fingers?"

"I've got neuro, neuropathy or whatever the hell they call it, in my fingers. For most people cold makes it hurt like crazy. Not for me. I put my fingers in ice cream or anything cold and after about a minute the pain stops. Puzzles the heck out of doctors, but it works. So, folks started calling me Cold Fingers Gelato. But you can call me CF." Cold Fingers pulled a clear plastic sandwich bag out of his pocket, put some ice from his water glass in it, zipped it up, laid it on the table, and put his right hand over the top.

"Where are you from, CF?"

"All over. Last place, Brighton Beach."

"Want a cigarette?" Cold Fingers bounced the cigarette pack across the table. Scooter smiled. Turned out he did have a pack. Brando's third-rate replica was now complete.

"Can't smoke in here."

"Okay."

"Why'd you contact me?"

"I heard you're the guy to talk to about startups."

Cold Fingers wasn't the only one interested in Scooter. If Scooter had been looking, he would have seen the wooden booth in the southwest corner of the room through the shadows. The shadows fell from a stone gargoyle protruding from the wall over the table. The faded Latin inscription under it was too hard to read except for the year, MCCLX Anno Domini—1260 AD. It looked like the Xenomorph, the monster from the film *Alien*, with its snail-like head, long teeth, and braided and twisted neck veins. The monster cast a shadow over the face of the person below, alone at the table pretending to write on the paper placemat. The pen, rather a chubby imitation of a pen, was always pointed in Scooter's direction. The shadows covered the person's features.

"You wanted to talk to me about a camera?"

"Yeah. So, you're 'sposed to be the dude that can make startups happen, right?"

"It depends. What do you have in mind?"

"I got hold of a very special camera. I need some business advice on locking it up in a company where nobody can find or take it."

"What kind of camera?"

"Let's just say a very special one. It mostly works, some of the time. But when it does … amazing. You're a lawyer, right?"

"Yeah."

"So, you can never reveal any secrets I tell you, right?"

"Yes, I would never do that. Who owns this camera company?"

"Me and my buddy. I set it up with one million shares."

"What happens to the equity if your partner drops out?"

"Ahhh … ahhh … he'd never do that; we're long-time buddies. And I'm not worried about money cause I bought it for $250,000 but just got promised one million from a guy in Cambodia for it. All cash, and he's in a hurry to invest by this Friday. I just sent him my bank account number so he can put the money right in. How about that?"

"Do you have a non-disclosure agreement or anything in writing with your buddy?"

"A what?"

"Do you have a lawyer?"

"A lawyer? Why?"

Time to straighten out Cold Fingers. Scooter felt his legal adrenaline surge. He imagined his tongue turning into a long, sharp fish knife. Time to filet this idiot.

"You need one because you just woke up too late at your own party and folks are running off with the punch bowl. That guy who's investing the money? He's probably not. He's laundering it and draining your account dry. You're committing Startup Suicide." Then Scooter backed off a little. He'd come on strong and he forgot for a minute who he was dealing with. "Let's get some food, and I'll walk you through some things." Scooter called Sonia over.

"The usual, professor? The crab cake special's looking good; big lumps of Bluefin with mustard sauce. And I saved you two scoops of butter pecan ice cream for later."

"You're amazing, Sonia! What would you like, CF?"

They had lunch and Scooter ran him through some of the basics on reducing risk and avoiding Startup Suicide by making sure to use non-disclosure agreements, never take money from the wrong sources, never wire money unless you call the recipient to confirm the account information, and much more.

Finally, Scooter said, "I'll send you an engagement letter with a memo with what we discussed. Once you've read that, give me a call if you have any questions."

Then the mood changed. Cold Fingers looked Scooter directly in the eyes and leaned right into his face.

"There's more," he said. "I want all your files on the Molly Bloom case. Those files are the key to finding the hidden mob money. I was one of Molly's top players who lost millions on her games and I need that money back," said Cold Fingers. "I know you've got those files, the ones that show where the money is."

The Molly Bloom case was one of the FBI's biggest mob cases in New York City. Molly was a real person and an Olympic-class skier. She left the skis behind to run the biggest high-stakes underground poker games in the United States and allegedly Ben Affleck, Tobey Maguire, and Leonardo DiCaprio were among her high rollers. Then, Molly made mistakes. You can legally host a private poker game where people bet. But it's a crime to run a game and take a share of the pot unless you have a gambling license. She allegedly did that, and financed losers and fell into taking drugs to keep up with her hectic lifestyle. FBI agents with automatic weapons came after her in a midnight raid and prosecuted a bunch of alleged mob figures who were players. Molly's Game, the 2017 movie with Jessica Chastain and Kevin Costner followed. But there were still questions about where the money ended up. Was some laundered into legitimate businesses? Folks still were trying to find company files for clues as to where the money was hidden.[4]

Cold Fingers was looking right at Scooter. Scooter had met some bad dudes over the years when he was a prosecutor at Justice. He'd seen that same dead look in the eyes before—a look that would scare cancer. It sent a chill through him. He discreetly searched his pocket for some Tums and popped three of them.

"Hypothetically, even if I had the files, I couldn't tell you or talk about them. The bar rules prevent disclosure of a client's secrets. I could be disbarred for that. Only the client can authorize the lawyer to release them. Get this. Even if the client is dead, the lawyer must continue to protect the files until a court allows their release. And in this case the client company no longer exists so there's no one to give me permission."

"I said I want those files. Don't make me say it again." He reached into his jacket pocket and fiddled with something as he continued, "My partner will be here in a week or two. You'll get me those files or bad things will start happening. Real bad things. And don't even think about telling the cops, your wife, or anyone about this, or … anak ku slab.

Scooter didn't know any Khmer but he was pretty sure he knew what Cold Fingers just said. And it wasn't good.

Scooter shifted in his seat. His left leg was twitching.

Cold Fingers got up abruptly and left.

Scooter paid the check, waited for a while until he was sure Cold Fingers was gone, and then left. The person from the other table followed.

"Hope you enjoyed your meal," Sonia said.

"Yeah, I got lots more than I expected!"

The waiter cleared the table. When no one was watching he picked up Cold Fingers' and Scooter's water glasses with a cloth napkin. Back in the kitchen he put the glasses in his backpack then went outside for a smoke. Two minutes later a black car rolled up from the next block and pulled over in front of the restaurant. The passenger window went down and the waiter gave him the bag. The car quickly drove away.

"I've got the package," the car's passenger radioed out on a secure frequency.

"Good work," replied the desk officer at the FBI.

***

Mark Twain once said, "Eat a live frog first thing in the morning and nothing worse will happen to you the rest of the day." Scooter should have eaten a live frog. He came home confused and scared. Five minutes later his phone beeped with a text from Cold Fingers. Scooter saw it and froze. "Me and my partner Crunch want to meet you at The TOMBS. Come alone. Four o' clock one week from today. Be there or else." Scooter felt his stomach knot up.

"Breathe, think," he told himself out loud. "What are my options? How far do I want to push out the boat? If I tell the police they'll probably move too slow or mess up and then CF will get me. If I don't play along, who knows what might happen. I need to stall. Maybe I can figure some way out of this mess." After a while he settled down and starting planning. "Why am I playing the victim? Just maybe I can turn the tables on this guy." "Yes," he said, "I'll work on that."

Later than night, Scooter finally fell asleep and started dreaming about The TOMBS. None of it was true of course, but his mind was still working overtime. What he remembered dreaming when he woke up was that:

There are 131 Carnegie rated "R-1, very high research universities" in the United States. Places where vital national security and high-tech research are conducted. Georgetown is one of those. With its DC location, advanced biomedical and other research, and the Walsh School of Foreign Service, the first US school of international affairs, it draws students and scientists from around the world. But some aren't just students.

The TOMBS is a central meeting place for students and faculty across the whole campus. A place where information flows as frequently as the beer. In 2001, after the Twin Towers attack, the FBI launched "Project W" at Georgetown. At least one waiter informant was at The TOMBS all the time listening for any conversations with national security interest. It was so successful that the Bureau expanded it to twenty-five more R-1 colleges across the country, until the word got out and it was all closed down... [Dear reader, sorry to interrupt, but remember this is fiction...!]

Chapter 3

LOCK UP YOUR INTELLECTUAL PROPERTY

Intellectual property has the shelf life of a banana.

—Bill Gates

Despite Bill Gate's quote above, before you sell any products or services, your value might only be you and your ideas. Later you will build a team and start producing something. But even before then, you need to protect your intellectual property (IP). Intellectual property includes what you've invented, your commercially valuable information such as vendor and customer lists, your company's name, and branding. You need to lock up your intellectual property like a bank locks up its money. Of course, you'll probably only win by succeeding in the marketplace, not by litigating against patent infringers. But IP protection often is essential and can add great value to your company. Investors will be interested in what intellectual property you have and if it is properly protected.

Note that you can't get any intellectual property protection for a mere idea (except for a trade secret). For example, to obtain a patent, trademark, or copyright you need something that is reduced to a physical form, such as written materials, data, design, artwork, any kind of machine or prototype, etc.

INTELLECTUAL PROPERTY AND IVANKA TRUMP'S LAWSUIT

Intellectual property extends to any kind of property. Take Aquazzura Italia SRL's lawsuit against Ivanka Trump's shoe design as an example.

Aquazzura's Sandal (left side) Ivanka Trump's (right side)[1]

In June 2016, shoe designer Aquazzura Italia SLR sued Ivanka Trump, It Collection LLC, and Marc Fisher Holdings, LLC, et al., in U.S. District Court in New York,[2] alleging that Trump's Hettie sandal at $145 was a "virtually identical"[3] copy of Aquazzura's Wild Thing's distinctive design, which cost $785. According to Aquazzura's complaint, this was the third time it had sued Trump's company for copying one of its designs. And Aquazzura claimed that the Wild Thing infringement was particularly harmful because of the shoe's popularity: "Following its launch [of its Wild Thing shoe] Aquazzura skyrocketed to fame in the fashion world. Its shoes are coveted by fashionistas and celebrities alike, and are regularly photographed and written about in high profile publications such as Vogue, Harper's Bazaar, Elle, and the New York Times, as well as in myriad fashion blogs."[4]

Trump and Fisher then filed a counterclaim asking the court to find that the shoes weren't subject to trademark protection because the Wild Thing design is in the public domain and was not trade dress (the design, shape and packaging of a product). Therefore, the court held that the design elements were not so distinctive that shoppers would recognize the shoe's fringe and strappy lace up as signatures of Aquazzura's brand.[5] On the other hand, an example of trade dress being present and enforced by the courts is found in a 2013 *Christian Louboutin* case. In that case, the court held that Louboutin's signature lacquered red sole shoes combined with contrasting color or colors on the rest of the shoe was trade dress.[6]

Who would have won the Trump case? We don't know because the parties issued a joint statement in Nov. 18, 2017, saying the case had been settled and dismissed with prejudice, which means that same case can't be brought again in that court.[7]

Ivanka Trump has had several ethical and legal challenges regarding her brands, including White House staff pitching her product in violation of government ethics rules. In March 2017, counsellor to the president Kellyanne Conway suggested during an interview with Fox News in the White House briefing room with the White House seal behind her that people "go buy Ivanka's stuff," and "this is just a wonderful line. Go buy it today, everybody. You can find it online."[8]

In response to this, Modern Appealing Clothing, a San Francisco boutique, filed a class action suit against Ms. Trump's firm, Ivanka Trump Marks, Inc., alleging that she received an "unfair advantage" from the Trump administration in promoting her brand. That case and apparently the ethics investigation regarding Ms. Conway's actions were dropped when Press Secretary Sean Spicer announced that Ms. Trump would follow ethics rules in the future.[9]

Also in 2017, Unicolors, a textile converter based in Los Angeles, sued Ivanka Trump's brand, seeking an injunction and damages, alleging that Trump had obtained swatches of its trademarked print and "made only slight changes to it before going into production with it on a jacket." Unicolors argued that Trump's jacket was selling well at T.J. Maxx and therefore Unicolor was losing money. Unicolor was aggressive in protecting its brand, with over forty lawsuits protecting this textile and some two hundred cases in California overall. That provided an opening for Ms. Trump to argue that Unicolor's suit was merely its usual mode of doing business. That case also was settled.[10]

Infringement cases can spotlight the pros and cons of aggressive marketing. On the one hand companies have an obligation to shareholders to grow the company and reasonably maximize profitability.

But marketing too aggressively can lead to litigation and damages—even treble damages in patent cases. And damages can be more than financial. If the company gets a reputation of breaking the law to make money or otherwise being unethical, then the business can suffer and it may be more difficult to hire, motivate, and retain employees. For a broader discussion of business ethics, see Chapter 7, "Methics"™—Management Ethics.

THE FOUR BASIC TYPES OF INTELLECTUAL PROPERTY (IP)

IP is a bundle of law that balances two conflicting public policy goals: 1) to provide inventors an incentive to create by giving them ownership in their inventions, while at the same time 2) giving the public maximum access to inventions to promote a competitive marketplace and grow the economy.[11] Intellectual property is protected by the U.S. Constitution.

Article 1, Section 8 of the U.S. Constitution authorizes Congress to enact patent and copyright laws: "To promote the progress of science and useful arts, by securing for limited times to authors and inventors the exclusive right to their respective writings and discoveries."

The Commerce Clause, also in Article 1, is the basis for federal regulation of trademarks and unfair competition. States retain concurrent jurisdiction to regulate IP under the Tenth Amendment, except states do not issue patents; only the federal government does.

There are four types of IP. They all are important to your company.

Trade Secrets

You should consider keeping some of your ideas, proprietary data, customer lists, and inventions etc. secret, particularly before they're more formally legally protected. These are called "trade secrets" and you don't have to file anything with the government to protect them, but you do need to keep them secret, because once they get out to others the protection is gone, and your legal remedies are limited. So, your designs or other IP should be kept secret until your products are released or you file a patent or you copyright them.

Copyrights

Your brochures and other documents automatically get a common law copyright when you create them, which can be enforced in court. But if you ever need to enforce your rights against infringers then you will need to successfully register the copyright with the US Copyright Office before you can prosecute an enforcement action.[12]

Trademarks

Your company's name, logos, and the names of any product lines or specific products (if they are important enough to trademark) should be trademarked to prevent others from using them.

Patents

If you are creating new types of products or designs, software, or processes, etc., you should consider filing for a patent. Patents are expensive but can add a lot of value to the company and help to attract investors.

IP and Your Business Strategy

There's a tendency to think of IP separately from your business strategies, but it needs to be fully integrated into your business plans.

More on all of this follows. For a summary of key provisions of these four types, see Illustration 2.

WHY IP MATTERS
IP Protects Your Ownership in Your Property

You need to keep what is yours and not lose it to competitors or others.

As an example, I was involved in a case where the CEO hired a contractor to develop software. The parties ended up in a dispute about compensation. The software developer took off to Asia. Because he owned the IP and had never assigned it (legally transferred it) to the company, he was entitled to use it for his own purposes. He started his own company and competed against the original CEO's company. I'll discuss how to prevent that later.

IP Adds Value to a Company

IP can be a valuable company asset; something as simple as a very short website domain name can be worth over $100,000. You can sell it or earn royalties from licensing it.

Investors Like Barriers to Entry

The world is flat. In some markets, you're virtually competing against the whole world for your products and services. If you have a patent, you can prevent others from selling, distributing, importing, etc. products and services that are identical to yours.

You Can License IP

Even if you don't manufacture, produce, distribute, or sell your product, you can license the IP to others to do those things. Often, that is an easier way to make money than going into the manufacturing, sales, and other aspects of business yourself. As a startup, your license usually will be worth more after you can show sales traction and proven commercial value. You might want to wait to get that before negotiating a licensing agreement to increase the value of the license.

Think about it like this. You're a movie producer. You want to sell or license an idea for a movie. That by itself isn't worth much. Then you add another element, like a polished script from a well-known writer. Now it's worth a little more. But if you can get Julia Roberts or Brad Pitt to star in the movie, it's worth a lot more and easier to license.

Investors Like It

Investors like additional revenue streams like IP royalties. They balance out income fluctuations from product sales.

It Helps Brand Your Company as a Market Leader

If you have the lead IP in your field, it's easier to be seen as a market leader; this gives you a leg up on the competition. You can tell others that no one can have a product just like yours and enforce any infringement of your IP, if necessary.

INTELLECTUAL PROPERTY OPTIONS			
Type	Description	Typical Uses	Term and Price; Fees are subject to change
Trade Secret	• Common law right • Can be stolen, so you must protect it. • Can reverse engineer around it. • Can't be commercially disclosed. • Can save on the expenses of patenting.	• Data, formulas • Customer lists • Manufacturing processes	• No expiration • No expense, not filed.
Copyright ©	• Common law ownership attaches when created and fixed in a tangible form. • Must have valid registration to enforce rights. • Apply: U.S. Copyright Office • Don't need an attorney.	• Original authorized works fixed in a medium • Books, pamphlets • Music scores and recordings • Film, photos • Software code, but must be in a fixed medium, e.g., printed out	• Generally: Life of author + up to 70 years; no renewal necessary • Price to self-file: Electronically: $45 and up + attorney @ $250 and up
Trademark TM, SM ®	• Name, symbol, device, or combination to identify, distinguish goods and services from another and the source • Registration requires a legal determination by U.S. Patent and Trademark office (USPTO); not an automatic filing. • Can take time and expense; use an attorney. • Apply to USPTO.	• Distinctive mark and/or words, phrases, logos, and designs • Helps create brand, customer perceptions of quality & service.	• No expiration • Need to renew. • Price: varies per class, plus attorney's fees, $500 and up
Patent Pat. Pend.	• Monopoly right to exclude others from making, using, offering to sell, & importing • Must eventually disclose to the public. • Takes time and expense. • First to file now usually wins. • Must apply to US Patent and Trademark Office (PTO) within one year after you offer it for sale in the US or make disclosures about it. • Must be new, non-obvious, useful, and described in enough detail to enable one with ordinary skill in the art to know how to make and use it. 35 U.S.C. Secs. 101-103. • Provisional and Non-Provisional • International – Patent Cooperation Treaty (PCT)	• Utility processes, methods of manufacture, business methods, methods of use, compositions of matter, & machines. • Design: ornamental aspects, trade dress • Plant and Plant varieties	• Utility Pat. - 20 yrs. from date issued • Design Patent – 15 yrs., plant: 14 yrs. • Price: Varies widely with number of claims, etc. Utility filing online. $5K-$6K plus attorney's fee of $8-20K

TRADE SECRETS
Definition of a Trade Secret

A trade secret is any confidential information, not known by others, which gives a business a competitive advantage. It typically includes things like:

○ Data, formulas, designs;
○ Customer lists; and
○ Manufacturing processes.

The owner of the trade secret can prevent others from using it if it was illegally obtained.

A classic example of a trade secret is the formula for Coca-Cola. John Pemberton, an alleged morphine addict and pharmacist, invented the drink in 1886 and the formula was not written down but passed by word of mouth. When the company was sold in 1919, investors received the written formula as collateral for a loan. Now, the formula is locked in a vault in Coca-Cola's headquarters in Atlanta and only two executives know the formula at any time, and they can't travel on the same plane.[13] Some have suggested that the formula is so simple that revealing it would merely prove how profitable a business can be when touting a trade secret. Keeping it a secret adds to Coke's marketing mystique.

The good news about a trade secret is that:

○ It is not filed with the government, so you save on legal expenses; and
○ You can sell and license your trade secret to others.

The bad news is:

○ It can be stolen, so you must take reasonable steps to protect it; and
○ Others can reverse engineer around it. Of course, that's true even if you have filed a patent or copyright.

Remedies

If a trade secret is stolen, you can file an injunction to prevent further disclosure of the trade secret, seek damages, and in some cases, criminal penalties for theft.

Under the federal Defend Trade Secrets Act of 2016 (DTSA),[14] trade secret owners can file lawsuits in federal court if the trade secret was used in interstate commerce. Prior to that, remedies were only available in state courts.

An example of an infringement case is *Waymo v. Uber Technologies*. In 2017, Waymo, an Alphabet/Google enterprise, obtained a preliminary injunction in federal district court against an engineer to prevent him from working on a similar project with Uber. He had allegedly downloaded fourteen thousand documents with 121 trade secrets.[15]

COPYRIGHT AND FAIR USE—CHARLIE CHAPLIN'S ONE MINUTE RESULT
Definition

A copyright is a bundle of rights held by the creator of an original work of authorship. This includes virtually any type of expression that can be fixed in a tangible medium, such as: a fashion item, books, audio visual works, computer software code, graphic works, musical arrangements, and sound recordings. However, it must have some degree of creativity. Just copying names from a phonebook, for example, would not be sufficient.

A copyright doesn't protect the underlying facts or ideas, only the expression of it in a physical medium.

Once you have a copyright, you have the exclusive right to make copies, sell the work, display the work, perform it, and obtain court relief to prevent others from infringing on your rights.

Things That Can't Be Copyrighted

- Names of products or services;
- Names of businesses, organizations, or groups (including the names of performing groups);
- Pseudonyms of individuals (including pen or stage names);
- Titles of works;

    ◦   Catchwords, catchphrases, mottoes, slogans, or short advertising expressions;

    ◦   Listings of ingredients, as in recipes, labels, or formulas. When a recipe or formula is accompanied by an explanation or directions, the text directions may be copyrightable, but the recipe or formula itself remains not copyrightable.[16]

The Fair Use Doctrine

You need the copyright owner's permission to make copies of copyrighted material for commercial purposes. However, under the "Fair Use Doctrine," copying for educational, non-commercial, and even some commercial purposes may be permissible. Whether the use is protected as fair use frequently depends on a four-factor test used by the courts. This test usually is very fact specific:

1. What is the use? Is the use commercial or not? Using the material for teaching is acceptable, absent other factors. Using it for commercial purposes is less likely to be approved.

2. The nature of the copied work. Copying a news broadcast may be okay but not a commercial movie.

3. The amount of the material used. This also is very subjective: "A television news program copied only one-minute and fifteen seconds from a seventy-two-minute Charlie Chaplin film and used it in a news report about Chaplin's death. Nevertheless, in 1982, a Federal U.S. Court of Appeals found an infringement. The court said that the portions taken were substantial and part of the "heart" of the film.[17]

4. The effect on the potential market when the product is sold. For example, use of a poor-quality thumbnail may be fair use. In *Kelly vs. Arriba* in 2003:

Plaintiff Leslie Kelly, a professional photographer, alleged that defendant Arriba Soft Corp.'s search engine infringed Kelly's photographs. Defendant operated a visual search engine that "crawled" the internet searching for images that it copied and then generated as smaller, lower-resolution thumbnail copies for display on a search results page. Defendant reproduced thirty-five of plaintiff's photographs and displayed them as thumbnails in response to search requests. Plaintiff appealed the district court's ruling that defendant's use of plaintiff's photographs in its search engine was fair use.[18]

The court held that it was fair use because the thumbnails served a different function that the original images. Also, while they were "artistic works" their use was "unrelated to any aesthetic purpose"—they were used as an index tool, and the lower-resolution thumbnail images did not harm the market for or the value of the plaintiff's images. [19]

Term in Force
Under the Copyright Act of 1976,[20] copyright protection is for:

- o   The life of the author plus seventy years; or
- o   Ninety-five years from the date of publication or 120 years from the date of creation, whichever is shorter if the author is an employer or the author remains anonymous.

Using a Copyright Notice
You can put a © symbol on your creations without filing with the US Copyright Office. A typical format is "© [year] [name of owner]." The word "copyright" also can be used. I generally recommend that my clients put the notice on their major marketing materials such as brochures and their website or other key places where the company or item is being introduced to others. There's no need to put it on everything, such as when your name is in a letter or e-mail. Using the copyright notice shows would-be competitors and others that you are going to protect your intellectual property, and suggests that you have a lawyer on hand to protect it. Having a copyright notice also counters an infringer's argument that it didn't know the material was copyrighted. But to enforce your rights, you first need to register the copyright with the Copyright Office. Registration also allows you to recover up to $150,000 plus attorney's fees without the difficult task of proving monetary harm in a lawsuit.

How to Register a Copyright

You can file to register a copyright with the US Copyright Office yourself without using a lawyer. The fees start at forty-five dollars for an online filing. Simply go to copyright.gov and follow the directions. The application is examined, which might take a month or so, and then you will be notified of its acceptance or of any issues to be resolved.

TRADEMARKS—OPRAH'S *O MAGAZINE* WIN
Definition

A trademark is a distinctive word, phrase, or logo to identify the source of a product or service and distinguish it from competitors.[21] A service mark does the same thing for services. Frito-Lay is a trademark for its products; UPS is a service mark for its delivery services. Often, the word trademark is used generically for both trademarks and service marks.

Trademark Law

Trademark law is a subset of unfair competition laws. The Lanham Act (15 U.S.C. Sec. 1051 et seq.) establishes the US trademark registration system and provides for judicial remedies in case of infringement. Most states also allow for infringement remedies. Getting a trademark gives you exclusive right to use your mark.

> TIP: THE FIRST TO FILE A TRADEMARK APPLICATION WINS (WITH EXCEPTIONS). SO, BE SURE TO INCLUDE THE EARLIEST DAY OF ITS USE IN COMMERCE; OTHERWISE, THE TRADEMARK OFFICE WILL USE THE LAST DAY OF THE MONTH BY DEFAULT.

Filing for a Trademark

Usually, the first to use the mark in a commercial context wins. That could include, for example, conducting sales or providing company information on the internet. Filing for trademark registration will help establish that first use. Registration fees with the US Patent and

Trademark Office range from $225 to $400 and vary with the number of business sectors or "classes" for which you are seeking trademark protection. I'd recommend using an attorney for filing because you can easily get bogged down in the complexities of classes and other requirements and not get broad enough protection or end up paying too much for protection you don't need. In addition, if you're filing for a logo, there are lots of complex rules regarding the specifications for the images you must submit.

Trademark Process

Once the application is filed, it will be given a serial number and you can check on the status of your application online or by phone. After some months, an examiner will be assigned to examine it. The examiner may approve it for publication in the USPTO's *Trademark Official Gazette* (TMOG) or issue an "office action," noting issues to be addressed, such as if it is too similar to another mark.

Similarity can be surprising. Even though a word is spelled differently, it may have the same sound when reading it, in which case your application might be rejected. Once any objections have been resolved, the application will be published and for thirty days anyone may file an objection ("opposition") to it. If there is no opposition, then it will be published in the *Principal Register* and the process is completed. If there is a dispute, it will be heard before the Trademark Trial and Appeal Board (TTAB) to resolve the issues.

There also is a *Supplemental Register* but it has fewer benefits. For example, trademarks on the *Principal Register* have a presumption of validity in court, unless proven otherwise. Trademarks on the *Supplemental Register* require you to prove that you own the trademark. In addition, after five years on the *Principal Register* your mark becomes incontestable for infringement purposes but those on the *Supplemental Register* don't have that status.

Some things cannot be trademarked. For example, if:

○ the trademark has been abandoned or is no longer in service;

○ is a generic name such as "computer" or "eyeglasses;"

    ○ is confusingly like another mark to cause consumer confusion; or

    ○ is a "weak mark"—that's hard to distinguish because it is like other marks.

Trademark Notice

You can put a trademark notice in the form of capital "TM" on the item to be trademarked before filing an application for the mark. It often is shown as a superscript or subscript and must be a large enough font to be readable. Once your mark is registered, you can then use the registered symbol a capital in a circle ®.

State Trademarks

You also can file for a trademark in a particular state. This could make sense if you're only doing business in one state. The filing fee is less than a federal filing. It also is usually a faster process than a federal filing. When approved, however, you are restricted to using "TM" rather than the federal "R" in a circle.

There are several advantages to a federal filing, however, including:

    ○ A state filing is only valid in the state in which you file; a federal filing provides protection across all US states and US territories.

    ○ Federal filings protect you from unauthorized imports.

    ○ Federal filings provide a basis to file in other countries.

    ○ You can file infringement suits in federal courts.

    ○ You can file before you use the mark.

Trade Dress

Trademark law also protects "trade dress," such as the distinctive shape of a Coke bottle or the Burberry plaid.

Christian Louboutin S.A. v. Yves Saint Laurent Case

One color alone can be enough to establish trade dress, the design, shape and packaging of a product. In 2008, Christian Louboutin, a Paris footwear designer, produced a shoe with a bright red, lacquered sole and received a trademark on it in 2011. In 2011, Yves

Saint Laurent released a collection of similar shoes. Louboutin filed a trademark infringement suit in New York alleging violation of the Lanham Act, trademark infringement, counterfeiting, false designation or origin, unfair competition, and trademark dilution. On appeal, Louboutin won. The Second Circuit held Saint Laurent had infringed, but only in those cases where the red lacquered sole contrasts in color with the upper part of the shoe. So red on red would not be an infringement.[22]

How Oprah Winfrey Won Her O Magazine *Trademark Case*
Registered trademark protection has its limits. In 2016, the U.S. Court of Appeals Second Circuit held that Oprah's use of the phrase "Own Your Own Power" in *O Magazine* and in her motivational events did not infringe another's registered service mark with the same words.[23] How was that possible?

Plaintiff Simone Kelley-Brown, owner of Own Your Own Communications, Inc. had registered that same phrase as a service mark in 2008 and provided motivational services under that mark. In 2010, Oprah started using that phrase in commerce and, in 2011, Kelley-Brown sued Oprah and Harpo Productions, Inc., Winfrey's production company, in the U.S. District Court. Kelley-Brown appealed. After a remand, ultimately, the Second Circuit held for Winfrey stating that the mark as used by Kelley-Brown was only "descriptive" (which is a non-trademark use) and was not "uniquely associated with its products in the mind of consumers."[24] Further, there could not be any confusion in the minds of consumers between Kelley-Brown's and Winfrey's use of the mark.

PATENTS—HOW BLOGGING CAN KILL YOUR PATENT'S CHANCES
Definition
A patent is a grant by the US Patent and Trademark Office (USPTO) for a limited period, to develop and use an invention. The protection from a patent prevents another from making, selling, importing, and distributing the product. There are no state-issued patents, only federal patents in the United States. Unless otherwise mentioned in this discussion, "patents" refers to United States patents.

Types of Patents
Utility Patent
Usually when we think of a patent, it's a "utility" patent. This is a new, non-obvious, and useful invention or improvement in a process, product, machine, manufacture, or composition of matter. It provides a unique way of operating or functionality.

Design Patent
A design patent protects a design that ornaments unique visual qualities of a manufactured item. For example, a new shape for a car fender, the Statute of Liberty (1879), or flashlight design that doesn't improve functionality. Unlike a utility patent, a design patent does not require annual maintenance fees to keep it in force. The same product may have both a design and a utility patent at the same time.

Plant Patent
This is a patent for a novel and non-obvious plant. It can be natural, bred, or somatic (created from non-reproductive cells of the plant). It can be invented or discovered (but only if it is discovered in a cultivated area). No maintenance fee is required to maintain a plant patent.

Utility and plant patents last for twenty years, and design patents for fifteen years.

Maintenance fees are required to keep a utility patent in force, and they are due after 3.5 years, 7.5 years, and 11.5 years.

Application Process
You should use a patent attorney when filing a patent application with the USPTO, rather than trying to do it yourself. The wording in an application is critical to getting the maximum amount of coverage and there is a lot of strategy involved in the filing. You want to get as broad coverage as possible for the patent. But the broader the coverage, the more likely it is that it will overlap on "prior art" (already existing technology) and not be patentable. As a result, patent applications often are structured with broad claims that are followed by a series of narrower sub claims in the hopes that at least

one of those narrower and more specific claims will be granted. So, unless you like doing your own brain surgery, don't try to do this yourself.

The patent application is filed with the PTO and then it's examined by a patent examiner. The examiner will review the application to see if it complies with the following and other requirements.

The invention must be new, non-obvious, useful, and described in enough detail to enable one with ordinary skill in the art to know how to make and use it.[25] To determine if it is new, the examiner will do a search of prior art in the relevant technical field, and the search will include, among other things, patents and other publications.

There is a non-obvious requirement. If A and B already have been invented and your invention merely combines them into C, the examiner would find that invention non-obvious and reject the application. The application may be objected to in part or totally rejected. Then you or your attorney will have an opportunity to discuss this with the examiner and see if an accommodation can be reached. You can also file an appeal with the Patent Trial and Appeal Board (PTAB). If you lose there, you can proceed to the U.S. Court of Appeals for the Federal Circuit or file a civil case against the PTO in US District Court.

If the patent is approved, it is published, issued, and you pay a fee. You'll also be paying your patent attorney. Those legal fees usually are based in part on the complexity of the filing and can range from $6,000 to $15,000 or more.

Those are a few of the IP basics; now let's talk about your IP business strategy.

BUSINESS ISSUES AND STRATEGIES—THE PATENT MINE FIELD STRATEGY

Who owns the invention, materials, or other "work?" Generally, if the work is created by an employee "during the scope of employment" the company owns the work, however this varies with state law. Otherwise the employee does. But these simple rules don't mean so much when lawyers are nearby. The rules have many exceptions. For example, "during the scope of employment" does not include intellectual property developed prior to employment, or done during the time of employment on an employee's own time and without use of the employer's resources.

Thus, to be safe, an employer always should enter into a written assignment of intellectual property agreement with the employee.

- The assignment should require that the employee assign to the company all intellectual property developed during the scope of employment and require the employee's full cooperation in prosecuting any filings or cases regarding it (usually at the company's expense); and the inventor should authorize the appointment of an attorney-in-fact to do those things necessary to prosecute the patent if requested by the employer.
- The assignment should specify in detail what inventions, if any, the employee has developed prior to employment or independently and whether the inventions relate to the subject matter of the employer's activities.
- If the assignment is entered into after employment, it should recite new, legally sufficient consideration for it or it might not be valid. Consideration could include a bonus, for example.
- Be sure to check and comply with state laws which can have additional conditions.

Regarding copyrights, there is a federal law stating that copyrighted material made by an employee within the scope of employment is owned by the employer and not the employee (17 U.S.C. §201(b)).

If the author or inventor is an independent contractor rather than an employee, you should take similar steps to protect the company's intellectual property.

The creator of the IP also should sign a non-compete and non-disclosure agreement (NCNDA). See an example of this in Appendix 3. This prohibits another party from competing against you and disclosing the confidential information.

That's all fine, but what happens if the other party doesn't want to sign these documents?

○ If it is an employee, you could put these requirements in any employment agreement or the company's employee handbook, and have the employee sign a document as proof that the employee understands and agrees to them. Signing can be a condition to employment and failure to sign can be grounds for discharge.

○ If it is an independent contractor, this language should be in your contract with the contractor.

○ When dealing with major investors, they often won't sign NDAs. They'll say, "I can't keep track of what I can and can't talk about." Then you will have to decide what and how much to disclose.

○ With customers and investors, you, of course, must tell them *what* your product or service is and what it does, but you can try to draw the line at *how* something works, which is your "secret sauce." In other words, here's what my product or service can do, but I'm keeping the details of how it does that confidential on advice of counsel. If you're entering serious negotiations that require further disclosure, it usually is more likely that the other party will sign an NDA.

○ Here are some practical suggestions to save money and get better results in your patent filing.

> **TIP: USE THE PATENT MINE FIELD (PMF) STRATEGY™ FOR A MAXIMIM VIABLE PATENT™ (MVP) WHEN FILING A PATENT APPLICATION.**

Extend and Stretch the Invention/Idea Before You File a Patent

Suppose your software developer has an idea. He writes it up. Don't just send it off to your patent attorney to be filed or you'll miss getting broader patent protection. Instead, get your team together and see if you can expand on the idea. Get everyone in a fun, creative, and relaxed mood. Find a room with a big white board or blackboard;

or use some of those big self-stick easel pads on the wall. Have your team brainstorm, with no rules except to capture any associated ideas. The crazier the better. What bells and whistles can be added to make it more likely your invention will be new and non-obvious? I once added language to a patent application for a power station that made part of it edible. Your goal is the "Maximum Viable Patent" (MVP). You want the most coverage you can get from your patent without making your patent application so broad that it won't be approved.

Think of this as a war game. Your goal is to create a wide "Patent Mine Field" (PMF) around your core invention to protect it from those who would steal your invention. Ask yourself, "What would my competitors do to try to get around these patent claims I've drafted? What kind of a patent claim would they file to do that?" Then draft more comprehensive patent language to prevent that. Then ask again, "Now what would competitors do to get around these even broader or more varied claims; and how can I expand my claims even further to protect against that?" Do this a couple of times before you send your draft patent ideas to your patent attorney to be put into proper form and filed. Hopefully, your patent claims now will be much broader with more features. Those additional features will make it more likely to be patentable as "new, useful, and non-obvious," and harder for competitors to get around your patent claims.

How Does Your Patent Relate to Your Business Plan?

Creating and protecting your IP should be an integral part of your business plan and business. Patents are expensive so your approach should be strategic and carefully thought through. For example:

○ What is the core intellectual property that you really need to protect? File for that ASAP. Remember that the first to file a patent application with the PTO wins the patent rights. I once filed a patent claim for a mobile power station and only beat out another claim from a European company by a few weeks. The world is flat. Patentable ideas spread like wildfire. So once your invention is developed, go ahead and file to get your place in line.

○ You'll continually think of new ideas that might be patentable. You can add those later by a new application or a "continuation in part" (CIP) application (in which a later application is linked to the first one) after your experience with customers shows you whether such features are worth the expense of a further filing.

Patent Search

Before filing a patent application, consider conducting a patent search. You can get some sense of what the prior art looks like by going to patents.google.com and doing your own search for free. Or you can use a patent search firm. You can find search firms on the internet, just search for "patent search." That may cost $500-$2,000 but could save you $10,000 or more if you file for a patent and get rejected because your invention was already patented. There's another advantage of doing a search. You'll get some ideas from other patents that can give you new ideas for your patents.

When you get the search results, have another white board session with your team. Make three columns. Column one is your proposed invention(s). Column two is what the search shows is already invented; you can't get a patent on those inventions. Column 3 is what's left that's new that you can include in your patent application. This way you can determine if there's enough in column three to make it worthwhile to file for a patent.

> **TIP: DON'T BLOG ABOUT THE SECRET SAUCE OF YOUR INVENTION BEFORE FILING A PATENT OR YOU MAY NOT BE ABLE TO GET ONE.**

One-Year Limit

You must file for a patent within one year of the first offer to sell your invention or within one year of your first public use or disclosure of the invention, such as any information in the public domain that makes your invention obvious. So don't blog about the details of your invention or otherwise publicly disclose it unless you don't plan to file a patent. Also, avoid disclosing your patentable idea before filing for a patent so that you can get a head start on the competition. Absent special circumstances, disclosing your invention under an NCNDA, however, is probably not a public disclosure, so if you need to you can share your ideas with third parties and potential customers under an NCNDA without triggering the one-year filing requirement.

Save Money with a Provisional Patent Application

The typical patent filing with lots of details, drawings, and claims is called a "non-provisional" application. There is also a "provisional" application (PPA). That's a simple document that merely demonstrates how to make and use the invention. Sometimes an inventor will have the patent attorney file raw notes and other random items regarding the invention. That might only cost $500 to $1,500. Once filed, you will get the all-important filing date to secure your place as the first to file for that invention.

The Provisional application is not published. Rather, it totally disappears in one year if you don't take any further actions. You have one year to file the "real" or "non-provisional" patent if you want to capture the earlier date of the provisional filing. The non-provisional will include a discussion of the state of the "prior art," an explanation as to why the invention is different from prior art, a description with details on the invention, drawings, and finally the "claims." The claims are the key parts that specify precisely what you are claiming as your monopoly for the invention and therefore what others are not allowed to copy if the patent is granted.

Fast Track Applications

Patent applications can take many months or years to be reviewed and approved, rejected, or rejected in part. There are several ways to accelerate the examination. These require filing a petition and may require a fee and limit the number of independent and dependent claims that can be filed. For example, PTO's "Track One Prioritized

Examination" aims to complete the examination within about one year and limits patent claims to four independent claims and thirty total claims. Fees for that range from $1,000 to $4,000 depending on the size of the entity filing.[26]

Maybe You Don't Want a Quick Answer!

On the one hand, getting a patent can be very helpful to raising money from investors or other partners. On the other hand, investors will be disappointed if your patent is rejected, so it might be better not to get an answer quickly from the PTO. Your patent attorney should be able to give you some sense of the strength of the application so you can decide whether to file for an accelerated examination.

Enforcement of Patents

If your patent is infringed, you can bring an infringement case in federal court. You need to consider that the other party might then challenge your patent as not having been properly issued. These cases often take years and can cost hundreds of thousands of dollars, so be careful before you start any litigation because it might be very expensive and hard to stop.

International Patents—Patent Cooperation Treaty (PCT)

Should you file internationally?

The PCT provides for a single filing and examination internationally that covers some 150 countries. Following examination, the examination report is sent to the countries in which you wish to file. Each country then decides on its own whether to grant a patent. This starts out simply but becomes very expensive when each country assesses filing fees. Then, after the patent issues, periodic maintenance fees must be paid as well.

So, before you file for international patent protection, be sure to ask your attorney how long it would take and how much it would cost. And think about why you are filing. Even if you have the right to sue for infringement in another country, the time and expense might not be worth it. Do you really want to be tied up for years of litigation in another country?

CONTRACTING WITH THE GOVERNMENT

Contracting with the government is beyond the scope of this book. Be sure to consult an attorney experienced with government contracting before doing it. A major issue is what IP rights to the invention does the government get and what rights do you retain? In general, you can retain ownership in your patents and other intellectual property when contracting with the government. However, the government will often want to receive a non-exclusive license to use that IP for government purposes. Some of the factors involved when you are negotiating with the government include:

- o Whether you own "background IP" (prior IP that isn't the subject of the current contract with the government) or "subject IP" (the invention that is conceived and reduced to practice in the performance of the government contract). The closer your IP is to subject IP the more likely it is that the government will want more rights to it because government funding and efforts were used to develop it.
- o How much of your invention does the government need to use? The more they need to use, the more they will want to control it, but this might give you more leverage in negotiating with them when they may really want to license your invention.

- You need to be wary of other government contractors who may be competitors that will have access to your IP. Government agencies often contract out their duties to private companies. Some of those may be your competitors.
- You should use an attorney before entering into any contracts with the government as the statutes and regulations are complex, such as the Federal Acquisition Regulations (FAR) for civilian agencies and the Defense Federal Acquisition Regulations (DEFARS) for military contracts.

**Examples of Intellectual Property Challenges:
"I Lost my Intellectual Property and Can't Get Up!"**

*Scooter helps a fashion heiress deal with intellectual property
piracy using patents, trademarks, copyrights, and other tools.
All startups drink from a firehose and struggle to maintain
life balance amid the chaos. Here's how Scooter deals with
this challenge.*

*With much seductive speech she persuades him.
With her smooth talk she compels him.
Right away he follows her,
and goes like an ox to the slaughter...
He is like a bird rushing into a snare,
not knowing that it will cost him his life.*

—Psalms 7:22-23

Early the next morning, he shook off his dream as he came up for
breakfast and saw Megan's car out front. She came in the front door.

She looked upset and her eyes were red.

"Are you okay? You look worried."

She didn't reply.

"What's the problem?"

"You remember I was worried about Mom? She finally broke
down and told me she was afraid that dad was having an affair with
his new secretary. She's very attractive, and twenty years younger.
I never would have suspected that of dad. He's not perfect, but if
that's true.... You'd better not ever, ever do anything like that!" Her
tears started.

"Don't worry, don't worry," he said. "Maybe it's not true."

Scooter took a long sip of coffee and poured her some as he
listened.

As they talked, he straightened the pictures over the kitchen
table. The cleaning ladies did a great job every two weeks but managed to move every picture in the house. Scooter didn't like anything

unbalanced, pictures or people. Pictures were a heck of a lot easier to rebalance.

But this was just the start of a very long day for Scooter. Just as he was pouring some more coffee, he heard something come through the mail slot by the front door and drop on the floor.

Scooter picked up the envelope. It was from a law firm. He hated getting mail he wasn't expecting from law firms.

"Sidley and Dallas," he mumbled. "Must be a thousand lawyers in that junk yard dog, Wall Street mega-firm. It's like a basement in a horror movie. Nothing good ever comes out of a basement." He was shockingly correct.

He quickly scanned the cover letter and the attached, 100-page complaint listing fifteen causes of action. He had just been sued for $100 million. One hundred million dollars!

The complaint came from a case five years ago. Scooter had sued Stay Safe Grocery, a national chain, for $25 million. Scooter's client, Sally Martin, had died from salmonella after eating their contaminated lettuce. The grocery store knew about the salmonella but kept selling it to make more money. Scooter won the case.

Now a new party had come out of the woodwork. The estate of John Martin. John was Sally's brother. The complaint said that John also was at Sally's house for a big party when Sally was poisoned, and he got sick too and died. That was news to Scooter. He didn't remember any of this. Scooter felt the blood rush to his head, and he groped for the nearest chair. "How could I have been so stupid to have missed this!" he said to himself. "I've committed gross negligence! I don't know how that was possible. The case took years; I thought I had everything covered! All those interrogatories, all those depositions, years of work down the drain and now this!"

"What's wrong?" asked Megan.

"I've been sued," he whispered.

"What for?"

"A new party popped up in the Stay Safe case. His estate claims I failed to include him in the suit for damages and the statute of limitations has run out, leaving his estate with nothing, so they're coming after me."

"You've got insurance, right?"

"Yes, I've got professional liability insurance, but the suit is for $100 million and my coverage is $3 million."

"$100 million! Ohhhh ... Scooter J. Magee! You're supposed to know what you're doing!"

Those words cut deep. Right to the bone.

"I'll figure something out. In the meantime, stop jumping on me for a second and let me think! Just for one second ... can you do that?"

Megan turned and left the room. He heard the bedroom door close and her sobbing.

Scooter, the Startup Expert, had made a stupid rookie mistake. He'd missed the one fact hidden in the thousands of facts in the case. The devil is always in the details.

"What have I done?" he cried. His professional reputation as a lawyer and his self-image were inseparable. They had been fused together by the constant heat and pressure from decades of law practice. A chunk of his professional core, his very core, was falling off.

He collapsed into his chair. He was scared.

Of course, he would fight this. Find a great malpractice attorney. But the legal fees would drain his assets. A case like this can take years of depositions, interrogatories, meetings, and endless legal bills.

What he feared as much was what it would do with him and Megan. Just when things were already going downhill. They had been going to France on vacation each summer for the past few years. The last time they went she fell in love with Le Canadel, a quaint coastal town in the South of France between Toulon and Saint Tropez. It was in the hills with amazing views of the water. From time to time, they had been looking online at small villas there and with the pandemic the prices were coming down. This finally was going to be the year they could afford to buy. But suddenly they'd separated. And now, suddenly the money might not be there anyway. He just sat there, slumped in his chair. He looked at the picture he'd just straightened. It was tipped again.

***

Washington Field Office, FBI
JW McKinney picked up the phone.

"Scarlett, JW here. Are you on the secure line?"

"Yes."

"Good job on your first assignment. Now you need to cozy up to Professor Magee. Whatever it takes. Find out all you can."

"What do you mean whatever it takes?"

JW smiled, while looking at her with eager eyes that could have undressed a mummy. "You're a good-looking woman, you know what I mean."

Scarlett was furious now. "Look, I'll get close to him but let me do it my way. Don't interfere with any funny stuff or you'll scare him away and we'll have to start all over."

Her boldness surprised him. "Yeah ... Yeah ... okay."

He filled her in on next steps. She said "Okay," and hung up. She had a bad feeling about where this was going but she was trapped. She wandered out on the balcony to get some air and watched the dark clouds moving in from the West, thinking about how to get even with the bastards at the FBI and CIA.

***

Three days later, Scooter still couldn't sleep. At breakfast, he just sat at the table, not eating. He was devastated. How could he hold things together long enough to fix this mess? If it wasn't bad enough to have the mob after him, now he's got a $100 million lawsuit. What is happening?!

For some reason, he thought about Five Miles. Then it hit him.

"I want a dog," he said aloud. "Actually, I don't just want one, I need one."

He remembered what author Ben Williams once said: "There is no psychiatrist in the world like a puppy licking your face."

So, that's how he found himself at the Arlington Animal Welfare League on South Arlington Mill Drive. He opened the door and a cheery young woman approached.

"Hi, I'm Caroline."

Scooter took off his cap and put it on the table by the door. Caroline was holding what might have been a dog or a big squirrel. It was hard to tell with its hair exploding in all directions. Thank God the big collar was at least holding some of it together. Caroline put it down lovingly in a nearby cage. Only a mother could love whatever it was.

"How can I help you?"

"I'm looking for a dog."

"Anything in particular?"

"Maybe something short haired, not too big, friendly."

They talked for a while. Then she got up the nerve to ask the make-or-break question.

"Are you allergic to poison ivy?"

"Say again?"

"Are you allergic to poison ivy? The plant?"

"Had it once, no big deal."

"Good, let me show you Sammy."

Caroline led Scooter down a corridor past rows of cats and turned the corner to the dog section. There was Sammy. He was a cute, light tan Cairn terrier. He instantly made eye contact with Scooter. When dogs and people make eye contact, it releases oxytocin in the dog—the same chemical that produces parent-child bonding in humans. Sammy was a charmer. Scooter was intrigued. Sammy kept looking at Scooter and gave a high pitched, but sad whine.

"What do you know about him?"

"He's very friendly, seems really smart. Came from Crooked Creek, West Virginia—along with a sandwich bag of poison ivy."

"What?"

"Seems his owner used to put poison ivy in his own salads to build up an immunity to it. He'd give a little to Sammy from time to time, and Sammy liked it a lot. He was raised on it. The good news is that the urushiols—the chemicals that cause the poison ivy rash—are an antidote to some foods like wine that usually are poisonous to dogs. But too much poison ivy can have some strange effects on dogs. It's not really understood. In Haiti, they used to feed poison ivy to dogs to increase their natural skills. People said they'd sometimes develop unnatural skills, too."

"Unnatural skills?"

"Yeah, that's all he told me, probably just idle talk or something."

"Any other dogs I should take a look at?"

"No, the last one left this morning. Since the last pandemic people are staying home more and looking for dogs and cats for comfort."

Scooter opened the cage and picked up Sammy. Sammy cuddled in.

Scooter made up his mind on the spot. "I'll take him."

Sammy seemed to understand that and wiggled for joy. Then he jumped out of his arms and bolted down the hall toward the door. Before Scooter and Caroline could get back to the entrance, Sammy had jumped on the table, grabbed Scooter's hat, and brought it to him. Scooter and Caroline looked at each other.

"How did he even know that was my hat? We were around the corner."

"Probably just a coincidence."

Caroline had Scooter fill out some papers, gave him a complimentary leash, and said, "Enjoy. Just call me if you have any questions." Scooter picked up some dog food and headed home, hoping that Megan hadn't changed her mind about having a dog. He walked up the stone steps to his house with Sammy in his arms and opened the front door.

Megan was over for their appointed "date night," where they were trying to get comfortable with each other again. She smiled when she saw Scooter's new companion.

"That's a surprise! Is that yours?"

"Yeah, I thought it would be fun to have a dog."

"He's kinda cute. Does he have a name?"

"Maybe Sammy, does that sound okay?"

"Yeah, I guess. I'll get him some water. Here, give me the dog food and we'll see if he's hungry."

Sammy lapped up the water and all the dog food. After dinner, they watched TV in the family room. Scooter polished off his quarter pint of Ben & Jerry's butter pecan ice cream. Sammy was sleeping. Things felt nice and more normal for a change. As Scooter's old boss Bud Lawrence used to say, "There's nothing better than a warm fire, your wife by your side, a drink in your hand, and a dog at your feet, reading words you have written."

Scooter opened the door to let Sammy run out into the fenced yard. Scooter watched him explore the big oak trees, munch on some fresh poison ivy by the azalea bushes, chase a squirrel, and then disappear into the shadows. Scooter came back and started thinking about the lawsuit and how to fight it. He'd check on lawyers in the morning.

After an hour or so Scooter opened the back door and called for Sammy. Nothing. He called again and again.

He turned on the flood light on the big oak tree in the middle of the yard and still no Sammy. So, he got his flashlight and walked around the fence that surrounded the yard.

"Maybe he tunneled under the fence, or something," he thought.

Then he heard something like a whine. It sounded far away. He went around the whole yard again. Nothing.

Scooter sat down under the big oak tree. Another whine, this time louder or closer, he couldn't tell which.

"Where's that coming from? I've looked all over."

Sammy gave a bark and Scooter looked up. Right above his head, Sammy was twenty feet up the tree sitting comfortably on a big branch.

"Good gosh. How'd you get up there? Is *that* the strange behavior from poison ivy Caroline at the pound mentioned?"

Sammy turned and slowly walked down the tree headfirst, all the way to the ground. He sat next to Scooter and nuzzled his head into Scooter's lap. Sammy looked up at Scooter with knowing, sad eyes. Scooter had just rescued Sammy from the dog pound. Scooter had just been sued for $100 million. Now, Scooter was too scared to even hope. He couldn't know it but Sammy was going to repay the favor and more.

The breeze picked up. It was warm and comforting. Nature's blanket. They sat there for a long time in silence and watched the clouds go past the golden moon. For a moment even in all the chaos, there was calm.

Meanwhile at the Global Surveillance Division (GSD)
Washington Field Office, FBI

"Boss, here are the results from Project W at The TOMBS. We got the Pencam video from CIA's Agent S and the prints on Cold Fingers and Magee. Hard to make out everything, but it sounds like Cold Fingers' got a high-tech camera like the one the CIA's after. Magee was somehow involved with the Molly's Game mob case; don't know how yet, so we should keep the tap going on him."

Jackson Tapper, division chief, looked up from his desk.

"Okay, good. Get that intel over to Bulldog at CIA right away. How's the wiretap on Magee working?"

"Pretty good. Not much so far. Talks about his new dog and the usual stuff around the house. We'll be scanning the data with Wordtrac, and I'll let you know if we hear anything of interest."

"Okay, and have DOJ ask the judge to authorize thirty days more on the tap. Wait a minute, he's got a dog?"

"Yeah."

"I've got an idea. Have you heard of the CIA's Project Tailgate?"

"Nope."

"I need to talk to Bulldog. Fill you in later."

***

"Hey Bulldog, you still looking for a dog for Project Tailgate?"

"You bet, Jackson, appreciate your call. This thing's got a lot of potential. Needs to go operational. The scientists keep wanting to test, test, test."

"I think I've got what you need, listen to this..."

***

The next morning, Scooter's phone woke him up at 7:00 a.m.

"Hello?"

"Mr. Magee?"

"Yes."

"Please hold for Scarlett Montevideo."

Scooter rubbed his eyes and sat up straight. *Good gosh*, he thought, the *Scarlett Montevideo?*

"Dear Mr. Magee, I'm so sorry to bother you so early, but this is Scarlett Montevideo, and I wonder if I might have a minute of your time. It's urgent," said the silky voice with a slight Latin accent on the other end of the line.

"I'm listening." She had his attention as he fumbled for his slippers.

"I've created my own line of designer clothes and need some advice on how to protect the intellectual property on the designs I've developed." Instead, he found himself intrigued. And her sultry voice started creating some images to match.

"Go on."

"I really need some legal and business advice. This is crazy short notice, but could you join me for dinner tonight? There's a pressing matter that I need to resolve."

This was intriguing. Scooter knew that Scarlett was a principal at Zapata, one of the world's leading fashion houses. The *New York Times* typically showed her at some elegant ball with one of those dark, handsome Latin types with perfect short beards; and she was never without her diamonds.

"Ah ... what's the pressing matter?"

"I've been selling my fall collection in Brazil, and now I want to bring it to the US. But I'm afraid I've made a big mistake by going public with these great designs before I've done anything to protect my intellectual property from the pirates with patents or something. They'll copy anything overnight, even use one of my own factories in Thailand to do it at night. Then, I'll start seeing the third-rate copies on racks on the sidewalks in New York and DC. It will kill my reputation, and I'll lose all that business."

"I see. All right. Okay, I can meet you tonight. Want me to make a reservation downtown?

"Thank you so much. No. I don't want anyone to know I'm meeting with you. So, let's meet somewhere away from DC, the Blue Moon Café in Shepherdstown, West Virginia. It sounds far but it's really only a little over an hour from DC. I'll see you around 7:30 tonight, okay?"

"Ah... Okay."

"Great, see you tonight."

Obviously, Scarlett wasn't used to people saying no to her.

Around noon, to prepare for the hour drive and just to take his mind off of things, Scooter picked up some tools, opened the bonnet on his Healey convertible and listened to the sound of the engine. When it was tuned right the car produced a melodious low growl— one of the best sounds in classic sports cars.

The downside was that the three carburetors always needed synchronizing. Scooter liked to do that the old school way with a cut-up garden hose. He put one end of the hose into the intake throat on each carburetor, one at a time, and put the other end to his ear. He listened carefully and went back and forth with the hose, adjusting each carburetor until their sucking sounds were all the same.. Then he locked the set screws down tight. The car was ready to go. Cars need to breathe right just like humans.

Around 6 p.m. he headed north along the Potomac River on GW Parkway to the Greenway toll road, then south around Leesburg on Route 15. After a while, the Lego-like rows of houses fell away in his rear-view mirror. Paraphrasing columnist Alexandra Petri, they were rows where you don't remember which house is yours, so you mark an X on the door. Except that everyone else has an X, or was it a Y? They were endless suburbs where the lawn must be mowed. Suburbs where you must get in a car to have fun, which is to get lost in Walmart with the giant bins of colored balls. Meaningless eye candy to dress up the big box stores in the same big box suburbs.[27]

The car was cruising now, with a low vibration like a Lazy Boy Massager. He was floating down the road. His mind was wandering. He laughed at himself. What had he been doing this afternoon leaning over the engine with a cut up hose stuck in his ear?

Then it came to him. Had he been working on the car or was the car working on him?

When the car was idling, the moving parts sounded like instruments. The exhaust was like a contrabassoon, blowing a low, resonating C. The overhead camshaft rhythmically clicked when it pushed the twelve spring-loaded valves up and down into the engine block. Two valves multiplied by each of the six cylinders produced a twelve-drum percussion instrument. And the carburetors, moving the air through the engine, were the wind section.

So, he wasn't just tuning a car; he was conducting a four-wheeled orchestra. One of the carburetor players was too loud or soft. Valve number two was clicking too loudly. When he tuned the sounds just the right way using a wrench for a baton, they all came together—synchronized. With a perfect touch, the car was transformed. It wasn't just playing music; it was singing its own complex and unique song. A car is a lot more than a mode of transportation.

Or ... was all this really about *his* balance instead?

Maybe that's why I'm sticking a hose in my ear, Scooter thought. *I'm trying to use precision tools to achieve my balance.* Then again, *maybe it's just a hose in my ear.* As Freud supposedly said, "Sometimes a cigar is just a cigar." But on some level using the hose and getting control over a couple of carburetors was evidence that he had a chance to control and balance his life.

He had seen the balance problem with his legal clients too. Some days were a triage operation. They'd call him when the egg was already scrambled. They expected miracles and demanded vengeance. "I want a junk yard lawyer who can teach those bastards a lesson and run them out of business." Scooter tried to calm things down, restore balance, and aim for justice. Justice is the goal; law is just the means. They were headed off the cliff with their selfish demands. He saw it long before they would. Lawsuits might be temporarily satisfying to the plaintiffs when they file a suit but that's only 1 percent of the mess that follows. There are depositions, countersuits, hundreds of thousands of dollars, years of stress, and appeals, until one side gives in, usually because they're out of money. Scooter would try to calm things down up front and see if they could settle. See if each side would give a little here, a little there, tune the parties, and reduce the clicking noises. Find the right balance on the scales of justice.

Scooter clearly needed to re-balance his life. He was unbalanced like a banging brick in a washer on spin cycle. He needed to get his balance back. End the chaos from Cold Fingers and the lawsuit And most important, work things out with Megan.

*∗∗

Somewhere North of Bakerton, West Virginia, he saw it and snapped out of his musing. Fifty yards ahead was a two-mile straight shot of road with a beautiful forty-degree uphill stretch in the middle. And no oncoming cars. Think Steve McQueen in *Bullet*, in his souped-up Ford Mustang 390 GT leaping over the hills in San Francisco chasing the bad guys. But Scooter wasn't thinking. He jammed the pedal to the floor. You can tell a lot about a driver by how much rubber is left on the accelerator pedal. His had none. The pedal smashed the electric switch under it that automatically downshifted the car. Simultaneously, the mechanical linkage popped open all three of the butterfly valves on the triple carburetors and the car inhaled a tornado of air, mixed it with high-octane fuel in the intake manifold, and blasted it into the six cylinders. The RPMs went from 2,500 to 5,000 and the speed from 60 to 70 to 80 mph. At 80, the spoke wheels started to sing a high-pitched whistle as they loosened and vibrated to match the engine's vibrations. Now Scooter felt alive: he was on that knife edge of danger where all his senses were enhanced. At 90, the left side mirror flipped upside down. It blew clear off at 110 but Scooter kept going until 120. Now the car was shaking and the steering was wiggling like a wet noodle. His 2,549-pound guided missile flew up the hill, and at the peak, all four wheels launched into the air, and he and the car went weightless. "Whoee!" he screamed at the top of his lungs. It was one brief moment of bliss to escape from his problems.

Scooter turned down the wick as he drove into Shepherdstown, the oldest town in West Virginia. German Street had a couple of blocks of family-owned shops and restaurants and there was usually someone playing music on the sidewalks. Thomas Shepherd got the whole town and a lot more from a land grant in 1734; West Virginia's first newspaper and book were published there. In 2000,

President Bill Clinton helicoptered there for the Syrian-Israeli peace talks. Hard to top that for a little town's history.

Scooter parked on Princess Street next to a big van. That and the silver Maserati behind it seemed out of place. He walked down the sidewalk past the 1790 Pump House at 107 Princess. The Pump House was a sort of nineteenth century laundromat. Water from the Town Run, one of six streams in the area, meandered through the middle of town. It used to run under the Pump House and the locals could do their laundry there while catching up on the latest news. Now, Town Run went along Princess Street, tunneled under the sidewalk, and disappeared.

"Wonder where that goes," he mused.

The Blue Moon Café, on a corner across from Shepherd University, was an ordinary looking, boxy building with big windows and a red tiled roof. He walked in. It had a cozy, friendly feel with big chalkboard menus, antique blue bottles of every size and shape on the windowsills, board games for kids, and happy chatter. And it had its own special character—literally. On a table in the left corner crouched a three-foot ceramic bearded elf with a blue shirt holding a welcome sign in his left hand. He was bending over and mooning the room—with his bare rear perilously close to an earthen pot with long-spined cactuses. "Ah," he chuckled, "blue shirt plus moon equals Blue Moon Café."

Altogether, the place was not as classy as he expected. "Why would Scarlett come all the way out here?" he wondered aloud, as he opened the side door to the outside patio. Then he saw why. There was a vast, rambling garden. Must have been twenty trees, from giant pines and oaks to red flowering trees presiding over different levels of lazy gardens. Wrought iron tables randomly gathered around the trees. Bougainvillea ran up the walls of the restaurant. Someone could have grazed a cow there and it would have fit right in.

Down some stone steps was the centerpiece, a sunken garden, surrounded by a curved fieldstone wall. Then, on the far right, the Town Run that had disappeared across the street bubbled up right there and ran happily along the garden wall until it disappeared into the ground on its meandering journey to the Potomac River less than a mile away.

Once his eyes adjusted to the shade, he could see that there was just one table, with a white tablecloth, set for two, in the middle of the sunken garden. And just one woman. She was more than enough.

Scarlett saw Scooter and smiled. She had him at the smile. She looked every bit like an heiress. Thirtyish, cute nose, glowing, flawless complexion, long blonde hair pulled off her face, blue eyes, and a dress that was way too low cut for Shepherdstown. The strappy black Prada sandals showed off her toned legs. The platinum and diamond stud earrings, at least twenty carats, topped off the shapely package. The diamond on the boot strap wasn't shy.

She held out her hand. "May I call you Scooter?"

"Sure. Is Scarlett okay?"

"Of course."

After some pleasantries, Tracy, the friendly blonde server with a big smile arrived and others kept coming. First, with a carpaccio of herb crusted baby lamb. Then, a fresh Maine lobster served on a silver plate floating on heart shaped ice. A goat cheese, walnut, cranberry, and pear salad with a light Dijon vinaigrette was next. By the time they were on the second bottle of Cabernet, they were laughing together and telling stories. Her stories were better, but she laughed at his anyway.

"Great wine."

"Yes, it's my favorite Napa, the 2012 Berringer Private Reserve Cab. The combination of wild cherry, plum, and raspberry is very subtle."

"The food was excellent too."

"Good. I sent my chef here this morning in his catering van to prepare everything. A friend owns this restaurant, and he lets me use it when I want to have a quiet place to go."

Scooter was feeling out of his league with Scarlett. She was like a Ferrari. Fascinating, but would need more tuning than triple carburetors. He was a long way from Diet Cokes at the Cowboy Café. Nevertheless, he was wondering if they had any butter pecan ice cream, but quickly put that out of his mind.

"What's your favorite movie, Scooter?"

"I like the classic, early James Bond movies with Sean Connery. The ones before they had too many explosions and special effects. Movies like *From Russia with Love*."

"Scooter, speaking of Russia, have you ever been to Brighton Beach? It's sure not fancy, but it's so earthy and real. Lots of interesting people and things going on there."

"Haven't been, but funny you should mention it. I just was meeting with someone from there."

"What about?"

"Oh, just a client thing, new product."

"Come on, tell me more! What kind of product?"

"Still finding out."

"I'd love to hear more when you do."

She looked disappointed. She was awkwardly quiet for a time and then abruptly changed the subject.

"So, Scooter, I need you to protect my new clothing line. What should I do? Am I too late to get a patent or something?"

Scooter was still dreamingly enjoying the scene, the 2012 Berringer, and Scarlett. He was trying his best to focus on business, not pleasure. Slowly he came out of Berringerville and his inner lawyer was awakening. In a few more seconds he'd be cruising along on lawyer-talk autopilot.

"Well, as I mentioned on the phone, your concerns were right on. You should have taken steps to protect your intellectual property before releasing your new fashion line to the public. There are four kinds of intellectual property: trade secrets, trademarks, copyrights, and patents. You'll need to do something on each. I can show you what to do."

Scarlett came back to the game. She leaned in across the table toward him. Her low-cut dress was working overtime. He could feel her warm breath and breathed in that and her scent. She put her soft hand on his, and purred, "I'd love you to show me just what to do. I think there's a lot we could do together."

Scooter didn't need the Rosetta Stone to translate that.

Then she leaned back, and her mood changed again. She started describing her new clothing line in way too much detail. Scooter broke in.

"Scarlett, time is of the essence to keep you out of trouble. You don't want to commit Startup Suicide. How about if I send you a quick memo tomorrow with the details of what you need to do, okay?"

"Great, here's my e-mail address and private cell number, Scooter. I would love to get together again after I've read your memo. My driver's here. Got to go." She squeezed his hand and gave him a smile. They stood up, she came around to his side of the table, she moved in closer to him, and as they made eye contact she slowly pressed her body into his and gave him a long-lasting hug to remember. Then she was off. But her mind wasn't.

What am I doing coming on to Scooter like this? she thought. *He seems like a nice enough guy; talked about his wife a lot. I don't know how much more of this I can do.* Scarlett got in her car, put her head down, and sobbed.

Scooter just sat there in the garden. A sliver of moon sent a glow through the trees. Everyone else had left except a few waiters smoking by the kitchen door. As he drove home he was filled with questions. What did this woman really want? Was she a "Wolf in Chic Clothing?"[28] What was that about Brighton Beach? Oh well, until he figured that out, why not just go along for the ride? After all, nothing's more tempting than temptation!

As he drove into his driveway he was too preoccupied to notice the car parked half a block away in the dark. Inside was a man talking on his phone eating Chet Chien, a fried banana dessert popular in Cambodia.

Chapter 4

BE SMARTER ABOUT PERSONNEL MANAGEMENT

Personnel matters present some of the most difficult problems for entrepreneurs and businesses. Many companies fail right off the bat because the founders don't agree on policy, financial matters, or have personal issues. Some of the best and worst decisions I've made have been in hiring and firing staff. One time, I hired a young engineer after meeting her for only fifteen minutes. I saw her resume, of course, but after spending a few minutes with her I just knew that she would be good, and she was. At the other extreme, I hired another employee who looked fantastic on paper. I had paid thousands of dollars for a headhunter, winnowed down the number of candidates over some months, and the headhunters and I agreed she was the strongest candidate. She checked every box and had all the right credentials and references. But she turned out to be lazy. Lazy is one thing that's hard to predict.

But an even bigger challenge for startups is the rapidly growing body of federal, state, and local regulations regarding every aspect of personnel matters. This includes hiring when you can legally do a criminal background check; promoting and firing employees without being discriminatory; and figuring out whether teasing becomes an illegal sexual advance.

In Appendix 4 is a table of contents from a typical employment manual. That will give you a sense of the variety and complexity of personnel matters. You really need to understand what to do and not to do to avoid liability because there are so many rules and penalties.

This chapter focuses on some of the most basic things you should know. But understand that this just scratches the surface. So, particularly when you're a startup, be sure to get expert human relations (HR) or legal advice until you feel comfortable with what to say and do with employees and others.

PARTNERSHIP AGREEMENTS AND ISSUES

Some of the most common startup and business problems are partner disputes, such as when one partner wants to fire another partner. Partner disputes can cripple the company, demoralize other employees, and result in arguments and even lawsuits. And lawsuits scare away investors.

While writing this, I had a call from a prospective client in a typical partner dispute. This woman, I'll call her Rosa, owned 50 percent of a restaurant company. Her partner Anna owned the other 50 percent. Rosa said, "I'm working twelve hours a day. Anna's doing nothing. She never even shows up. She sends her husband to the restaurant instead, and he's worthless too. He only comes when he wants to. How do I get rid of both of them?"

I asked Rosa if she had any kind of a written agreement with Anna such as a partnership agreement that said who's in charge and when her partner could be fired. She didn't have anything. I expected this. Many entrepreneurs think that all they have to do is make the legal filing to create the company (like filing for Articles of Incorporation with their state) and they're done. They don't get a business license, create bylaws, or have partnership or employment agreements. Then they're stuck. Once you grant shares of stock to someone, it's very difficult to get them back, absent fraud or other unusual facts. Rosa tried to buy out Anna's 50 percent share in the company but Anna wouldn't even discuss this. Rosa would be stuck unless she hired a lawyer, threatened to sue, and found some grounds to litigate. Then, maybe Anna would decide to sell to get out of the suit. If the case were tried, figure a year or two to trial, another year for an appeal, and lots of legal fees and frustration.

It would have been so much easier if Rosa and Anna had signed a partnership agreement. That could have spelled out Anna's duties and how she could be fired or required to give back or sell her stock.

A partnership agreement is much like a typical employment agreement but with more emphasis on hiring, firing, and compensation issues.

Here are some of the partnership-related hot button topics that should be included in a partnership agreement. These provisions are a lot easier to agree to if they're done as soon as possible after the company's formation. Otherwise, once the company starts making money it will be much harder for the partners to agree.

Duties of the Partner

It should be very clear what the partner is expected to do and not do. For example, specify the partner's title, such as chief marketing officer (CMO), and to whom the partner reports and supervises. A job description should be attached spelling out a detailed list of duties and how those duties could be adjusted as required.

Control

Generally, providing joint or equal control such as fifty/fifty voting rights creates unnecessary tensions. It's usually better if one person or a board of directors or several other partners have the final say in case people can't agree.

Compensation

The type and amount of compensation also should be very clear, whether it's salary, commissions, bonuses, stock, or stock options. For example, the agreement might say that the partner is eligible to be in the company's stock option pool for potential stock options but that stock options are awarded at the sole discretion of a majority of the partners. The criteria for awarding stock options should be spelled out in the company's stock option plan documents.

Hiring and Firing

Under what circumstances may the partner be fired and by whom? By a majority or two-thirds vote of the shareholders? Sometimes partners, particularly founders, will insist that they cannot be fired (absent willful or criminal actions) unless there is a unanimous vote of the board or all the other partners, and that they have an opportunity to be heard before being fired.

What Happens to Partner's Stock or Stock Options When They Leave or Are Fired?

From the company's perspective, it would be good if the company had the right to reclaim some of the stock that the partner hasn't gotten yet (not yet vested) when the partner is terminated. The company could have a vesting schedule for the partner earning stock or stock options. For example, the company might set a target that over twenty-four months the partner could receive up to 15 percent of the company's "issued" (actually granted to shareholders) or "authorized" (stock allowed to be issued by the company whether or not issued to any stockholder) stock, which would vest at the rate of 3 percent of the total each calendar quarter. This vesting would only occur if the partner met the milestones set forth in the job description or partnership agreement. If the partner left the company before the required twenty-four-month period, perhaps the partner would only receive some portion of the vested stock and none of the non-vested stock. This would protect the company from giving away too much stock while providing an incentive for the partner to stay and help the company succeed at least over the twenty-four-month vesting period. To prevent a former employee from competing against you, you could provide that the former employee would forfeit his/her stock back to the company if the employee competed against the company in violation of the employee's post-termination NCNDA with the company.

Termination Terms

Upon termination of employment, there should be a mutual release by the company and employee of all claims that could arise from matters during the term of the partner's employment. The company and the partner could agree not to disparage each other and could agree on a statement that the company would use if the partner wanted a reference for employment purposes after termination.

Assuming the partner and company can agree on these or similar terms early in the company's life, the likelihood of misunderstandings and litigation will be reduced.

HIRING
Job Description

The first step in filling a new position is to prepare a job description. This requires you to focus on what skill sets you need in the job, the work to be done, and what percentage of time is devoted to each work component. Like a partnership agreement, it should include:

- The job title and to whom the position reports and/or whom the person supervises;
- Duties so that there are no misunderstandings when discussing the job with the potential employee;
- Salary or a salary range;
- Any opportunity for other compensation such as bonuses or stock options;
- Benefits such as health insurance, accident insurance, dental, etc.;
- Travel requirements;
- Vacation and paid time off (PTO);
- Other requirements such as physical capabilities required on the job; and
- It should recite that employment matters and the employee are governed by the policies in the company's employee handbook as amended from time to time.

While it's tempting to make the job description sound great, you're better off being realistic. This will help avoid getting candidates who drop out when they find out what the job involves; and will reduce your legal liability from an employee who might claim that he/she was misled about the position.

Once you have the job description, you can try to find someone with as close to your requirements as possible. But there's another option. Sometimes you find a fantastic person and then decide that he or she can be trained on the job for skills that aren't there yet but can be learned on the job. In that case, you're molding the job around the person rather than fitting the person into the job. Once you go through that process, you should also create a job description with the new scope.

Using a Recruiter

You could do much of the hiring work yourself. For example, you could post an ad on the web and get the word out to colleagues. This could save you money. But you will end up with a far narrower search than if you use one of the many online or in-person recruiting services, such as LinkedIn, Indeed, or ZipRecruiter. ZipRecruiter claims it will post your job on many sites, screen millions of candidates for your desired attributes, and encourage curated candidates who rank high to apply.[1] But there are challenges for the 90 percent of employers that use such services. Post-pandemic, ZipRecruiter reported that 55 percent of job candidates wanted a job that would allow them to work at home. And job seekers have challenges too. Because those computer-based services use algorithms to screen candidates, many candidates fail to get jobs because one key word answer in the computer scanning process can kick them out as candidates. For example, nearly half of employers quickly reject candidates who haven't work in more than six months.[2] But a candidate might have had a one-time problem that caused that and would be perfectly qualified for the job. Despite the challenges posed by job site screening techniques, try to use in-person interviews as much as your time permits.

> **TIP: MAKE SURE YOU GET WRITTEN CONSENT BEFORE RUNNING A BACKGROUND CHECK.**

Background Checks

Once you've narrowed the field of prospective candidates, you should do a background check on the top ones. It makes sense to do that even before interviews so that if you have questions about what's in the background check you can ask about it in person rather than over the phone. That way you can get a better sense of the person's demeanor. It's also helpful to have more than one person doing the interview. This protects you from claims that you were discriminatory or abusive, etc. in the interview and it provides another perspective on whether to hire the candidate.

There are many federal and state rules about how to perform background checks. You need to be familiar with the specific rules for your jurisdiction. For example, here are some of the federal and local rules that apply in Washington, DC. But don't rely on the following provisions because they may change and may be different in each state. Be sure to get good legal advice in this complex area and other personnel matters.

The Fair Credit Reporting Act (FCRA)

This 1970 federal law (15 U.S.C 1681) was enacted to promote the accuracy and privacy of consumer information in consumer reporting agencies' files and to protect consumers from inaccurate information in their credit reports. It is enforced by the US Federal Trade Commission (FTC), the Consumer Financial Protection Bureau (CFPB), and by private litigants.

It also provides rules for employers screening job applicants. Employers *must*:

- Get written permission from the applicant or employee to run a credit report;
- Explain to the person being screened how the credit report is to be used;
- Not misuse the information;
- Provide a copy of the credit report if the person is not hired or is fired; and
- Provide the person being screened an opportunity to dispute the information before making an adverse decision.[3]

If a consumer's rights under FCRA are violated, the consumer can recover:

- Actual or statutory damages;
- Attorney's fees;
- Court costs; and
- Has a private right of action for employees to sue for punitive damages and willful violations.[4]

Arrest Record Laws

In Washington, DC, employers may not require a job applicant to supply an arrest record at the applicant's expense; but the applicant may voluntarily obtain the arrest record and authorize the employer to review it.[5]

Credit Information

Under the Fair Credit Employment Amendment Act of 2016, Washington, DC employers may not use a job applicant's or employee's credit information when making an employment decision.[6]

Ban-the-Box and Fair Hiring Laws

These laws, found in many jurisdictions, get their name from job applications that ask the question, "Have you ever been convicted of a crime?" Then the applicant must check a box "Yes" or "No." Under these laws:

- Employers only may inquire about criminal convictions and pending cases, not past charges;
- There must be an individual assessment of each applicant prior to an adverse action; and
- Candidates have the right to access relevant records the employer has used in making its determination.[7]

Assuming you are ready to hire the candidate, the next step is to prepare a letter offering employment, including the start date, compensation, and the position description.

> **TIP: MAKE SURE YOU'RE FAMILIAR WITH THE MANY EEOC REQUIREMENTS.**

PROHIBITED EMPLOYMENT PRACTICES AND EQUAL EMPLOYMENT OPPORTUNITY COMMISSION (EEOC) COMPLIANCE—AVOIDING VIOLATIONS

Beginning with the job search, it's easy for employers to make serious mistakes. Even if you have a personnel expert on staff, you should know what you can do without breaking the law. This will help protect you in case you accidently say or do the wrong thing. Title VII of the Civil Rights Act of 1964 as amended[8] sets forth the major federal rules regarding discrimination in the workplace. These rules are enforced by the Equal Employment Opportunity Commission (EEOC). You can find those rules at eeoc. gov. There are state and local rules that govern as well. I'd suggest that you prepare a summary of these rules and go over them with your key staff to avoid liability. Here are a few high points. EEOC states:

> [I]t is illegal to discriminate against someone (applicant or employee) because of that person's race, color, religion, sex (including gender identity, sexual orientation, and pregnancy), national origin, age (40 or older), disability or genetic information. It is also illegal to retaliate against a person because he or she complained about discrimination, filed a charge of discrimination, or participated in an employment discrimination investigation or lawsuit.[9]

EEOC's requirements for those in those listed "Protected Classes" must guide your actions from the time you place an ad for a job until the employee finally leaves your company and even after that.

Job Advertisements

It is illegal to place an employment ad that shows a preference for anyone because of race, color, religion, sex (including gender identity, sexual orientation, and pregnancy), national origin, age, disability, or genetic information. For example, you can't place an ad for a "female" or "recent college graduate." And if you primarily rely on word-of-mouth recruitment from a mostly Hispanic work force that may violate the law if it can be shown that almost all new hires are Hispanic.[10] In some jurisdictions, it is illegal to ask about past salary. You are not allowed to ask about an arrest record or involvement in political demonstrations. But it may be legal to ask about convictions. You also can ask about a person's age if it is a minimum requirement for the position such as driving a truck.

Job Assignments, Pay Reviews, and Promotions
It also is illegal to consider the status of persons in the Protected Classes for job assignments, salary reviews, promotions, disciplinary actions, and discharge. For example, you are not allowed to hire and recall a younger person or lay off an older one because of age.[11]

Employment References
You may not give a negative recommendation based on the fact of someone being in the Protected Classes previously listed.

Reasonable Accommodation and Disability
You must "provide reasonable accommodation to an employee or job applicant with a disability, unless doing so would cause significant difficulty or expense for the employer."[12] For example, you might need to provide a ramp for a wheelchair user or a reader for a blind person. You also must reasonably accommodate an employee's religious beliefs and practices unless doing so would cause difficulty or expense for the employer. This might include allowing an employee to swap shifts to attend religious services.

Harassment
It's also illegal to harass an employee. This includes slurs, graffiti, offensive or derogatory comments, verbal and physical conduct, "unwelcome sexual advances," and requests for sexual favors. Simple teasing is allowed. And the advances generally must be unwelcomed. But harassment becomes illegal if it creates a "hostile or offensive work environment or if it results in an adverse employment decision."[13] Sexual harassment itself is usually a civil matter resulting in fines and penalties and isn't a crime. But some acts of sexual harassment could be criminal acts such as assault and battery, false imprisonment, or rape.

Filing an EEOC Complaint

It is a relatively simple process to file a complaint with the EEOC. It can be filed in person or by mail with a nearby EEOC office. You can call the EEOC for the location of the nearest office, and the information to be included in the complaint is detailed on EEOC's website EEOC.gov. A complaint must be filed with EEOC within 180 days from the date of the alleged violation. This 180-day filing deadline is extended to three hundred days if the charge is also covered by a state or local anti-discrimination law. For Age Discrimination in Employment Act charges (ADEA)[14] only, state laws extend the filing limit to three hundred days.

Once an EEOC complaint is filed, EEOC will notify the organization within ten days and a web portal will be set up for communication between EEOC and the organization. EEOC will then investigate and witnesses may be called. Cases can be resolved through mediation, settlement, or litigation.[15] EEOC typically seeks to return the complainant to the same condition as if the violation had not occurred. EEOC can impose compensatory and punitive damages, and penalties up to $300,000 may be assessed for violations of Title VII discrimination violations.[16] Damages could be more if the EEOC sues in court.

EMPLOYMENT AGREEMENTS AND COMPENSATION
Employment Agreements

Employment agreements are used more frequently with C-suite or other senior officers or employees who are more critical to the company. These agreements will have many of the items in their job description but will include other items as well such as more details about compensation and termination. Senior-level candidates are likely to negotiate these items as well as salary. An example of some of the terms in a basic employment agreement is in Appendix 4.

Compensation

Because startups usually don't have much money, it's common for their compensation to be a salary plus other compensation such as commissions, bonuses, stock options, warrants, or equity in the company. Sometimes there's only a promise of compensation after sufficient funds are raised. Make sure you don't casually make any oral promises because if the employee relies on them they may become an "implied-in-fact" contract and legally enforceable.

Commissions

Commissions are used a lot with sales and marketing jobs. Because of the importance of getting sales, sometimes the sales and marketing employees make more money than the CEO.

Commissions typically are based on a percentage of sales made after subtracting refunds or returns. The company may want to base the commission on profits from sales rather than the gross amount of the sales. This provides a lot of opportunities for the company to load expenses on to the sales, which cuts the profit number and lowers the commission to be paid. Of course, salespersons understand that and are likely to challenge it.

Some commissions vary with the size of the sale. For example, the percentage of the commission often decreases as the dollar amount of the sale increases. A commission on the first $10,000 of gross sales might be 15 percent, the next $100,000 could be 10 percent, and anything over that, 8 percent.

Commissions also could be paid on repeat sales with the same customer, rather than just for the first sale. Some commission contracts limit or reduce commissions for the same customer after some period of time, such as after twenty-four months.

Bonuses

A bonus is a specific cash payment to recognize good performance on a specific task. Some companies pay bonuses only at the end of the year when they can see how much money is available for the bonus pool. Paying bonuses as soon as possible after the good performance can do more for morale.

One advantage of a bonus for the company is that it doesn't usually get rolled into the employee's base salary when it's time to provide an annual or other salary increase. That saves the company money.

Stock Options

A stock option is a written offer by the company to the employee or other recipient of the right (but not the obligation) to purchase or receive a specific amount of stock over a specified period at a specified price upon the occurrence of an event.

For example, the company may offer the employee an option to buy a thousand shares of stock at a discount to the current market price, at any time over the next five years provided that the company achieves $1 million in sales or raises $1 million in new investment. When the employee triggers the option to receive the stock, the employee "exercises" the option rights.

Both the company and the employee can benefit from stock options. The company benefits because it provides an incentive to the employee to support the Company and to stay with the company at least until the option can be exercised—a form of "golden handcuffs." The company benefits when it can require that the option can't be exercised unless the recipient is still an employee of the company. And, because stock options only convert into stock when all the option conditions have been met, if all the option expires without being exercised, then the company can do whatever it wants with the stock. For the employee, options can become very valuable if the company does well and can even create a windfall for the employee if the company goes public and the price of the stock soars.

The company's list of who the stockholders are and how many shares each has, is called a "stock capitalization table" or "cap table." That often lists the total stock available as if all the options were exercised. That is called a "fully diluted" cap table and provides full transparency to shareholders and investors as to how many shares are and will be issued.

There are two types of stock options: "qualified" (QSOs), also called "incentive stock options" (ISOs), and "non-qualified" (NQFOs). They are treated differently for tax purposes. Profits the employee might get from QSOs are taxed at the capital gains rate, which is lower than the ordinary income tax rate. To get this capital gain treatment, the employee must hold the stock for at least two years after receiving the option and one year after exercising the option.

Employers sometimes prefer NQSOs because they can more rapidly deduct their costs as an operating income expense. Also, with QSOs the exercise price can't be lower than the fair market value of the stock when the option is issued. NQSOs don't have that restriction and therefore provide more flexibility for the employer.[17]

To issue stock or stock options, the company must be a corporation because only corporations have "stock." Limited liability companies (LLCs) have shares of equity, but they are called "membership interests," not stock, although the term "stock" is sometimes used generically to include both.

THE "EMPLOYMENT AT WILL DOCTRINE"

The "employment at will doctrine" or simply the "at will doctrine" is a provision that allows an employer to terminate an employee "at will," meaning at any time for any reason. It also allows the employee to end employment at any time if there are no other federal or state laws that would prevent that. It typically applies when there is no contract provision to the contrary, such as a fixed term of employment or a thirty-day notice requirement prior to dismissal. Some states have enacted exceptions to the at will doctrine. These include a covenant of good faith exemption, which requires that the employee can only be fired for good cause or refusing to take a polygraph test.

> TIP: MAKE SURE YOU HAVE A GOOD PAPER TRAIL BEFORE
> TAKING AN ADVERSE PERSONNEL ACTION.

TERMINATING EMPLOYEES AND OTHERS WITHOUT GETTING SUED

If you need to take an adverse action against an employee, make sure you have a solid paper trail that justifies the action. If you terminate an employee, the employee may contest your action with an EEOC complaint or lawsuit. In either case, the employee's history and your records will be part of the record and examined closely.

Your records should show due process throughout your actions. A good paper trail might look like this. You meet with the employee and discuss the need for improving performance. You provide a written list of what needs to be done by specific dates. You send the employee a written record of this meeting and ask the employee to acknowledge receipt of it. If the employee then meets your requirements, the matter is satisfactorily resolved. If not, you could do the same thing again, this time with a warning that unless the employee meets your requirements by a certain date, then the employee may or will be terminated. You also send a copy of this to the employee and require that he/she confirm its receipt.

If you need to terminate the employee, you might have your attorney do this or have a witness along with you when the employee is terminated in case the employee misrepresents what you say. The employee should be asked to leave immediately, clear out his/her desk, and turn in keys and any other company property. Prior to the meeting you could cut off access to company servers. To smooth over the process as much as possible, you could agree that if the employee asks for a job reference you will merely disclose the employee's time of service in the company. Sometimes a month or two salary severance packages could be granted. To receive that, the employee should sign a mutual release of all claims. There are rules governing severance agreements, etc., so be sure to consult with an attorney on the process you use.

EMPLOYEE HANDBOOK

Your company should have an employee handbook that spells out key personnel matters such as benefits, hiring and firing procedures, and conflict-of-interest policies. The table of contents for a typical employee handbook is in Appendix 5. At the end of this Appendix, you will see an acknowledgment form. You should have your employees sign an acknowledgment that they have read, understood, and agree to comply with the employee handbook. This helps to avoid misunderstandings and disputes. If the employee doesn't want to sign the form, you should consider not keeping this employee.

Examples of Employment Issues And Solutions:
Do-Si-Do Or Let 'Em Go!

Scooter describes what should be in partnership agreements among business owners, and how listing their rights and duties prevents misunderstandings and litigation.

When Scooter came home from an electronics store the next morning with some equipment for his Key Bridge project he saw Megan's car there. And another car was parked in the driveway too. As he came in the front door, a man was putting the collar back on Sammy. Megan was laughing and smiling at something the man had said. Scooter hadn't seen Megan smiling in a long time. She turned to Scooter and her smile faded as she saw his puzzled look.

"This is Jimmy from the dog pound. He came to check on Sammy."

"Okay ma'am, he's all set, I gave him a shot and checked him over."

"Yup, even trimmed around his eyes," said Megan, looking at Sammy who was lying on his side. "He's been acting a little different since the shot," she said, concerned.

"Nothing to worry about," the man said as he left the house. "That's normal after a shot."

He crossed the yard and walked a few minutes to a plain unmarked van several blocks away. "All set, the chip's in the dog," he called in to Bulldog. "A few hours from now the first live feed from Sammy should be coming to you."

Scooter and Megan were at the kitchen table. Sammy was nearby. Scooter leaned over to pet Sammy. *Huh*, he said to himself, *nobody from the pound said they were going to pay us a visit.* "What did the guy say his name was?"

"Jimmy," said Megan.

"Feel funny."

"What did you say?" asked Scooter.

"I didn't say anything," Megan replied.

"It sounded like it came from Sammy."

"You're hearing things," said Megan.

"Guess so. Anyway, I've got lunch at Salamander today. Some partners fighting over their restaurant and want me to help solve their problems. I'll leave here around 10:30."

"You mean that fancy resort in Middleburg?"

"Yeah."

"Who are they?"

"Three women. Speaking of women, I've got a new client, Scarlett Montevideo."

"Montevideo? You mean that South American bombshell with the diamonds everywhere?"

"Yeah. She's worried about losing her fashion line to pirates."

"Did you meet her?"

"Yeah, we had dinner." Scooter immediately realized it was a mistake to mention this, so he preempted her next question. "It was her idea."

"Dinner? Oh…" Megan was expressionless on the outside but not on the inside.

***

Scooter always enjoyed the ride to Middleburg—the open fields, horse farms, and the big sky had a calming effect on him.

While Scooter was looking for calm, Megan was looking for clues. When Scooter left, she went to his jacket on the chair and checked the pockets.

"Nothing in the pockets. Something's going on. I can just feel it," she said aloud.

Then she went to his clothes hamper and found the shirt he wore the night before with Scarlett. Then she wished she hadn't. It smelled of perfume—something exotic, expensive. She sat down and buried her face in her hands. Their separation truly may have lost Megan her husband.

***

After a while, Scooter turned right on to Route 50 and ten minutes later he came up the hill into Middleburg, a village halfway between Bull Run, where the first major battle of the Civil War was fought, and the Blue Ridge Mountains. On the right was the historic Red Fox Inn and Tavern that had been there since 1728 and was still going strong. He turned right and soon was driving through the three hundred acres surrounding the Salamander Resort and Spa. The road led right up to the front door and he handed the keys to the doorman. Scooter walked inside, down the hall with red-framed antique prints of fox hunts, and into the Wine Cup Gold Bar.

The bartender looked up, "Mr. Magee?"

"Yes."

"Your guests are on the terrace through the white doors. The last table on the right."

"Thank you."

As he went outside, he could hear them arguing even before he saw them.

"Hello," said Scooter.

They finally stopped arguing and stood up.

"Mr. Magee, I'm Toni." Toni looked like a former WWF wrestling diva with her leathery skin, green camo tee shirt, broad shoulders, hair down to her elbows, and boots up to her knees. The silver chain hanging off her big black leather belt told Scooter that she was in charge. Scooter was starting to wonder what he was getting into.

"I'm Natalia," said her sister in the salmon colored, low-cut, tight-fitting dress, "and this is Karen," who looked shy in her blue plaid flannel shirt and jeans.

"Good to meet you."

The waiter came by and they ordered lunch.

"So how can I help you ladies?"

Toni spoke first. "We each put one hundred thousand dollars into Suzie's Restaurant in Sterling, Virginia. I've been on the West Coast for the past two years and just came back. My sisters have run the place into the ground, and I want my money back and out of this mess."

Natalia jumped in, yelling, "That's nonsense, Toni, you haven't done anything for two years, while Karen and I have been working our tails off, getting up early every day to open up. We buy all the food, handle the bills, and manage the staff. When's the last time you cut up green beans at 6:30 in the morning? We've kept the restaurant alive through a pandemic but it's barcly breaking even. Even if we had money, which we don't, there's no way we're going to pay you a cent. You owe us money for all the work we've been doing while you've been carrying on with Joey and all those other guys at the gym in LA."

The waiter was coming around the corner with the salads but quickly backtracked. Karen didn't say anything. She just looked like she'd rather be at the dentist's.

Scooter's phone rang. "Excuse me for a second." Scooter walked off the terrace onto the lawn.

"Mr. Magee?"

"Yes."

"JW McKinney, Washington Field Office, FBI here. Do you have a minute?"

"I'm in a meeting. What's this about?"

"I don't want to discuss this over the phone. Could I come by your house sometime real soon to talk?"

"Ah ... okay." They set up a time and Scooter hung up. *Good gosh*, he thought. *This doesn't sound like the usual FBI call for someone's employment background check. First the death threat, then the lawsuit ... what is* this *all about?*

Scooter pulled himself together and returned to the women just as Toni was moving her chair back so she could swing her arms around better. The shouting went on for a while. Scooter let them blow off some more steam and then he broke in.

"Hey, folks, look, I get the picture. Nobody's happy. Give me a few minutes and maybe I can help. Let me ask a few questions. Do you have any kind of written partnership agreement among yourselves that covers any of this ... who's responsible for what, salaries, your share of the income and expenses, and when you can buy out another partner?"

They all looked at each other.

"Okay, I'll take that as a 'No.' Do you have written records of the time and money that each of you spent on the business? Here's where I'm headed. First, you always should get an agreement in writing before you start any business venture. It should cover who's going to contribute what to the business in time and money, what is expected of each partner, and how a partner can be fired or bought out. That's helpful because each person can have different expectations of what the arrangement was. One of the biggest causes of business failures and lawsuits is simply a failure to communicate; and most of that can be avoided by just getting things in writing. If you'd like, I can guide you through this process and hopefully get to a point where each of you feels that it's a pretty fair solution."

The sisters mostly calmed down as they were eating, except when Toni let out a string of profanities at one point, and Scooter spent the next hour going over his advice. Finally, he was done and too distraught by the FBI's call to do anything more with them. He needed some time to think.

"So, it's been a pleasure meeting you," he said. "I'll send you some draft documents to review. I'm confident we can figure this out. In the meantime, if you have any questions give me a call."

Scooter waved to the women and left as fast as he could without looking like an escape artist. On the drive home, he tried to focus. Scooter was attacked by reality. *I just met with CF so the FBI's call might be about him*, he thought to himself. *CF told me not to talk with the FBI. Now I'm meeting with them. If he finds that out he's going to think I called them and he'll come after me. But if they ask me about CF and I don't answer they can charge me with withholding evidence. Either way I'm screwed.*

One Week Earlier
CIA Project Tailgate
Undisclosed Location near Ft. Meade, MD

The Secret is Out. Russia Weaponized and Trained Dolphins and Whales.

"In fact, one of their trained animals actually got caught spying on NATO ships ... Both the Soviet Union and U.S. Military have trained Beluga whales for military purposes, as well as a large number of dolphins, sea lions, and seals ... they're capable of killing an enemy on their own with a special dolphin muzzle with a spike.

The *National Interest*, March 5, 2022.[18]

Smarter Than You Think: Renowned Canine Researcher Puts Dogs' Intelligence on Par with 2-Year-Old Human.

TORONTO—Although you wouldn't want one to balance your checkbook, dogs can count.

They can also understand more than 150 words and intentionally deceive other dogs and people to get treats, according to psychologist and leading canine researcher Stanley Coren, PhD, of the University of British Columbia."

—American Psychological Association[19]

Deep in the woods at Site MX2 near Ft. Meade, Maryland, the CIA had failed again. For three years and $20 million of "black budget" money, it had worked to create a Bionic Spy Dog (BSG). BSGs certainly seemed doable. Dogs were smart, cameras could be imbedded in them, they respond well to commands, and if Alexa can talk, then the CIA should be able to imbed them with chip-based speech. It was just a matter of putting all the pieces together. Then the CIA would have a spy dog that could speak—at least a few hundred words.

They'd made a lot of progress. They found a way to inject a nanochip into a dog. Then it could respond to directions from Langley, record voices, gather video, enable the dog to speak a few words, and send the data in a continuous stream to Langley.

They did that by injecting an electrobiochip (EBC) into the blood stream using a standard hypodermic needle. The EBC was a $250,000 experimental nanochip infused with human stem cells. It was so small that it could pass through the blood-brain barrier into the brain just like small-molecule drugs. Once in, it attached itself between the Broca area of the brain that turns ideas into words and the frontal and temporal lobes of the Cerebrum that control speech. It also picked up signals from both eyes at the optic chiasma—the point in the brain where the nerves from both eyes come together. That allowed the CIA to see through both of the dog's eyes. And the human stem cells developed near the speech areas of the brain combined with the chip's advanced AI machine-learning capabilities meant that the dog could even increase its vocabulary over time.

The problem was that when the EBC transmitted to Langley, the outgoing signals interfered with the normal functions of the brain, creating unpredictable electrical interference and seizures. No dog had survived the test more than two months. Dog FJ-282 was the latest. But dogs were staying alive longer than before. And their speech capacity was up to two hundred words, although when they talked it sometimes sounded like a cross between Ray Charles and growls.

Dr. Heinrich Johansson, chief project scientist, was reviewing FJ-282's autopsy with his team.

"We're almost there. I can feel it. Two-hundred-word capability, the chip's transmitting well, and passed into the brain in only two hours. The video's pretty good as long as we keep the dog's hair away from the eyes. We just have to find the right power level for the nanochip to stop killing the dogs. For the next dog, let's lower the power by 5 percent. Then, add a kill switch to the chip that can sense a seizure and pause it."

Derek Martin, lab researcher, was skeptical. "Doctor, we can probably do that but 5 percent? That's probably not enough power reduction to save the dog. How do we know that 5 percent less won't just kill the next dog?"

"We don't, but it's the only way to find out. We'll just have to keep doing this until we can get maximum output with minimum lethality. That chip has a lot of functions to perform so we can't cut back the power much more. Our scatter diagram from past tests indicates that we need somewhere between 5 and 20 percent less power. I don't want to give up performance by lowering the power more than 5 percent at a time. If the dog ...you know... we'll run another test at 10 percent less. Look, FJ-282's a sheltie and shelties are prone to epilepsy anyway so that might be part of the problem. Would be nice if the dogs didn't die every time we ran a test, but they're just dogs. Think how many dolphins the guys next door are killing to catch up with the Russians and their killer dolphin program. The bottom line is Langley won't wait forever. Either we find the solution or they will kill our program. Langley wants our BSG to be fully operational ASAP. Let's get this done!"

Later that Day at Project Tailgate

"Good gosh, Derek, Bulldog just called. Get the latest chip ready. Langley wants to use it right away!"

"Doctor, what do we know about the dog they're using it on?"

"Nothing."

"We've only tested it on female shelties. They're good size dogs; FJ-282 was twenty-eight pounds. If it's a smaller dog, there might be a bigger risk."

"I know, but we can't do anything about that. Just get me the chip."

"It's ready, but I haven't put in the kill switch in case the dog has a seizure."

"Derek. I won't say it again. Get me the chip! Langley needs it this afternoon. Sounds like they have a limited window for a secret insertion."

"Okay." Derek grimaced as he thought to himself, *I hope my kids never find out what I do. They love their sheltie.*

***

Megan came by the house and was at the kitchen table when Sammy started. First it was a growl then he started barking louder and louder.

"What's happening, Sammy?"

Sammy kept pacing toward the basement door and then back to Megan.

"You want me to go downstairs?"

He barked, and it sounded like "Yes."

Megan followed him to the door, and just as she was going down the stairs, a brick smashed through the kitchen window and landed on the floor near where she had been sitting.

"Sammy, you saved my life!"

She grabbed her phone, called Scooter, and told him what had happened.

"And while you're coming home, I'll call the police."

"No, no, no, please don't."

"Why not? Someone's trying to hurt us!"

"I know, just make sure the doors and windows are locked. Please don't call the police. I'll be there right away."

Ten minutes later Scooter ran into the house.

"Megan?" No answer. He looked around everywhere. Finally, he saw Sammy in front of the storage closet in the basement. He opened the door, and Megan was sitting in the dark. A baseball bat was in her hand. She was sobbing.

"Megan, are you okay?" Her lip was trembling as she looked up.

"What in the world is happening?" she cried. "I was almost killed. Does that woman have anything to do with it? I looked at the brick. It had 'You know what you need to do' on it. What's all that about?"

"Someone's just mad. It happens sometimes with clients. That's what happens when you're a lawyer."

"Why does that shirt you wore the other night smell like perfume?"

"Megan, come on, nothing happened, it was just dinner."

"Nonsense, I'm not stupid, you're hiding things from me. I don't believe you!" Megan got up, went into the bedroom, and slammed the door.

Scooter sat at the top of the stairs near the bedroom door and waited—for a long time. Finally, Megan came out. She didn't look at Scooter and walked right by him.

"I can't take this anymore," she said, her voice trembling. "I'm scared. It's not safe here. I don't know what's happening and you won't tell me anything."

"Look, it will be okay, just give me a little…"

"No!" Her voice turned firm.

He watched helplessly from the top of the stairs as she squeezed past him and hurried down the stairs. Her last word was the "crack!" when she slammed the front door.

He went into the bedroom and sat on the bed. Scooter hadn't smoked for years but now he desperately wanted a smoke. He went downstairs and rummaged through some drawers until he found an old pack of Camels. He pulled one out, lit it, and took slow, deep breaths savoring the poison. Then he had two more while just staring at the wall. The sun was going down now and he was getting tired. He shuffled back up to the dark bedroom and fell backwards on the bed, exhausted. It was all too much.

What have I done? What's happening? he cried to himself.

This wasn't the first time he had wondered what he had done with his life. Or maybe it was what his law practice was doing to him and Megan. Sure, lawyers sometimes did good things. Over the years he had helped lots of clients and had his share of wins and losses. And it wasn't his fault that clients got into trouble and needed him to bail them out. He did what he could once they'd scrambled their eggs. But he was in no mood to think happy thoughts about lawyers.

Lately he was feeling like he was just "Mr. Transactions." Just a high-paid mechanic attached to clients who were lashed to the endless treadmills of commerce. He used law as a hammer to nail his client's rights, a saw to cut off others' rights, and an oil can to keep the transactions smoothly flowing from inputs to outputs and outputs to profits. "Get the fee *up front*," his law professor said the first day in class. Years later, he'd been there, done that. But then what was left *out back*?

And what *was* the point? Did it matter if there *wasn't* any point at all as long as the profits kept coming? Law is the means and justice should be the end. But maybe justice is just something invisible, forever revolving around in a far-away orbit powered by the sun of its own happy illusions, unrelated to reality. And maybe justice and reality are on separate orbits that never will meet.

Lawyers... he thought, *there's a mess: they cash in on it, then they clean it up and make money. There's no end to it. They book-end your life and are all over the middle. They're writing the prenup before you're born and handle your estate when you're gone. They create their own orbit.*

He went on for a while wallowing in descending eddies of self-pity. Slowly, the tide of sleep washed over him and drowned it all out.

Years later, the US Psychiatric Association would identify Scooter's feelings as typical elements of Middle-Aged Lawyer's Syndrome (MALS), label it a disorder with 16.5 major variations, and call it "quite common in the legal profession." But even if Scooter had known that it wouldn't have made him feel any better, especially if he had known how many fake treatments would be peddled each year to cure it and how much money lawyers made from class actions fighting those phony cures in thirty-four states.[20]

After a while he woke up, shook himself off, wandered downstairs, and drifted out to the Healey—the one friend he still could rely on. Healeys may growl but they never talk back. As he got into the driver's seat, he never noticed what was in the back seat. Scooter found himself driving around Arlington and into DC, not caring where he was going. By habit he came down Canal Road into Georgetown and parked by The TOMBS, got out, and walked to the Exorcist Stairs. *Why is all this happening?* Cold Fingers was after him, Megan had left, and he was in a terrible lawsuit. Now the FBI had "business" with him. He had no clue what to do. Everything was going downhill. He was becoming roadkill.

At CIA's Project Tailgate

Agent Frank Early, CIA, was alone again on night detail in a bland government-furnished office in an undisclosed location. He was supposed to be watching Scooter's house through Sammy's eyes, but he was more interested in the ball game on the portable TV he'd brought from home. Then he heard a crash and Megan Magee scream as the brick came flying through the window. Frank jumped and spilled his third cup of coffee in his lap. He mopped it up worriedly. Cold

Fingers was apparently coming after Scooter and the CIA needed to keep Scooter alive if they were going to get to the Cambodian camera.

Frank kept watching as Scooter came home and Megan left in tears. After a while he saw Scooter getting ready to leave the house. Just as he was ready to tell Sammy to get in the car with Scooter, Sammy ran out the pet door at Scooter's house, jumped into the back of the convertible, and kept out of sight. Scooter never saw him. When Scooter parked at the Exorcist stairs, Sammy got out and followed him from a distance.

**

Scooter looked down the steep black concrete stairs. No one was around. Off in the distance he could see the taillights of the cars crossing Key Bridge from DC to Arlington and hear the hum of the traffic on Canal Road below. A mist was floating up off the Potomac, causing halos on the lights across the bridge.

Maybe this was how it was meant to end. He was out of options. He could jump or fall down the steps. It didn't matter; either way he'd be gone. But at least the nightmares would be over and he'd be at peace. Scooter walked to the top step, grabbed the cold black railing with his left hand, looked down, and leaned forward. Suddenly he heard Sammy barking and yelling "No, Scooter, No, Scooter, No, No!"

Scooter turned around in surprise. "Sammy! How did you get here?"

"In car, on back floor."

"Am I going crazy, or did you just talk to me?"

"Sammy learn to talk some. After big man give me shot."

"Good gosh! You mean the man from the adoption center?"

"Yes. Sammy still feel funny after shot. No like."

This was all too much. Scooter didn't have the strength to try and figure this out. He just collapsed on the curb. Sammy sat next to him. They just sat there quietly for a few minutes. Finally, Scooter pulled himself together.

"Let's go home."

Sammy hopped in and rode shotgun with his paw on Scooter's right arm all the way home. They walked into the kitchen.

"Thanks, Sammy. It's late, I'm going to bed."

Sammy looked up and smiled. Then he said, "Me want a Piña Colada."

"What?"

"A Piña Colada, the one with a cherry on top and an umbrella."

"Where'd you get that idea?"

"Sammy watched TV reruns of *Hawaii Five-O*. Everyone drinks Piña Colada."

"Sammy, you can't have alcohol, it's poisonous to dogs. And I don't trust the lady at the Welfare League who said you have immunity to alcohol."

"Please?"

Sammy just saved my life, he thought to himself. *So, I guess I need to do this. It's crazy, but not any crazier than anything else lately*!

"Look, how about this, tomorrow I'll go to the store and get some Piña Colada mix and cherries. I'll leave out the rum and you won't even notice the difference. I don't have any idea where to get the umbrellas so you'll have to do without that, okay?"

Sammy's tail was wagging, "Okay!"

Sammy trotted over to his dog bed in the living room, turned around a couple of times, lay down, and fell fast asleep dreaming about the cute little black terrier he met at the Welfare League. Scooter poured himself some wine. Funny, he was feeling better now, almost reinvigorated. He started thinking.

Sammy's talking ... maybe that's a clue to whatever's happening. He went to his computer and researched talking dogs and the government. Not much there. Then he found some oblique references to CIA's research on spy animals. *Ah ... maybe the CIA's interested in me because of the Cambodian connection with CF. Somehow they know about that, but how? Are they involved with Sammy's talking?*

Scooter kept trying to make sense of it all until he dozed off in his chair. The phone woke him up. It was Scarlett.

"Scooter, sorry it's so late, but what are you doing tomorrow? The weather's supposed to be great, and I've got a fun idea."

"What's ... what's that?"

"Are you okay? Your voice sounds a little funny."

"Yeah, I'm okay."

"Well, I'm on the Board of Friends of Jug Bay. It's a wetlands sanctuary in Maryland about an hour from DC. Beautiful, quiet spot on the Patuxent River. They're having a cocktail event with soft shell crabs at 4:00 after their board meeting. We could eat and then I'll show you around a little."

"Wow, that sounds good. I'll see you there at 4:00."

"Perfect, goodbye!"

He hung up. *Wait a minute*, thought Scooter. *That's a coincidence. Scarlett seemed interested in my Cambodian client when we met, now she calls me up and wants to meet again socially. Is she some link in all this?* It was late, but Scooter went back to his computer and started researching Scarlett and her company. There were several stories about the company struggling following recent allegations over tax investigations that included "top officers of the company." Some more research showed that Scarlett was number two in the company but had unexpectedly left Brazil and had vanished. *Interesting ... something's definitely going on here; I need to figure this out.*

* * *

The next day Scooter was heading east on Route 4 in Maryland toward Jug Bay. As he crossed a bridge, he looked down at the Patuxent River. The Patuxent, the longest river in Maryland, ran 115 miles from west of Baltimore all the way to the Chesapeake Bay, sixty miles South of Washington, DC. Captain John Smith first mapped it out in 1608; and the British launched their troops from the Patuxent in 1812 when they attacked Washington, DC and burned the White House and the Capitol.

A few minutes later Scooter turned into the small parking lot and got out. He saw the Jug Bay Visitors Center fifty yards ahead.

What he didn't see was the man with the Yankees baseball cap sitting in the grey Honda at the edge of the lot, watching him.

The barbecue smelled great! There were about a hundred happy people cracking crabs, drinking beer, and cooking burgers. As Scooter approached Scarlett, she looked good. Very good. She filled out her hot pink sweater in a way that saved his imagination a whole lot of work. She was sporting tan slacks, tan boots, and a diamond on the strap that flashed in the sun. Her long blonde hair was pulled back with a blue headband. He was walking faster now.

Meanwhile in the parking lot, the man was talking. "This is D1, are you there, D2?"

"Yes, in position at the end of the yellow trail."

"Good, targets are here. Come back fifty yards this way, turn right into the woods off the trail, and keep out of sight. I'll let you know when it's time."

"Got it."

Scarlett saw Scooter and ran up to him.

"I'm so glad you could come!"

"Me too. Have you eaten?"

"Nope, I was waiting for you. But are you okay? You look tired."

"Yeah, client stuff," Scooter said. "Clients always expect me to fix things. I understand that's what they pay me for so I'm not complaining but sometimes I'd like someone to fix my problems..."

She interrupted him, "Well, today, that's me! Let's forget all that and just have some fun." They settled in at a picnic table with some other board members, cracked crabs, and had a beer but passed on the cheesecake.

"Let's get out of here," Scarlett said after a while. "I want to show you the sights. Let's take the yellow Otter Point Trail that leads to the big bay."

"Works for me, lead on."

Ten minutes later they were all alone a quarter mile down the Otter Point Trail and crossed the old railroad bed. They had only seen one other person. Some guy with a baseball cap one hundred yards back. Scarlett had put her arm through Scooter's as they walked.

The woods had that musty scent of fall, and squirrels were chasing each other up a tree. Scarlett was kicking the leaves.

"I've got a surprise for you," said Scarlett pointing to the river. "It's down there." They turned right, off the marked trail onto a narrow, half-hidden dirt path. Scooter walked ahead of her to pull the branches back. They cracked as he did. About fifty yards down the hill a sagging wooden boardwalk meandered out into the river and disappeared off to the right. An old brown shack, ten feet square, was built onto the boardwalk.

"What is that? It looks like a duck blind."

"Scooter! You're in a wetlands sanctuary! No hunters allowed," she said laughing. "It's a swamp blind. You go in there and the animals can't see you but you can watch them. It's my favorite place in the Sanctuary. Not many people even know it's there. Come on, let's go in."

She grabbed his hand as they walked up to the heavy wooden door and pulled down the latch. It opened with a squeak. He looked in and saw a simple bench. That was it.

"I'm surprised how clean it is in here."

Scarlett wasn't.

He closed the door a little and they sat down inside. They were right next to each other now, looking west over the river. A perfect formation of large birds flew by.

"Canada Geese," said Scarlett. "See their white cheeks?"

Scooter nodded.

Billowing white clouds were lined up in the sky in a silent parade, and the sun was just starting down. It was beautiful and peaceful. But better than that, whatever Scarlett was wearing smelled good and reminded him of their dinner. She put her hand on his thigh. He didn't take it off.

"What do you think?" she asked softly.

"Nice," he said. "I could get used to this."

"Yeah." They just sat for a while.

Back in the woods D2 checked in. "I'm in position now. It's 4:50, ready to do it."

"Okay, but be quiet and don't get caught."

Back in the blind, Scarlett started to fidget. Something was bothering her.

"You okay?"

"No. Scooter, I'm not. I've got something to tell you. I'll just do it. You know I've been asking about your client with the camera."

"Yeah."

"Well, there's a reason."

"What do you mean?"

"Okay, here goes. That camera is a spy camera. It has some amazing capabilities that make it very dangerous to the US and our allies."

"How do you know that?"

"I work for the CIA."

Scooter looked at her. She seemed to be telling the truth. It could be possible but still, it was crazy.

"The CIA? What's that about?"

"You need to tell me what you know about your client and the camera so the CIA and FBI can get it back. You should want that too—it's a matter of national security."

"I can't do that. I can't reveal my client's secrets, you know that. The Virginia Bar would pull my license in a flash!"

Scooter wasn't ready to tell her that he had been researching her or anything else. He had to be careful. His mind was whirring now, trying to look at this from all angles. Was Scarlett telling the truth? Was this CIA stuff true? It made some sense. If it were true this would help him get rid of Cold Fingers. He was afraid to go to the police because Cold Fingers said he would kill him if he did. Ultimately, he thought, the decision makes itself. The death threat drives the decision. He needed to follow Scarlett's plan. The bonus is that maybe he could get some balance back in his life after all this chaos.

"Scarlett, I don't know what I'm dealing with here. Are you wired?"

"What! No, of course not."

"Are we being watched?"

"No."

For the next few minutes he asked a lot more questions and she answered them. Then he spoke up.

"Look, I just don't know if any of what you're saying is true. If it is, you need to get me iron clad assurances with the CIA and FBI. I'm tired of all these games. Can you do that?"

She was ready for him. "Yes, I figured you'd want that. I've arranged for us to meet with the FBI and CIA and they can get a judge to issue a sealed court order authorizing your disclosure. Under the VA Bar's rules, you can disclose a client's secrets once they get a court order. The FBI and CIA are ready to work with you to make sure it's done right." She reached in her purse and handed him a piece of paper. "Call this number tomorrow and the FBI will explain the details. And, it's already been cleared with Bill Jenkins, the Bar's ethics counsel."

Scooter started to feel a lot more comfortable. Neither talked for a while. Scarlett gave him some time to think.

"It's getting warm in here," she said, as she pulled her sweater off over her head and slowly smoothed her hair. She looked down and saw the top button on her blouse was undone. She caught Scooter looking and smiled. "Scooter, you're supposed to be watching the wildlife!"

"I am, trust me, I am!'

Scarlett laughed and turned toward Scooter with that same look he saw at the Blue Moon Café. The same look that got to him. "I'm sorry we got caught up in all this. Maybe when things aren't so complicated we could get to know each other a whole lot better."

"Yeah ... And if this checks out with the CIA and FBI, I'll tell them what I know about my client and the camera. It should help me get out of this mess with CF. I've just got to get out of that."

Now Scarlett seemed relieved too. She smiled, leaned toward Scooter, and slowly put her arms around his neck and pulled him to her. Her fragrance was running the show now. Scooter put his arms around her. They were both breathing heavily. She was pressing against him. Her hands were moving now. His hand was gently moving up under her blouse. She sighed. He was fumbling over the buttons on her blouse, wishing they were Velcro when...

Crack!

"Did you hear that?" Scarlett asked.

"Sure did," said Scooter. "Maybe someone's out there and stepped on a stick or something." He pulled away and scowled. "I thought you said we weren't being followed." Scooter really didn't know what to believe now.

"I did, I did! I don't know what that was!"

They walked back to the visitor's center. Neither talked.

They stopped near the parking lot. "Scooter, look, I know this all sounds crazy. Just call the FBI tomorrow and set up the meeting. We'll get the court order and everything will be fine. CF will be out of your life, and you'll have done the right thing for your country."

She kissed him on the cheek and Scooter left. He didn't know what to think, and he also didn't notice the Honda following him back home.

***

At 9:00 a.m. the next day, Scooter called the FBI at the number Scarlett gave him.

"Hello, this is Scooter Magee. Scarlett Montevideo gave me this number to call. Is this the FBI?"

"Yes. Can you spell your name and hers for me, please?"

He did.

"Just a minute." It was a lot longer. There was some static down the line and then the voice asked, "What's this about?"

Scooter explained.

"I'm sorry, but I don't know who you are or who Scarlett is. We have no record of either one of you."

"But she said you would know."

"We don't."

"Oh ... okay, thanks," Scooter hung up.

"Son of a biscuit!"

Scooter dialed Scarlett.

"I'm sorry but this number is no longer in service."

Chapter 5

HOW TO SHAKE THE MONEY TREE—LEGALLY

"Honey, the SEC's Calling About Your Stock Offering."

Your startup's like a car. You, the entrepreneur, are the driver, the shareholders are the passengers, and money built the car and fuels it. Money is important to any business but especially to a startup. Until you get income it looks like everything's about money. It's trite, but the major reason that startups fail is that they run out of money. Of course, there are an unlimited number of ways for that to happen, but money is key, so let's talk about how to get it in compliance with the complex federal and state fundraising laws.

You shouldn't have any illusions about how hard it is to raise money. One of my clients with an excellent product put together a great investor package but it took over one hundred pitches to various investors and a year to raise just the first $100 thousand. When I was raising money for a company, I went to an old friend who had just cashed out a family business and told me about the $50 million check he received. I asked him for a $100 thousand investment. Finally, after weeks of back and forth, I only got $10 thousand from him. Raising money is a challenge, but you can increase your odds of success by following these steps.

HOW MUCH MONEY DO YOU NEED?

The first question is how much money do you need? Ideally you should raise enough money so that you can operate for twelve to eighteen months (the "runway") and be able to focus on other things besides worrying about money. It's not always possible to get all the money you want at once, so you should have a plan for operating with your target amount and a plan B or C for a lesser amount as a backup.

One way to figure out how much money you need is to build a simple pro forma profit and loss statement or "P&L." "Pro Forma" means "for the form" and it's a financial forecast based on your assumptions and predictions. This will show revenues (income), expenses, and the difference, which is profit or loss. Once you know your expected income and expenses you can determine how much money you need to break even and make a profit from your expected sales over what period of time. If your draft P&L shows you're not making a profit over a reasonable period such as three to five years, depending on the type of business involved, then you need to raise revenues, cut expenses, or get additional funds. See the next table and Illustration 3 for what a pro forma P&L looks like. A few practical tips for creating your P&L follow.

Time Period Covered

No one can accurately predict financial results for five years. That's okay because a Pro Forma P&L is just a credible estimate. Going out three to five years will give investors a sense of your company's projected growth over time and a potential exit strategy. I'd suggest that you show the first year's numbers quarter by quarter because things change so rapidly in the first year and many of the startup expenses, such as accounting, legal, etc., will be one-time expenses as the company launches.

Include All Expenses

One of the most common mistakes in startup financial forecasts is underestimating expenses. No matter how well you plan, it seems like there are always more expenses and you don't want to run out

Pro Forma Profit & Loss Statement (P&L)			
	Yr. 1	Yr. 2	Yr. 3, Etc.
"Revenue" or "Sales"		$200,000	$ 300,000
Sales Product A	$ 60,000		
Sales Product B	$ 40,000		
Total Revenue	$ 100,000		
Less Cost of Goods Sold (COGS)	$ 80,000	Cost just for producing the product - no co. overheads	
Gross Margin $	$ 20,000	Total Revenue less COGS	
Gross Margin %	20%	Gross Margin $/Total Revenue	
Expenses			
Payroll	$6,000		
Marketing	$2,000		
Rent	$2,000		
Etc.			
Contingency (10% of above exp.)	$1,000		
Total Operating Expenses	$ 11,000		
"Net Margin" or "Net Income"	$ 9,000	Revenue Less COGS and Op. Expenses	
Net Income %	9%	Net Inc./Total Revenue	
EBITDA	$ 9,000	Earnings Before Interest, Taxes, Depreciation, and Amortization (EBITDA)	
Less: Interest, Taxes, Depreciation, Amort.	$ 2,500		
"Net Profit" or "Earnings"	$ 6,500	EBITDA less Interest and Taxes, etc.	
Net Profit %	6.5%	Net Profit/Total Revenue	

of money. Expenses will vary depending on your business and other factors. For example, urban law firms in big cities are usually more expensive than those in smaller towns.

Accounting

You could estimate accounting expenses for the first year at around $3,000. You may need an accountant to set up your financial books and records and answer questions, such as "Are patent costs a capital cost or an expense?" And you need funds to prepare your tax return and handle payroll.

Legal
Basic Corporate Legal Advice
Legal expenses might range from $3,000–$5,000 or more. Typical needs include:

- register the company with state authorities;
- prepare governing documents such as an operating agreement (for an LLC) or bylaws (for a corporation), and an Organizational Action in Writing appointing a board of directors, electing officers, and authorizing other basic startup actions;
- prepare personnel agreements for founders and key employees and non-disclosure agreements; and
- draft standard purchase orders and contracts.

Intellectual Property Legal Support
This includes general advice on trade secrets, copyrights, trademarks, and patents.

Trademarks

If you file for a trademark for your company's name and logo or for specific products and services, you should ask your attorney whether to conduct a trademark search before filing for the trademark. That's to avoid the time lost and expense of having a filing rejected because the name or mark is already registered. The cost for a search is under

$1,000. Filing for the trademark (or service mark) itself costs $1,500–$2,500 in legal fees plus the US Patent and Trademark Office's (PTO) fee of $250–$400 for each category (class) in which you file, plus legal support if the PTO raises questions about the filing.

Patents

If you have an invention, it may be worth filing a patent. See chapter 3 for details. Consider hiring a patent search agent to conduct a patent search before filing a patent. This will reveal other inventions like yours that are "prior art" (something already invented). If your invention is already patented, you can't get a patent. A patent search can avoid wasting money on a patent application that will be rejected. The estimated cost for a search is $500–$1,200. A provisional patent filing costs around $750–$1,500, while a non-provisional application could range from $6,000–$12,000 or more depending on the number of claims and complexity of the invention. See chapter 3 for the different types of filings and a discussion of patent terms and strategies.

Contingencies

Consider adding 10–20 percent to your other costs to cover contingencies. It can be frustrating if you can't make sound business decisions because you've underestimated expenses and run out of money.

> **TIP: BE SURE TO INCLUDE A 10-20% EXPENSE CONTINGENCY IN YOUR PRO FORMA P&L.**

Revenues

How do you estimate revenue (sales income) in your P&L? Revenue is simply the number of units sold multiplied by the sale price per unit over a specified period. For example, a thousand widgets sold over one year multiplied by ten dollars each = $10,000. You will need to add overhead expenses to that such as rent, accounting, legal, printing, travel, etc. Then add a percentage profit you hope to achieve and the total is your sales price or forecast of revenue.

The volume of products sold will affect the cost of each unit. Over time the cost per unit should fall as the sales volume increases. In any event your optimum sales price ultimately will be determined by the market.

How Much Money Should You Raise?

If your P&L shows a good profit and growth prospects, you might not need to raise any more money. You can self-finance from profits to grow the company. This is good because you won't go into debt with loans or give up equity in return for external funding. Here's an example of how revenues, expenses, and profits might look.

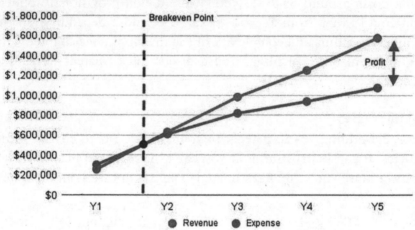

On the other hand, if you have a good product there will be competition for it and you might want to grow faster to get and maintain a leading position in the market. As with a dog sled, the lead dog has a better view! In that case, you can prepare a P&L that shows revenues and expenses at a higher level. Then seek additional funding for faster growth. How much funding is determined by the difference between increased costs to ramp up production compared to the revenues you can get from sales over the same period. Revenues will take time to be realized so the external funding can be used to cover the higher expenses from increasing your production and overheads such as marketing, until revenues catch up.

At the other extreme, if your P&L shows a loss right off the bat, then you will need to raise prices, cut expenses, or raise money to survive.

FUNDING SOURCES: SELF-FUNDING, ANGELS, CROWDFUNDING, AND MORE

There are many potential startup funding sources, including:

- personally funding your own company
- loans
- friends and family
- angel funding
- crowd funding
- business incubators and accelerators
- venture capital funds
- private equity
- government and foundation grants
- cryptocurrency, block chain, and Bitcoin financing
- raising funds internally from sales

Each funding source has a different profile of companies and products or services it likes to fund, based on factors such as what geographic region you're in, what products or services you're offering, and the level of funding required. The investors' websites will help answer those questions. The websites usually show the kinds of companies and products in which they like to invest and what you need to provide to them to be considered. Government and foundation grants post detailed instructions on the web on how to apply for funding.

Internal Funding From Profits

In an ideal world, your company would generate enough cash flow from sales to generate all the funding it needs. That way you wouldn't have to give up equity or incur debt. But this isn't possible for a startup with minimal or no profit. So external funding is necessary.

Personal Funding

Many entrepreneurs start this way. They use their savings, credit cards, or other personal funds to fund startup expenses. This avoids selling equity. But it can also damage your personal finances if the company struggles, so you might want to set limits on how much debt you are willing to incur.

Bank Loans

Usually, banks won't issue loans to startups unless there are personal or other guarantees or collateral. That is because a startup's assets are negligible. Even if they are more substantial, a personal guarantee is usually required.

A few years ago I was talking to a former US senator whose family owned a string of banks. He said that despite that, the banks still required him to personally guarantee his business loans. That could have been because he was considered an "insider" to the bank where more rules might apply. Nevertheless, it's an indication of how routine personal guarantees are. A bank loan that's personally guaranteed is simply another type of personal funding involving one or more guarantors.

Bank loans can be attractive, particularly if you're using a low interest rate secured line of credit, such as a home equity loan. That has some of the lowest commercial interest rates you can get. There also are non-bank commercial companies that loan funds, but their rates are typically higher.

Funding from Founders, Friends, and Family

Pick your partners and founders carefully. You may be spending more time with them than with your significant others. Would any of them have sufficient funds to loan or invest funds in the company? If so, this is one of the best and least expensive sources of funding. But it also can backfire if they are unhappy with how things are going and leave the company. Mixing friendship with business is filled with risks that can be uncomfortable or worse. No matter how many times you tell them, "Make sure this is money you don't mind losing because this company really is a gamble," if you lose their money, it can create an uncomfortable situation. They won't be happy and you'll be embarrassed.

Angel Funding

An "angel" or "seed investor" is a high net worth investor who provides funding to startups. Usually, an angel won't provide funding over 10 percent of the angel's net worth. Angels typically help to fund startups that need more money than might be available from friends and family but less money than from venture capital funds.

There is no specific definition of a "high net worth individual." However, there is an SEC definition of an "accredited investor." Only accredited investors are allowed to make certain types of investments under Securities and Exchange Commission (SEC) rules. This ensures that those investors have sufficient financial resources to withstand losing their investment. An accredited investor has:

- earned income that exceeded $200,000 (or $300,000 together with a spouse or spousal equivalent) in each of the prior two years, and reasonably expects the same for the current year; or
- has a net worth over $1 million, either alone or together with a spouse or spousal equivalent (excluding the value of the person's primary residence); or
- holds in good standing a Series 7, 65, or 82 license.[1]

Angel Groups

Some angel investors also work in angel groups. There are hundreds of angel groups across the country. Angel Capital Association provides an online list of those at angelcapitalassociation.org/directory/. In angel groups, individual angels meet to hear investment pitches from entrepreneurs and then they may join to pool their funds into an investment. For example, five angels might pool $10,000 each into an LLC as the investment vehicle to make a more meaningful $50,000 investment in a company.

Crowdfunding

Crowdfunding is a finance method usually done on an internet platform in which many individuals can make small investments or contributions. It is used for charitable campaigns (such as GoFundMe) or for companies seeking to raise money such as Kickstarter and Indiegogo. The SEC has issued rules regarding how much an individual can invest via crowdfunding in any twelve-month period depending on net worth and annual income.[2]

From the entrepreneur's perspective, crowdfunding provides a wider number of individual investors. Entrepreneurs pay a fee to the crowdfunding platform and then create a campaign. That can consist of a short video explaining the startup and getting friends to invest to show fundraising momentum. The startup can offer prizes to investors to help built interest. Often, the funds sought are under $100,000. In some cases, entrepreneurs use crowdfunding simply as a market research and market building tool to gauge reaction to their product or service and get customer feedback.

If you're raising funds on a crowdfunding platform, ask 1) what fees you will have to pay; 2) whether you need to reach 100 percent of your funding goal to receive any of the funds; and 3) whether you will need to issue equity to the investors in return for their funds.

If you are an investor, note that these investments are highly speculative, illiquid, and you may not be able to cancel your investment. There also is no way to determine the actual value of your investment and there are only limited disclosures of critical company information. Finally, there is a possibility of fraud and there is no assurance that the company's management has the necessary business experience.

Business Incubators and Accelerators

Business incubators and accelerators are organizations that provide mentorship and training programs for startups. While there is some overlap in their functions, there are differences. Incubators often provide office space, basic training in business skills, and limited exposure to financing and networking opportunities. They can be long-term and charge for these services.

Accelerators also provide education and training, plus they add access to investors. They are used after incubators have provided basic startup tools to entrepreneurs. Their programs are a fixed term for a few weeks and may end in a "demo day" when companies pitch to investors. Accelerators are more likely than incubators to directly assist with financing and offer it in return for a share of equity. Some accelerator programs are free, but most accelerators charge for these services and fees can range in the thousands of dollars. Be sure to carefully explore how much accelerator programs cost and how much time they will take. You'll be giving up weeks of your time and may have to pay hotel and travel costs. Also make sure they cover the subjects you need help with so you don't waste your time. Some accelerator's claims about meeting with high powered investors and getting funding can be exaggerated, as well.

Venture Capital Funds (VCs)

Venture capital funds are money management funds that invest in early-stage companies. Their funding can come from private equity, family offices (a private wealth management firm that provides financial services to ultra-high-net-worth families), corporations such as insurance companies, and sovereign wealth funds. VCs typically look to invest in companies that have shown successive quarters of high growth and profitability, and they are interested in investing from hundreds of thousands to millions of dollars. They need to show their own investors profits from companies they fund that are significant enough to "move the needle."

Private Equity

Private equity is capital that's not listed on a public exchange. It consists of investors and institutional funds that invest in companies. Often, private equity funds have limited partners (LPs) who own 99 percent of the shares and general partners who own the other one percent, have full liability, and operate the investment. Because the funds aren't listed on public stock exchanges, the companies they invest in can avoid the price volatility of public trading. They usually invest with millions of dollars.

Private Sector Grants and Loans

Foundations and other private organizations such as the John D. and Catherine T. MacArthur Foundation, Ford Foundation, and Gates Foundation have grant programs that can be excellent sources of funding. With a grant, you don't need to give up any equity or incur debt. Billions of dollars of grants are given away each year by thousands of foundations. There are many online directories and databases for finding grant sources that will make it simpler to match your needs with the type of grants offered by foundations. These sites may ask about your location, amount of money requested, ethnicity, gender, etc., and then provide lists of foundations that could match your needs.

Create a Charitable Tax-Exempt Company to Work in Concert with Your For-Profit Company

If you are a for-profit startup, you might consider creating a tax-exempt non-profit foundation such as a 501(c)(3) "charitable organization." This would allow you to obtain grant funding in addition to money you receive from the sales of your product or service. Most foundations only give grants to non-profit organizations. That means that, if you're a for-profit company, you need to pay a fee to an intermediary non-profit organization to receive grant funds. Those fees are around 6 percent of the grant amount. To avoid the fees, you could establish your own non-profit foundation that could then do the grant work directly, such as perform R&D or analysis that's useful for your for-profit company.

To form a 501(c)(3), you need to file an application with the IRS.[3] Their rules require that the foundation must be operated for exempt purposes, none of the earnings may enure to any individual or shareholder, it may not participate in political campaigns, and a substantial part of its activities cannot be used to influence legislation. Depending on the IRS's workload, you could receive approval in approximately six months.

Government Grants and Loans

Federal, state, and some local governments have thousands of grant and loan programs. I've had clients that have gotten millions of dollars of federal loans over many years for startup research and commercialization and made a lot of money without ever selling anything except their expertise in getting loans! I'll just focus on federal programs here because they provide the most money and many federal programs also overlap into state programs by providing funding for them.

The federal government provides over $1 billion of loans and grants each year to businesses. Most government agencies have grant opportunities focused on their program area. For a list of those, go to Grants.gov. If you're interested in a particular program area, you can go to that agency and get on their e-mail list for announcements of grant and loan opportunities. For example, the US Department of Energy's website energy.gov lists loan, grant, and financing programs, and other support resources for startups and small businesses.

The Small Business Administration (SBA)

The SBA, sba.gov, is the central federal agency for small business support. It has a wide variety of programs including business guides, federal contracting information, loans with lenders, links to investment capital sources, and matching funds for investors.

SBA's Small Business Innovation Research (SBIR) Program

SBIR is one of SBA's more popular programs. It helps small businesses conduct research and development (R&D) by funding through contracts or grants. The project must have a strong potential for commercialization and meet US government R&D needs. It is particularly useful for R&D projects that are too high risk for private capital investors. Applicants must be small businesses with fewer than five hundred employees owned by individuals who are US citizens or permanent residents. Billions of dollars are awarded through SBIR programs in some eleven federal agencies.

The SBIR program has three phases:
- **Phase I.** The Startup Phase gives awards to establish the technical merit, feasibility, and commercial potential of the proposed research/research and development (R/R&D)

efforts and to determine the performance of the awardee before providing further federal support in Phase II. Phase I awards are $50,000–$250,000 for six months (SBIR) or one year for the Small Business Technology Transfer Program.

- **Phase II.** These awards continue the R/R&D efforts initiated in Phase I. Funding is based on the results achieved in Phase I. Phase II awards are generally $750,000 for two years.
- **Phase III.** Commercialization. Phase III awards are for commercialization objectives resulting from the Phase I/II R/R&D activities. But private sector or non-SBIR federal agency funding must be used for Phase III awards.

SBA's Small Business Technology Transfer Program (STTR)[4]

The STTR program is like the SBIR program. But with STTR the small business applicant must be teamed with a non-profit organization, such as a federal laboratory or a university and (with some exceptions) the program must be focused on technology transfer from the non-profit to the small business. There are other differences, as well.[5]

Cryptocurrency, Block Chain, and Bitcoin Financing

Cryptocurrency is a virtual, digital currency operated by decentralized computer networks using "block chain" technology. It is secured by advanced cryptography (algorithms) which prevents counterfeiting and duplicate transactions. A "block" is a file containing one or more transactions, like a journal entry. A "block chain" is a series of blocks or a "chain" of every transaction in the chain that anyone authorized can view. Because cryptocurrency is not issued by a central authority or bank it avoids or reduces government interference and manipulation and is a preferred channel for illegal fund transfers like money laundering and tax evasion.[6]

The secure payments are transacted in "tokens," or virtual ledger entries. They are not "legal tender" because they are not backed by a government. The earliest block chain cryptocurrency was Bitcoin. Now there are thousands of other cryptocurrencies ("altcoins") that are "mined" by operators. "Mining" is the process of creating new bitcoins and verifying block chain transactions by running highly complex computer programs.[7]

Cryptocurrency Issues and Regulation

It's only a matter of time until cryptocurrencies will play a larger role in financing startups and more mature companies. One advantage is that these transactions avoid bank fees and can be done privately. A typical transaction might involve a physical or intellectual property asset like real estate or a patent. That could be turned into a token, split into an infinite number of pieces, and sold to investors. One major hurdle is that, as usual, technology is way ahead of the law. It's not yet clear under what conditions federal and state securities regulators will allow cryptocurrency to be used in investments. However, early SEC actions show some compliance concerns, such as when cryptocurrencies were used without following proper SEC registration processes.[8]

The IRS has defined cryptocurrencies as a digital asset and property rather than a fiat currency. This allows investors to be taxed for federal income tax purposes at capital gains rates, which are typically lower than ordinary income tax rates. Microsoft, AT&T, Burger King, and many other major businesses are now allowing payments with cryptocurrencies and this trend is likely to continue.[9]

Cryptocurrencies are used to finance initial coin offerings (ICOs). This is the cryptocurrency's version of an initial public offering (IPO). With an ICO, investors can buy into the offering "and receive a new cryptocurrency token issued by the company."[10] Unlike an IPO investment, the token may or may not represent an equity stake in the company and investors may participate simply in the hope that the token will appreciate in value. These transactions are not regulated by the SEC. As long as an IPO, private offering, or ICO follows SEC and state regulations for securities offerings, investors may pay for their investments using cryptocurrencies.

There are a number of problems with cryptocurrencies that have led to calls for regulation and have inhibited its growth. They can be used to hide dark money used in drug trade and other illegal transactions. Large mining operations can create noise from some types of fans that are used to cool banks of computers. This can disrupt neighbors and lead to lawsuits. And a tremendous amount of electricity is required to power the computers that create them. For example, "The process of creating Bitcoin globally, consumes around 91 terawatt-hours of electricity annually, more than all of the energy used by Finland, a nation of about 5.5 million."[11] Depending on the fuel source used to produce that electricity, it can produce carbon emissions that impact the environment and have an adverse effect on climate change.

President Biden's 2022 Executive Order on Cryptocurrency

In a 2022 Executive Order,[12] President Biden presented a comprehensive strategy for the federal government's treatment of cryptocurrency. This was the "the first ever, whole-of-government approach to addressing the risks and harnessing the potential benefits of digital assets and their underlying technology." The order noted that the "rise in digital assets creates an opportunity to reinforce American leadership in the global financial system and at the technological frontier ... but also has substantial implications for consumer protection, financial stability, national security and climate risk." The order won't "have any immediate effect on how cryptocurrency is regulated ... and will instead set in motion a slower regulatory process that will take years to bear fruit,"[13] as the SEC and Treasury Department and other agencies develop and issue regulations.

Non-fungible Tokens (NFTs) One of the growing uses of block chain is non-fungible tokens (NFTs). They are minted physical works of art that include secure data about the work and allow original works to be identified and protected from unauthorized copies. They include "a record of its ownership, instructions about its care and display, and stipulations about how much money should go to the artist when it's resold."[14] NFTs don't create a new financing method, but they can reduce sales prices by eliminating the middlemen in art transactions. For example, galleries' purchase costs are rarely transparent so they can more easily set sales prices with big margins. On the other hand, NFTs are all about pricing. Sometimes galleries even require buyers to purchase more than one work of art to maintain high prices for artists and higher fees for galleries. Block chain can eliminate such transactions.[15]

Money Milkshakes™

It can take a long time to land investments or wait for a government grant. And many grants are highly competitive. So it makes sense to seek and combine funding sources. Think of it as "money milkshakes." You've got two milkshakes and you can drink out of a straw with both to double your funding sources. Another advantage is that multiple money flows could offset each other in terms of timing, so as one dries up the other keeps paying. That gives you a "financial flywheel."

Funding Isn't Always About Funding

One of my construction company clients wanted to bid on a big construction job but didn't have the funding to staff up for it. So, we created a joint venture with a major construction firm to manage the more expensive part of the project and my client did the rest with his existing resources. Both companies then shared in the profits, which provided leveraged profits for my client. In other words, what looked like a funding problem was a resource problem that was solved with a joint venture. Once the project got going, my client was generating enough money to take on bigger projects. Problem solved. In such arrangements you need to look out for who has management control and over what aspects of the project to prevent internal disputes.

THE FUNDING CYCLE

As your product or service develops, hopefully it will evolve from a concept to research and development, Alpha and Beta designs, and then to a product or service with commercial value.

The Valley of Death

There is an especially perilous period that begins when you're working full time on your company and ends when you get to the financial break-even point. This aptly is called "the Valley of Death." This is the stage when you may have exhausted your funding sources but still don't have revenue. Your "burn rate" for expenses may be too high to continue operations.

To avoid this, you can: 1) raise more money; 2) cut expenses (you should have been tracking those to give you more lead time to raise money if necessary); or 3) suspend operations until you can get more funding. Suspending operations is particularly disruptive and you may lose critical personnel who won't work without pay. Remember, when you're raising money you always need more money than you think. So, make sure your financial resources will last long enough— maybe twelve to eighteen months depending on your product development cycle and sales cycle—so that you can make it through the Valley of Death and into the promised land of profitability.

Funding Stages

Pre-revenue funding is called "seed funding." Then, when you are profitable and need more financing startups typically move through additional investment stages defined by the dollar amounts needed. Those investment rounds are called "series," e.g., Series A, B, and C. In rare cases, you might even "go public," which means that your shares would be listed on a public exchange. Being publicly traded can add turbulence to the company's operations when stock prices are volatile. But you will be able to raise much more money from the unlimited number of potential investors/stockholders. There could also be further public stock offerings called "follow on offerings." See Illustration 4 for how those events look graphically.

MAKING THE INVESTMENT PITCH: TEASERS, SLIDE DECK, AND BUSINESS PLAN

Now that you've determined how much money you need and possible funding sources, it's time to make your investment pitch.

"Deliver the Mail"

I won't discuss what you need to do for loan or grant applications because each of those programs specifies the application requirements and they vary widely. But there is one thing to keep in mind

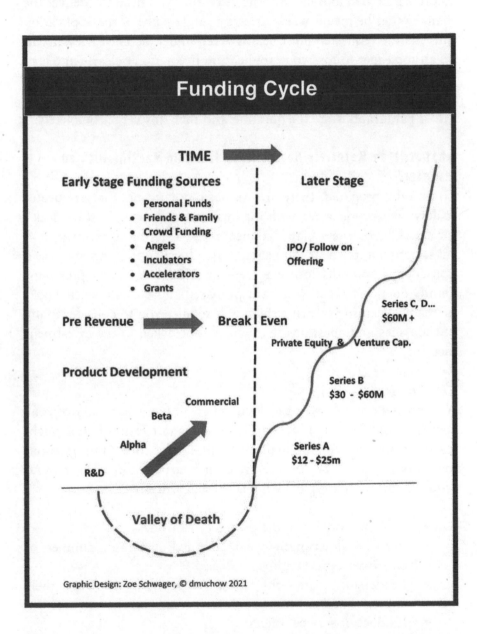

Funding Cycle

TIME

Early Stage Funding Sources

- Personal Funds
- Friends & Family
- Crowd Funding
- Angels
- Incubators
- Accelerators
- Grants

Later Stage

IPO/ Follow on Offering

Pre Revenue ➡ Break Even

Series C, D...
$60M +

Private Equity & Venture Cap.

Product Development

Series B
$30 - $60M

Commercial

Beta

Alpha

Series A
$12 - $25m

R&D

Valley of Death

Graphic Design: Zoe Schwager, © dmuchow 2021

on those and most applications. One of my federal contracting consultants pounded into me over the years that you need to "deliver the mail." What he meant was that every single piece of the application information requested must be answered in detail. The reviewer will be all too eager to toss your application if you don't clearly and specifically answer every question. So even if the application is in narrative form, when you answer, take it a sentence at a time, make that into a paragraph, state the question and then answer it completely.

What Written Materials Do You Need for Your Meeting with an Investor?

To be fully prepared, there are six basic documents that are useful to have when you meet with an investor: a "teaser," "slide deck" (or "deck"), business plan, balance sheet, offering agreement, and subscription agreement. You should also have your company's form non-compete non-disclosure agreement (NCNDA, see chapter 1 for details on that). Once you have prepared those documents, you'll be ready, because preparing them will require you to consider many of the issues and questions that you will be asked in the investment meeting.

The "Teaser"

A teaser is a one-or-two-page document that has a summary of your company and funding request. This is the short form of your pitch. It can be attached to an e-mail as the first piece to send to potential investors to see if they're interested in hearing more. There is no required format but typically it has these features:

- A picture or two of the product or business
- Business description—year founded, location, number of employees, product line
- Leadership team—titles and background showing their expertise and experience relevant to this line of business
- Product or service offered
- Technologies/special value added
- The opportunity your product provides

- Market and marketing plan
- The competition and how you plan to compete against it
- Risks and risk mitigation
- Financial projections—this can be just three spreadsheet-type rows: pro forma revenues, expenses, and EBITDA (Earnings Before Interest, Taxes, and Depreciation) for three to five years
- Funding request and "use of funds"—how the investment funds will be spent, for example, to provide expanded marketing and operating expenses

Slide Deck (or "Deck")
This takes the same types of categories as in the teaser and expands on them. Create around ten slides, with similar categories as the teaser. Some tips:

- Have them done professionally; they should look good.
- Use pictures and diagrams. For example, for financial projection use a graph to show growth over time, the company's financial break-even point, etc. See Illustration 5 for an example.
- Text should be limited to just a sentence or two on each slide—let the pictures do the work for you—you can then talk from them. The idea is to create interest so the investors will want to hear more.
- Keep the number of fonts limited so it looks clean and pick colors carefully for readability.
- Keep the text large enough so that everything can be read by someone in the back of the room.
- Include a comparison chart showing how your product has more features, is better, cheaper, faster, etc. than the competition's product.

Business Plan
The business plan should be around fifteen to twenty pages plus any appendices that might be useful. Don't make it longer. Remember who's going to be reading it—an overworked associate with stacks

of these on his or her desk. Keep it simple and easy to read with tight wording, outlines, an executive summary, and an overall professional look. For ideas on formatting a business plan, you can find templates on the internet including ones that will be specific to your kind of business. They ask questions for you to answer and make it easy to keep it focused.

Do you really need a business plan? On the one hand, some investors don't ask for them, especially those who know you personally. They feel comfortable after seeing your slide deck and asking questions. It's also true that because events move so fast, your plan is outdated soon after you create it. On the other hand, it forces you to think more deeply about your business and provide more information to investors. It will include short biographies of your key partners that show your team knows how to run this railroad. And it shows that you really understand the competition, the risks you face, and how to mitigate them. And importantly, it provides ready-to-go answers to the questions that you'll be asked by potential investors. For those reasons I'd recommend that you create one.

Write your teaser first, then the slide deck, and finally the business plan. That makes it easier to keep all three consistent, and it helps you stay focused as you write the business plan because you already have the outline from the slide deck. I know folks that have spent months working on their overly long business plan and kept trying to perfect it but never got done. Avoid that!

For an example of a business plan table of contents and a balance sheet, see Appendix 6. Your plan can be shorter and will be different, of course, depending on whether it's a product or service, etc.

Offering Memo

An offering memo ("securities purchase agreement" or SPA) is the document that describes your offering to investors. The SPA includes a description of the company, its business, the type of equity offered, and the rights of each class of equity offered, such as "common" shares and "preferred" shares. You should understand the differences because some investors will want a particular type of share.

Preferred or "preference shares" have priority rights to dividends and assets upon dissolution as compared to "common stock." Their disadvantage is that preferred shares often don't have voting rights that common shares have. There are various flavors of preferred shares with differences relating to dividend rights and then conditions when they are converted into common shares.[16]

SPAs also include warranties by the buyer and seller, restrictions on the transfer of the shares because they are not listed on a public exchange, and disclosures of risks to the purchaser. These risks might include market risks, the risk that management has not worked together in this type of a venture, your competition, product failure risks, etc. These risk disclosures, which can be extensive, are particularly important to the company because they mitigate potential shareholders' claims that the company failed to disclose investment risks including that the investor could lose all of its investment.

The Subscription Agreement
This is the contract for the purchase of your equity. It includes the price for the number of shares sold and any requirements that investors must meet to invest. For example, you may want to set a minimum investment dollar amount, such as $10 or $20 thousand for a required minimum number of shares so that you don't have too many small shareholders. When you get larger investors, they often prefer to buy out smaller investors to simplify the capital structure. Also, some companies limit investors to "accredited investors" who are more sophisticated and have sufficient resources so that they can withstand losing all their money. (See the definition of and discussion about accredited investors later in this chapter). In theory at least, this makes it less likely they will sue you if things go badly; and if they do sue, you'll have a better chance of winning.

VALUING YOUR COMPANY AND RETURN ON INVESTMENT (ROI)
You need to value your company. Investors will want to know how much you think it's worth. Then they will try to cut that amount before investing.

There are several ways to value a company. These include book value, market capitalization, enterprise value, discounted cash flow, and EBITDA. But it's likely that as a startup your balance sheet doesn't look very good, your revenues are weak, and your market capitalization value (number of shares multiplied by share price) is based on selling shares to only a few investors. One of your best arguments for value is based on future growth. Your conversation with an investor might go like this:

> **NewCo:** Our sales are $100,000 this year and profits are $30,000. We conservatively project that in three years sales will be $300,000 and profits $150,000. In our industry a multiplier of fifteen multiplied by sales is used to calculate a company's value. That gives our company a market capitalization value ("market cap") of $300,000 x 15 or $4,500,000, so we're willing to offer 10 percent of our shares for 10 percent of $4,500,000 or $450,000.

Let's assume that the investor agrees that the company could be valued on sales three years out (that's a big assumption)!

> **Investor:** Forget that. I don't like valuations based on sales, just on profits. After all, the bottom line is all that counts. So based on profits, three years from now, NewCo is only worth its profits of $150,000 multiplied by fifteen or $2,250,000. If I'm going to buy 10 percent of the company, then I'll give you $225,000 in return for 10 percent of the company's total equity (10 percent multiplied by $2,250,000).

You'd negotiate for a while and maybe end up somewhere in between your ask and the investor's bid.

Calculating Earnings per Share

You'll also need to know how to calculate earnings per share (EPS)—what one share of your company is worth. Earnings per share is simply earnings (profit or EBIDTA) divided by the total number of shares of equity. Parties generally use the total number of shares that have been "authorized" by its articles of incorporation. Shares that have been authorized but not yet issued are "treasury stock." When the company sells stock, it becomes "issued" or "outstanding."

If the EPS calculation includes shares that will be issued in the future because of a "conversion" such as warrants and options, the shares shown are "fully diluted."

Finally, to calculate return on investment (ROI), which is the profit the investor would make on its investment over a given period, see the next chart.

RETURN ON INVESTMENT CALCULATION ROI		
To Calculate Return on Investment (ROI)		Usually Stated as a % so You can Compare This to Other Investments
Dollars this Shareholder Invested	$5,000	
Total Dollars Invested by all Shareholders	$100,000	
Thus, This Shareholder's % of Equity in the Co.	5%	$5,000/$100,000
Assume that the Company Paid out all Net Profits for the Year as "Dividends."	$7,500	Usually, Co. Wouldn't pay out all Profits—It would Invest for Growth
$ Paid to Shareholder: 5% x $7,500	$375	5% of $7,500
If Company has 100,000 Shares Issued	100,000	
Then, the No. of Shareholder's Shares is:	5,000	5% x 100,000 Shares
Income/Share	$ 0.08	$375 Dividend/5,000 Shares Owned
ROI - Return on Investment	8%	$0.08 x 5,000 Shares = $400. $400 in Dividends/$5,000 Invested = 8%
ROI = Income from Investment/Cost of Investment. Note that ROI must refer to some time period. To adjust for that you could use rate of return (ROR), net present value (NPV), or internal rate of return (IRR) calculations. https://www.investopedia.com/terms/r/returnoninvestment.asp		

> **TIP: PUT A SECRET CODE ON YOUR OFFERING DOCUMENTS SO YOU CAN TRACK WHO MIGHT HAVE LEAKED THEM.**

Special Confidentiality Concerns

Your business plan discloses a great deal of your "secret sauce"—your product, strategy, market, and other confidential, commercially valuable information. Your competition would love to have this. So, if possible, get an NCNDA before sending your business plan and offering to anyone, number each copy sent out, and have the recipient sign a Business Plan Confidentiality Agreement page and return it to you. See an example of that in Appendix 6. For extra protection, you also could put an extra word or a secret mark in the plan when sending it to someone. That way, if it ever gets out and you're injured by that disclosure, you could prove who received it.

GET INSIDE THE INVESTOR'S HEAD

What does your investor want? Sometimes an investor just wants to make as much money as possible and that's it. Once I was making a pitch for a company and an older man came up to me afterwards and said, "Son, I've been investing for a long time. I don't give a blanky blank if you're selling apples or advanced tech. Just convince me that I can make three times my investment in three to five years. If so, I'm in and so are my friends."

On the other hand, some socially conscious investors don't care about profit at all. They just want to do something good for the world. Try to figure out what the investor is looking for.

INVESTMENT EVALUATOR

When I look at investing in a startup, here are questions I'd ask. Investors will ask similar questions when you meet or during the due diligence review before they invest, so make sure you have good answers for them.

Illustration 1
BASIC STARTUP STEPS, 0-60

✓   **Develop a Plan.**

✓   **Get a Partner With Money.**

✓   **Build a Balanced Core Team.**

✓   **Form a Business Entity.**

✓ **Use Non-Disclosure (NDA) and Non-Compete Agreements.**

✓ **Protect Your Intellectual property (IP).**

✓ **Get Personnel Documents In Place.**

✓ **Choose The Best Way To Compensate Employees.**

✓ **Create a Board Of Directors, Board of Advisors.**

✓ **Extensive Market Research – Define What "It" Is.**

✓ **Design a Minimum Viable Product, Field Test it.**

Note: These are the Earliest Startup Steps Before Marketing and Sales. Many steps can be done in parallel or different order.

Illustration 2

	INTELLECTUAL PROPERTY OPTIONS		
Type	Description	Typical Uses	Term and Price; Fees are subject to change
Trade Secret	• Common law right • Can be stolen, so you must protect it. • Can reverse engineer around it. • Can't be commercially disclosed. • Can save on the expenses of patenting.	• Data, formulas • Customer lists • Manufacturing processes	• No expiration • No expense, not filed.
Copyright ©	• Common law ownership attaches when created and fixed in a tangible form. • Must have valid registration to enforce rights. • Apply: U.S. Copyright Office • Don't need an attorney.	• Original authorized works fixed in a medium • Books, pamphlets • Music scores and recordings • Film, photos • Software code, but must be in a fixed medium, e.g., printed out.	• Generally: Life of author + up to 70 years; no renewal necessary • Price to self-file: Electronically: $45 and up + attorney @ $250 and up
Trademark TM, SM ®	• Name, symbol, device, or combination to identify, distinguish goods and services from another and the source • Registration requires a legal determination by U.S. Patent and Trademark office (USPTO); not an automatic filing. • Can take time and expense; use an attorney. • Apply to USPTO.	• Distinctive mark and/or words, phrases, logos, and designs • Helps create brand, customer perceptions of quality & service.	• No expiration • Need to renew. • Price: varies per class, plus attorney's fees, $500 and up

INTELLECTUAL PROPERTY OPTIONS

Type	Description	Typical Uses	Term and Price; Fees are subject to change
Patent Pat. Pend.	• The right to exclude others from making, using, offering to sell, & importing • Must eventually disclose to the public. • Takes time and expense. • First to file now usually wins. • Must apply to US Patent and Trademark Office (PTO) within one year after you offer it for sale in the US or make disclosures about it. • Must be new, non-obvious, useful, and described in enough detail to enable one with ordinary skill in the art to know how to make and use it. 35 U.S.C. Secs. 101-103. • Provisional and Non-Provisional • International – Patent Cooperation Treaty (PCT)	• Utility processes, methods of manufacture, business methods, methods of use, compositions of matter, & machines. • Design: ornamental aspects, trade dress • Plant and Plant varieties	• Utility Pat. - 20 yrs. from date issued • Design Patent – 15 yrs., plant: 14 yrs. • Price: Varies widely with number of claims, etc. Utility filing online. $5K-$6K plus attorney's fee of $8-20K

Illustration 3

Pro Forma Profit & Loss Statement (P&L)

	Yr. 1	Yr. 2	Yr. 3, Etc.
"Revenue" or "Sales"		**$200,000**	**$ 300,000**
Sales Product A	$ 60,000		
Sales Product B	$ 40,000		
Total Revenue	**$ 100,000**		
Less Cost of Goods Sold (COGS)	**$ 80,000**	Cost just for producing the product - no co. overheads	
Gross Margin $	**$ 20,000**	Total Revenue less COGS	
Gross Margin %	**20%**	Gross Margin $/Total Revenue	
Expenses			
Payroll	$6,000		
Marketing	$2,000		
Rent	$2,000		
Etc.			
Contingency (10% of above exp.)	$1,000		
Total Operating Expenses	**$ 11,000**		
"Net Margin" or "Net Income"	**$ 9,000**	Revenue Less COGS and Op. Expenses	
Net Income %	**9%**	Net Inc./Total Revenue	
EBITDA	**$ 9,000**	Earnings Before Interest, Taxes, Depreciation, and Amortization (EBITDA)	
Less: Interest, Taxes, Depreciation, Amort.	**$ 2,500**		
"Net Profit" or "Earnings"	**$ 6,500**	EBITDA less Interest and Taxes, etc.	
Net Profit %	**6.5%**	Net Profit/Total Revenue	

Illustration 4

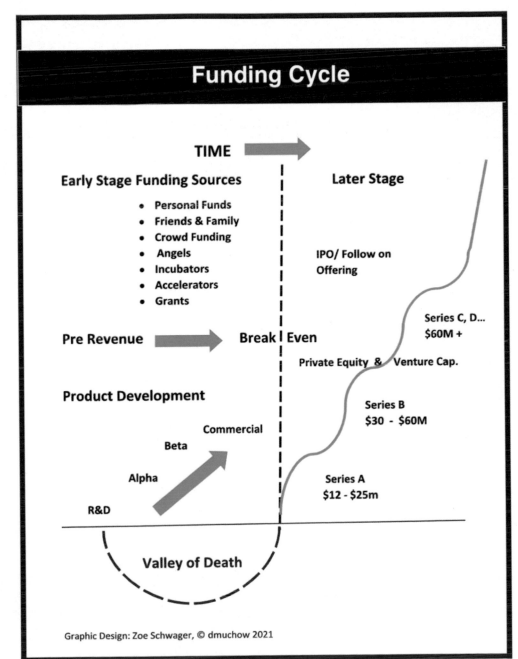

Graphic Design: Zoe Schwager, © dmuchow 2021

Illustration 5

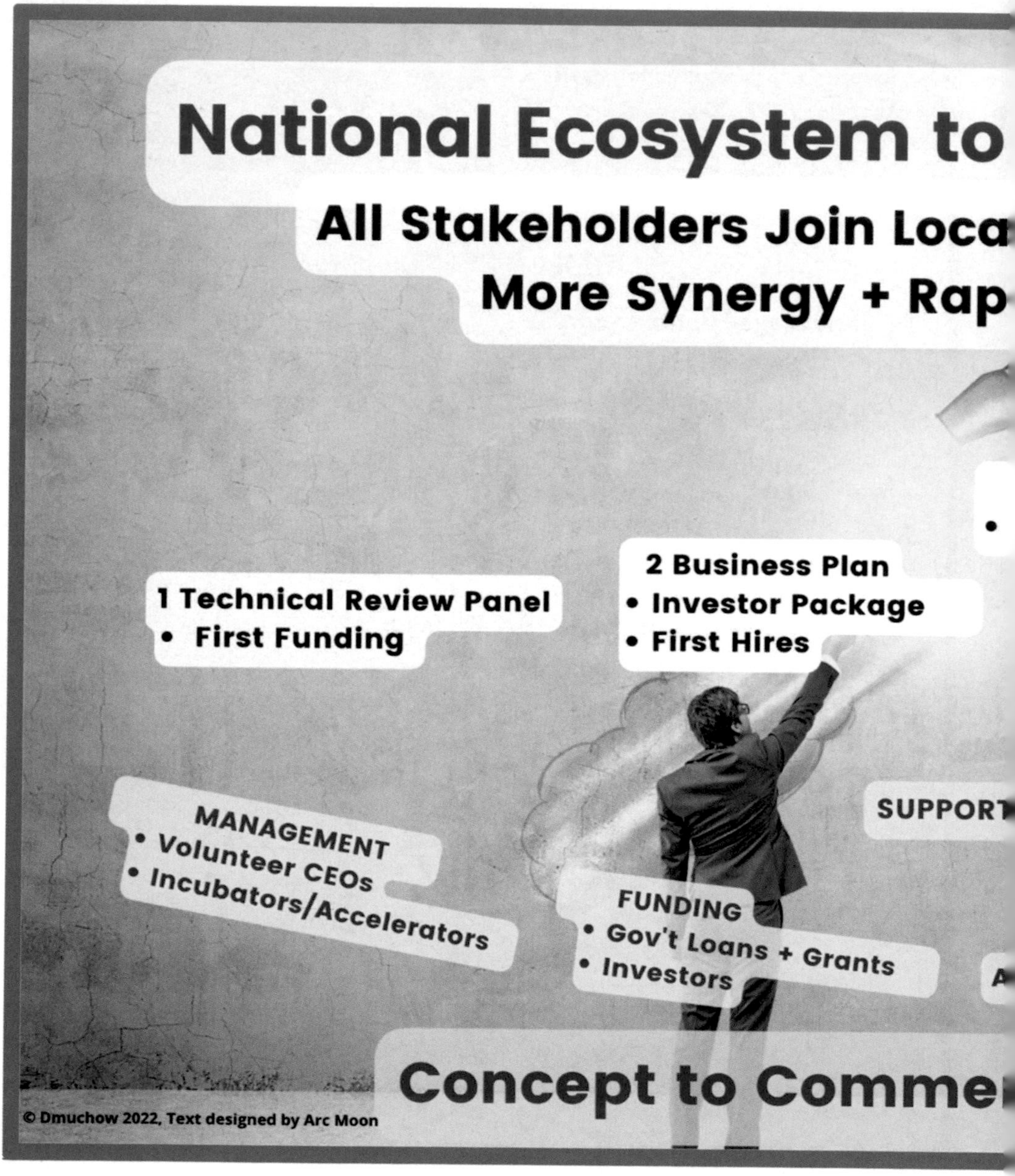
National Ecosystem to
All Stakeholders Join Loca
More Synergy + Rap
1 Technical Review Panel
• First Funding
2 Business Plan
• Investor Package
• First Hires
MANAGEMENT
• Volunteer CEOs
• Incubators/Accelerators
FUNDING
• Gov't Loans + Grants
• Investors
SUPPORT
Concept to Comme
© Dmuchow 2022, Text designed by Arc Moon

upport Startups (NESS)

artup Centers (LSCs) for
ommercialization

4 Prototype
• Testing On Site

5 Marketing +
NewCo's FIRST SALE

ent
NewCo

AKEHOLDERS:

POTENTIAL
CUSTOMERS

MARKETING
SUPPORT

AL

TECH

NTING

alization in 90 Days!

Rocket/man concept: ismagilov by Getty Images

Illustration 6

The TOMBS Restaurant, Georgetown, Washington, DC, Scooter Magee's Favorite Restaurant

> **TIP: GET A STRONG MANAGEMENT TEAM IN PLACE.
> A GOOD TEAM CAN SELL A PET ROCK. A BAD TEAM
> SIMPLY FALLS LIKE ONE!**

Management Team

This is usually the most important factor. Some investors place 50 percent of their investment decision on the CEO and team. Make sure you have your team in place or know what other additions in key positions you'd like to have before raising money. It makes it easier to get funding.

- Is management experienced in running this kind of a railroad? What is their track record (no pun intended), education, and expertise?
- Is management focused?
- Is there an experienced board of directors to provide guidance and open doors to markets or other company needs?
- Is there legal, financial, marketing, technical, and other necessary expertise available?

Corporate/Legal

- Has the company been legally formed? Are all the documents ready for due diligence?
- Does it have an operating agreement (for an LLC) or bylaws (for a corporation), business license, and an IRS federal employee identification number (FEIN)?
- Is it in compliance with SEC rules; and has it registered its securities offering (if necessary) in the states in which it's making an offering?
- Are there any legal or regulatory actions pending or likely against the company or its principals?

Sales

- What are current/projected sales?
- Can you show successive quarters of increasing revenues and/or profits?
- If no sales, can you show any traction from customer interest?

The Product, Market, Marketing, and Sales

- Give me your one-minute elevator pitch.
- What is the value added by this product or service? Is it better, faster, cheaper, safer, easier to use, environmentally superior, etc.?
- Is there a real problem to be solved, or is this just another variety of the same thing, like just another cell phone app?
- Potential market size:
  - What is the market? How do you know?
  - How much market research has been done? What does it show? Is it current? What's the quality of the market research?
  - Timing—how long is the window of opportunity for this product/service?
    - What is the level of difficulty in penetrating the market and rapidly scaling?
  - Competition:
    - What is the competition?
    - How crowded is this space?
    - What is your product price point vs. the competition's? (Better get this one right!)
    - How hard will it be to compete, and for customers to switch to this product/service because of embedded technology, or inertia, etc.?
  - Market Strategy:
    - How do you plan to penetrate the market?
    - What are your plans/budget for marketing, publicity, and sales?
      - How labor intensive/expensive will this be? Need sales teams, etc.?
      - Business-to-Business (B2B) marketing over the internet—for example, if your product is sold directly to another business rather than a personal end user
      - Civilian and/or government market?
      - If sales are international:

- What are the country risks—regulations, tariffs, political, currency conversion, other risks?
- Who's on the ground in the other country? Quality control?
- Export-Import bank or other financing?

Product Development Status
- How close to commercialization is the product/service?
- Any test or market results? What do they show?
- Technology risk? Will it work/scale up without failure?

Intellectual Property (IP)
- What is your "secret sauce"? How unique; how valuable; how likely is a patent?
- Patent search? What are the results? Patent filed?
  - Have you checked the internet for competition?
  - Will you file a fast-tracked patent? Estimated patent issuance date?
  - Will you file domestically and internationally?
- Trademark and Copyrights—Have you filed trademarks and copyright applications? Status?
- What other IP does the company have or can develop?

Financing
- Is there a business plan? How realistic is it?
- What are your reserves for contingencies?
- What's your monthly burn rate?
- How much funding is needed and by when?
  - Is there a fallback position? Can you cut the funding amount needed if necessary?
- Are the company's milestones reasonable?
- Can you get a minimum viable product (MVP) or prototype up and running to show investors and potential customers? If so, when?
- Can you get endorsements or joint ventures?

- What are your likely funding sources?
- Can you show any real expressions of interest, such as letters from potential customers, saying that they will buy the product if it works, etc.?

What Is Your Exit Strategy?
- Grow the company and stay to manage it?
- Exit or cash out in three to five years?

LEGAL REQUIREMENTS FOR OFFERINGS: SEC, BLUE SKY LAWS, AND JOBS ACT

> TIP: NEVER SELL EQUITY WITHOUT LEGAL ADVICE. MISTAKES CAN RESULT IN FEDERAL, STATE, CIVIL, AND CRIMINAL PENALTIES.

Securities Regulations
Federal and state laws govern the sale of equity for investment purposes. When you offer to sell equity, you are offering to "sell securities." At the federal level, the SEC regulates securities sales ("offerings"). Each state also regulates the sale of securities within the state.

The most important thing to know about this complex scheme of regulation is that you need legal advice before making an equity offering. The SEC's rules for startups are like Swiss cheese with trap doors for holes. These rules are evolving rapidly as regulators try to keep up with new kinds of offerings including crowdfunding and cryptocurrency transactions. The following is only a brief overview to alert you to some of the issues involved.

SEC Regulation
Under the Securities Act of 1933,[17] the Truth in Securities Act, securities offerings must be registered with the SEC, with the exceptions discussed next. That was to "require that investors receive financial and other significant information concerning securities being offered for public sale; and prohibit deceit, misrepresentations, and other fraud in the sale of securities."[18] While the SEC requires

that the information provided be accurate, it does not guarantee it. Investors who purchase securities and suffer losses have important recovery rights if they can prove that there was incomplete or inaccurate disclosure of important information. Registration involves filing information on the company and the securities offered along with certified financial statements.[19]

Fortunately for startups, there are exemptions to registration for:

o   private offerings to a limited number of persons or institutions;
o   offerings of limited size;
o   intrastate offerings; and
o   securities of municipal, state, and federal governments.

You must apply for any exemptions and only make an offering in compliance with federal regulations.

The JOBS Act

In 2012, the Obama Administration signed the Jumpstart Our Business Startups Act of 2012 (JOBS Act)[20] that further reduced regulatory requirements for offering securities.

Under Title II, the SEC eliminated the Rule 506 ban on solicitation and general advertising for issuers of securities. Now companies may raise an unlimited amount of funds under Regulation D (the regulation that requires registration of securities).[21] Issuers also may "generally solicit and advertise their offer online and elsewhere but those investors must be "accredited investors" only.[22] The SEC also allows a smaller company to raise up to $1.07 million from both accredited and "non-accredited" investors.

Title III (the Crowdfund Act) allowed companies to use crowd-funding to issue securities but imposed rules regarding how much an individual can invest during any twelve-month period. This varies depending on net worth and annual income.

State Regulation of Securities

State securities laws are sometimes called "Blue Sky" laws.[23] They apply to both for-profit entities selling securities and non-profit charitable solicitation companies. They require registration when securities are offered or are about to be offered in the state or when a sale is concluded. Many have exemptions from registration for smaller offerings. If you are offering to sell securities in a state, make sure you are complying with them. Registration fees can run in the hundreds of dollars and there are annual fees as well. So, you may want to limit the number of states in which you solicit investors to save money.

GOOD MONEY, SPIDER WEB MONEY™, AND FISHHOOK MONEY™

Getting funding is not just about getting dollars. It's more complex. When you get money, you're usually getting something else with it. It can be something good, like a dependable partner, or something bad, like money with strings that limit your actions (what I call Spider Web Money™). Sometimes it's even worse, when you accidently take money from questionable sources that are using your company as their private laundry operation. You're like a fish that takes the worm but gets the hook (Fishhook Money™). Let's look at how to avoid "radioactive money."

Good Money

While it's not always possible, try to get "good money." Good money is money with the fewest strings attached that does the most for the company. For example:

Long-Term Investor Money
Look for money from long-term Investors who understand that it may take time for you to reach profitability and don't bother you all the time about how the company's doing.

Strategic Investor Money
Another good source is money from strategic investors who add value to your company in addition to money. This might be a company that provides products you need, distribution services you can use, or introductions to valuable customers or investors. For example, if you could get money from a prime contractor who would help finance you and give you a continuing book of business that would be ideal.

Sometimes investors will pay more than market prices for shares in your company because it helps them strategically as well. I represented a company in Washington, DC that was trying to sell its property. Our real estate broker had provided an analysis of comparable market prices. But fortunately, a foreign investor was willing to pay a much higher price than the local market price simply because it wanted to have a foothold in the nation's capital for strategic marketing purposes.

Money with Fewer Strings Attached

Unless it's a gift (and sometimes even then), the money you raise will come with strings; some are obvious, some are not. Sometimes investors will offer more money than you want. Their fees are based on the size of their investment so they'll make more money that way. Also, they want you to have enough or more than enough funding to succeed. They need you to succeed or they will have to answer to their own investors financing the deal behind them. Sometimes investors want a bigger share of equity than you want to surrender.

Funding is often provided in stages, called "tranches." Make sure that you're getting enough funding up front and at each time period when you need it. Investors might tie their funding tranches to performance milestones such as revenues or profit margins to be met by certain dates. Then, if you miss those milestones, they might have the right to withhold funding or even oust you and bring in other management. Make sure you have your lawyer review funding documents so you don't get any fine print surprises.

Bad Money

If you're raising money, you'll usually need to give up something. And the more money you need the more you may have to give up.

TIP: WATCH OUT FOR PERSONAL GUARANTEES.
A PERSONAL GUARANTEE IS LIKE A HAND GRENADE.
IT LOOKS SAFE UNTIL YOU ACTIVATE IT AND THEN
IT EXPLODES.

Personal Guarantees
Lenders (excluding close friends and family) usually will require personal guarantees or collateral. A personal guarantee is like a hand grenade. It's safe until you activate it and then it explodes. It can take your personal finances down with it. If you can't afford to pay the guaranteed amount, you could be sued or even have to file for bankruptcy. So try to avoid those if you can.

Money Laundering
To criminals, startups look like a laundromat for their dirty money. To "launder" funds from criminal activities, criminals like to invest in legitimate, low-profile companies that can produce cash or asset growth without arousing suspicion. Entrepreneurs usually need money but might not have checked out their investors' sources.

> **TIP: CHECK OUT YOUR INVESTOR. YOU HAVE POTENTIAL CRIMINAL LIABILITY IF YOU ACCEPT FUNDS USED IN CRIMINAL ACTIVITIES.**

You have potential criminal liability if you accept funds used in criminal activities. For example, prosecutors might believe that you are a co-conspirator or partner in criminal activity if you have access to any of the money related to a crime. Under federal law, the government can seize your property even before you are charged with a crime. Even family members can have their assets seized for your actions. And US laws have jurisdiction outside of the country. For example, if your company is located in Panama and uses a US bank, those bank assets can be seized by consent, a search warrant, or a seizure order. However, if you can prove that you had no knowledge of the assets being related to criminal activity, you would have a strong defense to a seizure action. For further details, see the US Department of Justice's Forfeiture Policy Manual.[24]

A sophisticated investor typically will do due diligence on you and your company before making an investment. This will include asking you if there are any legal or regulatory issues pending against your company. If so, it's much harder to get funding.

The reputation, character, and integrity of your team and your investors are critical to success. So don't commit Startup Suicide by taking tainted money or working with the wrong people. If shady characters give you money, they also may want to be involved in management or be on the board, and you definitely don't want someone who is less than honest in those positions.

Know and Research Your Investor

Before accepting any investment funds or hiring someone, do internet research on your investor. Use more than one browser because browsers have different content and ranking algorithms. You can also use one of the leading public records and people search websites such as Checkmate, Intelius, or Truthfinder. These contain vast amounts of data from federal, state, and other government records, like addresses, phone numbers, marital status, liens, and lawsuits. On occasion the information is conflicting and not accurate, so be careful about accusing anyone if you find adverse information.

Get Consent

Be careful about using those websites for checking on employees and running criminal background checks because jurisdictions like the District of Columbia require written consent from the person being investigated before running the check and there are penalties of up to $5,000 for violating their detailed procedures.

Check Resumes

Ask for a resume and references from the person being investigated. Check those references. You could call schools to see if the person attended where they said they did and be sure to ask about the year of attendance, because the person you're investigating may be using someone else's record.

Verify Information Before Depositing the Funds

Don't accept any funds before checking out the source. If the investor in question gives you a check, don't cash it until you're satisfied everything is okay. Cashing it means you've accepted it. You also can have your lawyer write language into your offering documents that allows a thirty-day (or other) period from when you've received the check until when you can return it before the investment becomes final.

> **TIP: DON'T USE A "FINDER" INSTEAD OF A LICENSED BROKER-DEALER TO HELP SELL YOUR STOCK, UNLESS YOU TALK WITH A LAWYER FIRST.**

Dangers in Using a "Finder"

A "finder" is a third party, not registered with the SEC, used to help sell your equity. Under SEC rules, you are allowed to offer your own securities or use an SEC-licensed "broker dealer," such as an investment banker, to sell them, but a finder cannot legally sell your securities.

The SEC requires that a broker or dealer in securities ("securities" means "equity" or "stock") must be registered.[25] A "broker" is "any person engaged in the business of effecting transactions in securities for the account of others." A "dealer" acts as principal and is "any person engaged in the business of buying and selling securities for his own account, through a broker or otherwise."[26]

A finder is likely to be "effecting transactions in securities" unless its activities are severely restricted by you.

How much a finder can do for you without violating SEC rules is unclear and SEC rulings and court rulings on this issue depend on the facts in each case. In general, the more deeply and often the finder is involved in the entire transaction, the more likely it's violating the law. Finder's activities can range from simply providing a list of potential investors, which is likely to be allowed, to being actively engaged in negotiating the sale of the securities, which is likely a violation.[27] The SEC has taken steps to clarify its position on finders.[28] Nevertheless, be sure to consult an attorney before using a finder because the law is constantly changing in this area. Violations could result in serious penalties and void any transaction.

Examples of Funding Strategies in Confidential Transactions
and How Criminals Launder Their Money

*Surprisingly, startups sometimes jump into multi-billion
dollar schemes with no experience. Here's an example
of that and how a deal can be structured to work even
when parties don't want to be revealed. Then Cold Finger
shows us how criminals finance their underworld deals
without getting caught.*

Scooter didn't have much time to figure out what had happened with
Scarlett. Baraz Azad, a software developer client who changed jobs
like he changed socks, was on the phone.

"Hi, Scooter, I need your quick help on a financing matter."

"Sure, what's up?"

"It's a multi-billion-dollar deal on pandemic surgical gloves."

"Sounds like a big job for a new startup."

"Yeah, but I'd love to pull this off. After all, even high school
startups are making millions, why can't I?"

"Let's hear what you've got."

"Okay, Florida is having another pandemic flare-up. Restaurants
and doctors go through a box of a hundred PPE gloves every day.
They all want quality gloves, Dixant Nitriles, mixed sizes. I'm working on a three-billion-dollar sale. I can buy Dixant's for $7.51 per
box of a hundred and then sell them for $12.50. The margins are
amazing!"

"Where are they coming from?"

"The gloves will ship direct from the factory in Singapore to a
bonded customs warehouse in Miami. We've got a signed agreement
with agents claiming they have access to the ultimate seller in Singapore and the buyer's agent with the money in Zurich. It's enough
gloves to fill up twenty-seven big cargo planes that will ship over
the next thirty days. But we've only got forty-eight hours to do the
deal or someone else will take the shipment because prices are going
up every day. Once a deal falls through, the gloves are snatched up
within minutes by anyone with cash. Lots of them are counterfeit

and many of the agents have a checkered past. One even called me up and asked if I knew a good criminal defense attorney! It's the Wild, Wild West out there. Phony lawyers, phony escrow accounts. I looked up one law firm's address on Google Maps and it was a trailer in the woods in Tennessee. It's all risky but right now, my big problem is with financing."

"Not surprising, lots of risk and big bucks."

"Here's the chicken and the egg problem. The seller won't ship the gloves until the funds are segregated and locked up by the buyer's bank just for this deal. But the buyer won't tie up three billion dollars in its account for more than three days to avoid losing—over $150,000 a day in interest—and won't release funds anyway until they confirm that the gloves exist, aren't counterfeit, and are released from customs and accepted in Miami. What can I do?"

"Can you deal directly with the ultimate buyer and seller?"

"Impossible. On both the buyer's and seller's side I'm just dealing with ghosts ... agents who are dealing with other agents. I don't even know how many more are up the chain to the ultimate buyer and seller. Every agent wants a cut and doesn't want to be jumped over, so they won't tell me who their upstream agent is or even who the ultimate seller and buyer are. I hear the gloves are for the State of Florida. That's tricky too. Rumor is the governor seized some right off the dock. I can't go direct to Dixant, the seller, because it sells through their tier-one reps and they work through big hedge funds. The hedge funds and agents are the ones making all the money here, while people who need them can't get enough gloves and are dying. Most of the deals fail and that means delays in getting the gloves to folks that need them."

"Okay, Baraz. For a complicated deal like this, we need to think about what each party wants and find a way to get that for them. Otherwise, they won't buy in. Even if they do, they'll jump out at the first opportunity unless they feel they've been treated fairly. And you need to avoid Startup Suicide and protect yourself in case this all goes south. So maybe we could structure the deal something like the following. Have all the agents sign a non-disclosure, non-compete agreement and send those directly to me, and I won't disclose their names to anyone else to keep their roles confidential."

"Yeah, that's essential, makes sense," said Baraz.

"Then, let's get all the agents on both the seller's and buyer's sides to sign an escrow agreement and a Purchase and Sales Agreement with all the terms for the sale, delivery, etc. I'll be the sole escrow agent. The purchase price will be sent in smaller-lot tranches to my escrow account by the buyer as each individual lot is shipped and accepted. That reduces everyone's risks. To make everyone more comfortable, do a small deal first."

"Wait, if everybody has to agree to the escrow agreement and who gets paid, how much, etc., how do you keep that secret from the other parties?"

"Each agent will sign a separate agreement with you and me. The escrow agreement will only refer to each agreement by an arbitrary title of those agreements. That way no agent will know who the other agents are or anyone's commissions except us. Then, because they won't know who the other agents are, no agent can be bypassed."

"Yeah, that sounds good. But how do we stop the seller providing counterfeit goods?"

"Once those documents are signed, have your rep on the ground in Singapore film a live video of the lots and the bar codes as they're loaded on the plane, with a live feed to the buyer's agent. Show that day's *New York Times* front page on the video. Every lot needs to come with a certificate from an independent third party, like SGS, certifying that the lots are not counterfeit and meet all the buyer's standards in the Purchase and Sales Agreement. They'll also guarantee the deal. Then the buyer should be comfortable enough to fund my escrow account.

"How does the buyer know it's picking up the right goods and not a counterfeit shipment?"

"Once the shipment reaches Miami, have your own rep and the buyer at the customs bonded warehouse film the arrival of that shipment, its bar codes, and the buyer's written acceptance of the lot. Those will be matched to the original bill of lading when the products were shipped. At that point, the ultimate buyer's and seller's attorneys could be revealed but only to me. I need to know who I can work with if there's a problem."

"When I receive written confirmation from the lawyers for the ultimate buyers and sellers that both are satisfied, I'll pay everyone confidentially out of the escrow account."

"But how do we protect ourselves if something goes wrong that we haven't thought of?"

"Make sure that the documents reflect using US law. And if the parties don't agree to a US venue, then make it in London using the Rules of the International Chamber of Commerce's Dispute Resolution Services."

"Sounds like a plan, thanks, Scooter."

"That should do it. Everything stays confidential. If anything doesn't go down right, the escrow funds go back to the buyer and the seller keeps the goods to resell. Give me the details on the parties and I'll draw up the agreements and send you my wire transfer information."

Most of the time startups don't need big law firms with their expertise in international transactions. Why pay Mayo Clinic prices for a headache when you just need some aspirin? But when legal and business matters are really complex it's time to spend the extra money to get the best advice.

***

How criminals fund their operations and get money to invest
in startups and other businesses.

Wrapping his mind around Baraz's complex problems allowed Scooter a few hours to forget his own troubles. But that didn't mean they'd disappeared. Scooter was trapped in "Solomon's Paradox." He doubted himself. He could make wise decisions for other people, but his judgment just wasn't getting him anywhere with his own problems. Maybe things just needed to marinate for a while, because he darn sure didn't have the answers.

While Scooter was mapping out a plan for Baraz, Cold Fingers was waking up in a cold sweat in his low-budget basement apartment on S. George Mason Drive, a few miles from Scooter's home in Arlington. Cold Fingers had made a big mistake. He only had ten more days to pay off Russian oligarch Boris "Nuts" Spassky or else. He borrowed one million dollars from Nuts' son Jerry Spassky for a cryptocurrency coin investment in "SkyCoin," the hottest thing since Bitcoin. Like any crypto investment, it was secured with a nearly impenetrable algorithm. Cold Fingers' investment was volatile but finally shot up from one million to two million dollars. Then, Jacob Abner, the reclusive founder of SkyCoin, was found dead in his New York penthouse, hung from his chandelier with a Gucci necktie. Foul play was suspected. The key to the algorithm died with him. No one could access SkyCoin and its value dropped to zero and was delisted on NASDAQ. Cold Fingers lost the whole investment.

Nuts went nuts. He gave Cold Fingers just fifteen days to pay off the one-million-dollar loan. Even if Cold Fingers could sell the spy camera it wouldn't get him enough money. Only ten days were left. When Nuts went nuts someone got wacked. Cold Fingers was next in line unless he could get the Molly Bloom money, rumored to be in the millions. So, he'd squeeze and scare Magee for information until he got it. If Magee didn't pay, well, Cold Fingers would do unto others what Nuts would do to him, but he'd do it first.

In the meantime, Cold Fingers also needed more money to survive. And he could use some money to invest in startups and other businesses to make money. So, it was time to go to a cemetery again. He hated cemeteries; they reminded him of how close he was to being there permanently. But his cemetery schemes netted him twenty thousand dollars or more a month so he kept doing it. First, he'd go to a cemetery and find TOMBStones with the names and dates from an infant's death. Infants don't have much of a public record except a birth certificate and a death certificate. Then he'd go to the state office that issues duplicate birth certificates and get one by claiming to be a family member who had lost the certificate. With the birth certificate, he could get a Social Security number. Bingo! That was the "breeder" document he needed in the "Infant

Death Identity" or IDI fraud. Now he could get as many credit cards or other documents as he wanted. That's how some terrorists secretly funded their operations and invested in startups and other businesses.[29]

Next he'd turn the credit cards into cash. Sometimes he got cash advances on the credit cards. Or he'd go to an airport, charge expensive first-class tickets to Hawaii on a credit card, and sell the tickets at half price at the back of the line. Once in New York, he went to camera stores on Broadway. He and the store owner worked out a deal. If the cards were good, he'd max them out and buy thousands of dollars' worth of expensive cameras. Then the owner would let him stand outside the store and sell them for cash.

The trick was to get lots of birth certificates and credit cards, each with a different name. He'd only use the credit card for a week or so. Then he'd switch to another name. By the time the police tracked down one name, he was using another. He became a "paper person." It's hard enough for police officers to catch a criminal when they know who it is. But when they don't, it takes a lot longer.

Cold Fingers could have used one of the many online counterfeit services to get the birth certificates and Social Security cards. But the IDI method was much safer. That's because when the police officers investigated the documents and credit cards, they were all real. States have been working to shut down this fraud by linking up birth and death certificates so that no one could order a birth certificate of a dead person as easily. But Cold Fingers knew where the cracks were in the system. And he had friends in the Social Security office.

***

Meanwhile, Megan was on the phone with her friend, Kristen Blake, recently divorced.

"Glad to hear that you're doing okay after the divorce, Kristen. I know that must have been tough."

"Yeah."

"Who was your divorce lawyer?"

"Johnny Evans, nice to me but tough as nails with Jerry."

Megan got a pencil.

* * *

That night, Scarlett was writing too. To Scooter. She threw another letter in the waste basket. This wasn't working. She was angry. "I can't believe the CIA set up me and Scooter by spying on us—I hope they didn't get any pictures of us together in the swamp blind. They never told me trapping Scooter was part of the deal." She stopped writing.

"I hate the CIA and the FBI," she said out loud as she paced back and forth across her living room. "I didn't do anything wrong! They don't know who they're dealing with! I'm Scarlett Zapata! If those tin-badge bureaucrats think they can push me around, they're in for a big surprise. Like Scarlett said in *Gone With the Wind*, 'As God is my witness, as God is my witness, they're not going to lick me.' And I hope they all burn in hell!"

Wait a minute, wait a minute... she thought, *maybe, just maybe I could ... Yes ... that just might work!*

Scarlett continued pacing the floor for a while. Finally, she turned her thoughts back to Scooter. "I need to tell Scooter this whole mess wasn't my idea. But I can't say too much or the CIA might throw me to the prosecutors." She felt like a traitor to Scooter. She liked him—more than she wanted to admit. But she didn't want to be a home-wrecker, but then again, he did say that he and his wife were separated. Anyway, he was a good guy.

She walk out to her terrace. She just sat there for a while, exhausted, watching the planes descend one-after-another down the river, lured to their destination, by the control tower. Their blinking lights faded into the haze covering the airport. Finally, she went to bed, but only later did she sleep.

* * *

Back at home, Scooter was trying to get the oil and grease off his hands and face from putting a faster 350 hp 5.71 Chevy Corvette engine in the Healey. He started with gasoline and a rag (luckily he was done smoking the Camels) and ended up scrubbing with Zeps Original Orange Industrial Hand Cleaner with grit. The grit in that always did the job. He wished there was a Zeps for the mess with Cold Fingers and the lawsuit.

Sammy was pacing the floor in circles. His vocabulary was evolving quickly. But his interest in Piña Coladas was growing even faster.

"Scooter, Sammy want a Piña Colada."

"Really? Oh … okay. Give me a minute and I'll fix one for you." Scooter poured a cold one into Sammy's bowl.

"Where's the cherry?"

"Good gosh, Sammy, can't you do without a cherry?"

"No, I already do without the umbrella."

"Hang on, I'll get you one."

Then Sammy stopped lapping and started growling.

The doorbell rang. Scooter looked out. Two guys. They looked official. White socks, black shoes. Definitely FBI. He opened the door.

"Mr. Magee, JW McKinney, FBI, here, along with Jason Kingston, CIA. Can we come in?"

"You have badges?" They showed them. "So, what's this all about?"

Jason started sweeping the room for bugs. JW spoke first.

"You have something we want. Information on a new high-tech camera from Cambodia."

"Why do you think that?"

"Because we've got a recording with you discussing it with Cold Fingers Gelato."

"Well, if you've got that, then you know even if it's true, I can't reveal any attorney-client privileged information."

"We get that, but we'd like to show you something. Look at these." They pulled three 8 x 10 glossy color photos out for him to see.

He looked at the three pictures of him and Scarlett in an embrace in the Jug Bay swamp blind. Scarlett had totally set him up. He winced. He never expected that from her.

"Maybe we should show these to your wife."

"So, Scarlett does work for you and tried to set me up! You bastards; you low-life bastards!" Scooter jumped to his feet.

Then he stopped, sat back down, and slowly broke into a grin, "Go right ahead and show these to my wife. She and I aren't exactly getting along these days. Go ahead. I dare you. It won't get you anything."

The agents tried to act as if they weren't surprised by his reaction, but they were. Things weren't going as planned.

JW looked over at Jason. "Should we...?" Jason nodded.

"Magee, there's something else. That $100 million lawsuit."

"What about it?"

"We can make that go away."

"What do you mean? How?"

"Let's just say that maybe we made that happen, and we can make it disappear if you help us."

"You bastards! You did that just to put pressure on me? You have no idea what that's done to me and my wife!"

"Look, let's get reasonable here. We both want something. You want to get out of the lawsuit and we want information on the camera. And we both want to nail Cold Fingers. We're on the same side on this."

"You have a funny way of showing it."

"Let's suppose you work with us. We'll get rid of the lawsuit, get you a sealed court order allowing you to give us the information we want legally, and we'll get Cold Fingers out of your life. What's wrong with that?"

Scooter sat down. "You'd put it in writing, right?"

"Yes."

"What other surprises do you have? Is this the whole story?"

"That's all of it."

Sammy started growling. JW looked over at him.

"What's that white stuff the dog's drinking?"

"Piña Colada," said Scooter.

"What?"

"Piña Colada."

"You got to be kidding ... that's got alcohol, you trying to kill him?"

"Relax, no alcohol."

"Oh ... weird, weird."

Sammy stood up on his hind legs, growled louder, and looked at JW.

"What about me?" said Sammy.

"What do you mean?" asked Jason.

"Somebody did something to me. I not be same as before..."

Scooter interrupted Sammy and leaned forward, "Wait a minute ... You guys don't look surprised that Sammy can talk. Want to tell us what all this is about?"

"Ah ... I was going to get to that ... okay." And JW explained what they had done with Sammy, giving him the chip and cutting the hair around his eyes to improve the video feed to the CIA.

"What are you going to do to fix Sammy back to the way he was?"

"Sorry, but we can't take the chip out; it's so small you can't even see it and we don't know exactly where it is. Even if we could find it, that would require taking out a chunk of the brain that might be too big and cause more damage. Look at the big picture here," he said, lowering his voice so Sammy wouldn't hear, "Sammy's just a ... a ... dog."

Sammy looked at JW and growled, "Sammy heard you. Sammy not just dog. Sammy dog that talks. Sammy tell world what you did. No deal 'til Sammy fixed. You make Sammy mad. Sammy want you fix me."

"You're serious? That dog's crazy," said JW. "Both of you are crazy. Magee, you'd give up everything just for a dog?"

Scooter had heard enough. "Sammy's right; he's not just a dog. He's a lot more than that to me. He saved my life. If you can't do what he wants, then I'm out."

"Magee..."

"Get out of here. Out!"

Jason and JW hesitated, then got up and walked out the door.

Scooter slumped down in his chair. Sammy looked up at Scooter and put his head on his knee and said softly, "Man is dog's best friend ..."

Scooter lay in bed awake for a long time. How could he protect himself and still help Sammy? But at least some things were in motion. It felt like the tables could be turning. He was finally getting some control out of the chaos. It wasn't clear how yet, but maybe things could work out. Unless, of course, Cold Fingers got to him first.

That was closer to happening than he knew.

***

The next day, Scooter was with his grandchildren, Zoe, twelve, Zadie, nine, and little Lilly, only three years old, at Glebe Road Park. Scooter was sitting by himself swinging. Sammy was nearby. Zoe came over to him.

"Are you okay, Poppy?"

"Yes, honey, just a little tired."

"Well, I'm sure you'll be okay. It's a beautiful day! The sun's out; the flowers are blooming. I love the universe, there are so many fun things to do!" And Zoe ran off to play with the other girls. Zoe, the always-happy Zadie, and little Lily were all running around in circles until they all fell down laughing.

Scooter sat there watching. They didn't have a care in the world. What happens to people when they grow up? He was tired. Tired of the chaos. Tired of the problems he couldn't solve. He needed to get back to normal. Get his balance back. He didn't know how. But then, he thought, just because you don't know the answer doesn't mean there isn't one. It was time to find that answer. Zoe was right: things can be good.

Then he noticed Sammy was acting kinda quiet.

"You okay, Sammy?"

"When Megan come home?"

"It might be a while."

"I miss Megan. Scarlett make trouble. You like Scarlett more?"

"No, Sammy. It will be okay, you'll see."

***

That evening, Scooter was working at the kitchen table with the TV on. Sammy was in the front hall when a plastic envelope came through the letter slot with a "clink" as the brass mail slot cover closed. Sammy jumped up and looked for Scooter. He hadn't heard it and was still working. Sammy looked out the window and saw a woman walking quickly to a silver car. She got in and drove away. Sammy smelled the letter.

"Must be Scarlett. Not good."

He looked again at Scooter who was still busy at the table, took the letter in his teeth, went out the dog door to the back yard, and buried it next to a rose bush.

He came back in when he heard Scooter calling.

"Sammy! Sammy, where are you? I've been calling you!"

Sammy came back in.

"Why is there dog hair in my earphones?"

Sammy looked down and said softly, "Me use them?"

"What for?"

"Frank Sinatra. 'New York, New York.' Sound better than iPhone speaker."

"Ugh ... Sammy...!"

Scooter was cleaning off the headphones when the phone rang. Cold Fingers was on the line.

"Magee, my partner, Crunch, has arrived. Remember, see you at The TOMBS at four o'clock tomorrow. Be there. No cops."

Scooter heard the click as Cold Fingers hung up.

***

Back at the CIA, Bulldog was furious when Jason Kingston told him what had happened at Scooter's house. "You idiot! You had the goods on Scooter and got bluffed by a Piña Colada-drinking dog? This is crazy! I'll talk with Dr. Johansson. Let's see if he can fix the chip or something. We need to get Scooter on our side."

***

The next day, Scooter was headed to The TOMBS. He was a block away when he saw Cold Fingers and a huge guy with a black skull cap leaning on a black BMW M Series—the fastest street-legal BMW. His heart skipped a beat and he panicked. He spun the Healey around hard in a U turn and took off toward home. Cold Fingers heard the tires squeal and recognized the Healey.

"Let's get him! We need to catch him, knock some sense into him, and show him that we mean business about getting the files," said Cold Fingers as they jumped in their car and followed Scooter. They could see him now one block ahead. Scooter turned right on to 35th Street, the street version of the Exorcist Steps. It dropped a good eight stories in one block and was paved with bumpy cobblestones that hadn't worn down much in two hundred years. The car bounced in the air as Scooter careened down the hill, hitting one of the fenders on a car parked on the left side. As Scooter turned right onto Canal Road at the bottom, Cold Fingers was right on his tail.

Scooter's Healey was fast with the new Corvette 350 engine, but probably not faster than their BMW. But this time Scooter was ready. He just hoped that the sensor he planted on Chain Bridge would work.

There were several cars right in front of Scooter. He floored the Healey and the front end lifted as the rear tires squealed and dug in. He was going 80 mph now and honking and swerving to get around the cars. His racing experience at Summit Point was paying off. Cold Fingers was just a few cars behind him. Scooter made it through a green light at Arizona Avenue. In a few seconds he would be at Chain Bridge. He was ready. But his timing had to be just right.

Chapter 6

THE SMARTER ROAD TO MARKETING AND SALES

If it's not on the wagon you can't sell it.
—Bill Cetti, Former Energy Company CEO

Amazing things will happen when you listen to the consumer.
—Jonathan Mildenhall, Former Chief Marketing Officer of
Airbnb

There are thousands of books on marketing and sales. Each contains many strategies and tactics. Some expand on basic topics, like the four principles of marketing called the "marketing mix"—product, price, place, and promotion.[1] Others provide new techniques for marketing using the internet and social media.[2]

This chapter won't repeat familiar marketing and sales theories and tactics. Rather it's focused on specific startup strategies and tactics. There are similarities between traditional marketing and sales and what startups should do. But in some ways it's different for startups. For example, startups need to develop a product or service fast, before they run out of money. For convenience I'll use the term "product" to include both "product" and "service." And there's only so much a sole entrepreneur or small startup can even do. Entrepreneurs drink from a firehose. They must juggle raising money, legal matters, accounting, personnel issues, and building a product all at the same time. So having a focused marketing-sales plan and executing efficiently on it are essential.

One of my clients was creating a new software program. While the program was still many months away from being written, she started hiring marketing consultants and sales personnel. Three months later her burn rate was too high; she ran out of money and the company folded. To avoid that, focus on producing a marketable product first before you spend too much money on the marketing itself. What you finally produce will help to define the marketing and sales strategy. You need to execute the right steps in the right order and not get thrown off track by anything else.

THE DIFFERENCE BETWEEN MARKETING AND SALES—LESSONS FROM A HEAD OF LETTUCE

What are marketing and sales?

According to the U.S. Chamber of Commerce, "in the simplest of terms, marketing is building awareness of your organization and brand to potential customers. Sales is turning that viewership into a profit, by converting those potential customers into actual ones."[3]

There is no bright line between marketing and sales. After all, a salesperson can also build the brand during a sale.

These days, lots of marketing and sales take place on the internet with little personal interaction. Selling in person is a whole different story. I learned that when I was a law student selling Fuller Brushes door-to-door in DC, riding around on my red Vespa motor scooter.

Fuller Brush was founded in 1906 and was famous for its door-to-door sales of brushes and household products, including hairbrushes with a lifetime guarantee (longer than my hair has lasted!). Billy Graham, Jack Nicholson, and Dennis Quaid were all salesmen early in their careers.[4]

Working in door-to-door sales was a real education. I met naked homeowners, high level government officials, and one person who got me a job at the Bureau of the Budget. And I learned a few sales tricks, like putting my quick-sales kit in a paper bag with a head of lettuce on top to get into apartment buildings with "No Solicitors Allowed" signs. That worked great unless the first door I knocked on was the manager's apartment!

After one afternoon of training, I took my quick-sales suitcase to the first house and rang the doorbell. A lady opened the door.

"Hi, I'm your Fuller Brush man."

"Oh, thanks," she said. "I don't need anything."

"Okay," I said. By then I was on my knees, opening the sales kit and giving her three small packages of shampoo *one at a time*. "I'll just leave you some free samples."

"That's very nice of you!"

Next, I handed her the catalog of products—note that this was the fourth time she had accepted a free shampoo sample from a guy on his knees. Maybe she'd feel guilty enough to buy something. She did and bought a bunch of stuff. More than half of the folks did after saying "No."

When selling in person, keep in mind that the potential customer's first response is usually "No, thank you." Don't let that discourage you. Consider it an invitation to negotiate a sale.

What I learned was that you should:

- Be polite and agree with the customer;
- Give some free samples to set the mood; and
- Then work on the sales stuff.

I also learned not to play outside of my ability. One customer at the door had a big soup stain on his bright red tie. I offered to use Fuller Brush's Super Spot Remover spray on it and watched the colors run down to his shirt!

The takeaway? Don't take the first "No" as an answer. Treat it as an invitation to sell. And don't use carpet stain remover on clothing!

Here's a startup marketing and sales road map for you. Prioritize speed and focus. You need to develop your product and get to sales while the money lasts. And do it while avoiding legal and other traps that can lead to Startup Suicide.

WHAT MAKES A GOOD PRODUCT OR SERVICE?

If you're starting at the beginning, you need to create a product. Maybe you've seen something that doesn't work well and think you can improve it. Or there's an inefficient service and you've got a better process.

What Makes a Good Product?

Great marketing can sell just about anything (think Pet Rock, a toy first produced in 1975, which was quite literally just a rock with eyes and a great marketing pitch).[5] For a reality check on your choice of product, see the Product, Market, Marketing, and Sales section later in this chapter.

CUSTOMER DISCOVERY—LISTEN, DON'T TALK!

Once you have a concept or prototype of the product, you should conduct customer discovery, also called market research.

Keep Market Research Costs Down

You don't need to develop the final product to do market research. Don't spend too much time or money building what you think the product will be before you do market research. One of my software clients was looking to raise $40,000 to develop the software for a cell phone application so she could show the app to prospective customers. She was having a hard time raising the money and was stuck. I suggested that she simply use Photoshop and create four or five pictures of what the screen shots would look like for the users. She did that and was able to get good customer feedback with minimal expense.

Talk with One Hundred Potential Target Customers

Yes, one hundred. You'll get valuable feedback to improve your product. Your concept might even evolve from a product to a service such as leasing instead of selling the product, offering it on a subscription basis, or licensing the intellectual property and letting others deal with the complexities of manufacturing and distributing the product. Remember, at this stage you only have a hypothesis as to what features the product should have and who is the ideal customer.

The CEO of a manufacturing facility I was using was frustrated over an OSHA inspection. He had a high bay facility with twenty-foot ceilings. There was some rebar (metal rods used for concrete forms) sticking about four inches out of the ceiling well over ten feet above any operations below. The OSHA inspector wanted the ends of those rods twenty feet in the air covered with rubber tips for safety purposes. What the safety purpose was remains a mystery. Licensing the use of your intellectual property avoids dealing with those kinds of regulatory and manufacturing plant issues.

Create Multiple Sources of Income

Another client was developing a cell phone app to be used internally for a business to train their people. That was one source of income. But there could be others, such as getting ad revenues on the app and offering a subscription to the public—think ninety-nine cents per month per user multiplied by a hundred thousand subscribers, which equals $1.8 million per year.

The owners of the Empire State Building also created a very profitable side business. The 2011 IPO SEC documents revealed that the observation deck in the building made more money than the office space.[6] Try to think of as many revenue streams as possible.

Tips on Conducting Market Discovery

Start by making a list of what you'd like to know. Should the product focus on ease of use, lower cost, or new capabilities? When you meet with potential customers, mostly listen. You want to get into their head and find out what they want and need. Don't try to sell anything. This is a discovery process, not a sales call. Keep it informal. You might ask:

- What product are you using now?
- What do you like or not like about it?
- What about the price?
- What else would be better or useful to you?
- If you could get what you want, how much would you pay for it and how many would you buy?
- Then take those answers and revise your concept as appropriate.

Product Development

Once you've refined your idea, develop a prototype to show a focus group of potential customers. This will give you a sense of your product's cost so you can set a sales price and a profit forecast for your P&L. Build a minimum viable product (MVP). Keep it basic and simple because it will continue to change as you get more customer feedback and improve the product.

Avoid Volume Production Until Your Product and Other Questions Are Answered

One of my clients called me and said he needed to meet right away to get out of a $250,000 contract he had signed with a manufacturing company to build a new kind of air conditioner. He had signed a contract with the manufacturing company before he had talked with any customers and didn't even know what the end product would cost. We got out of the contract, but this could have been a disaster. Never start volume production of a product until you know what the customer wants and what the price point needs to be to cover costs and make a profit.

> **TIP: NEVER GO TO MARKET WITHOUT EXTENSIVE TESTING.**

TEST, TEST, TEST

Once you have a working model or prototype, put it through strenuous testing. Start testing it with friends or a small group, then a larger group—just like new restaurants use a soft opening to identify and smooth out the glitches. Get feedback. Fix what's not working. If you're developing a device, don't just test it in the lab under controlled conditions. Test it in the environment where it will be used. Stuff happens in the field that you can't imagine. Consider seagulls. When deploying solar power systems for the Navy along the coast in Djibouti, the Navy officer asked me if the solar panels would withstand the sea gulls in the area. I figured he meant they would leave droppings on the panels and cut their efficiency. "No," he said, "the seagulls go into the water and pick up shellfish. Then they fly up high and drop them to crack them open on solar panels!" We upgraded the panels. One of the power stations had hollow metal tubes to support the solar panels. They soon turned out to be great hornet's nests! There's no way to predict what might happen in the field.

The military does a great job with testing. They test to failure. They'll drag a product for deployment to a war zone through the water and then see if something falls off or rusts. They'll shock test it on bumpy roads and drop test it to see what breaks. When we were testing solar and wind power stations, we relied on the spec sheets from a manufacturer which showed that a key electronic component would continue to operate at up to 110 degrees Fahrenheit. Temperature tolerance was important because the products had to be used anywhere on the planet from the Arctic to Africa. We tested the unit at the Army's Aberdeen Testing Grounds in a climate chamber. It did fine in cold, but when it got to around 100 degrees the units started failing. It turned out that the manufacturer had never tested the units to such stringent requirements, although the spec sheets said that they would work under those conditions. That resulted in losing a big contract. Don't rely on manufacturer's spec sheets. They may not be correct so run you own tests.

The first time a customer uses your product it must work. If it doesn't, you've lost a customer you'll probably never get back. I see this problem all the time with clients developing software. Developing software is frustrating. Month after month, errors in coding creep up and changes must be made. Those changes lead to other glitches. Understandably, entrepreneurs just can't wait to launch their product. Sometimes, they don't have enough money or time to stop and sufficiently test it, so they just start selling and cross their fingers. It usually backfires. Drop down menus don't drop, fonts are wrong, the program freezes, and error messages start popping up. You don't need a software guru to tell you that you've lost a customer when that happens.

While we're on the subject of software, one of the most common problems is that the entrepreneur signs a software development contract that's created by the developer and provides little protection for the entrepreneur. For example, it might say that it will develop an application to do x, y, and z. But there's no remedy in the contract in case the software doesn't work, and no language as to how fast any errors will be corrected. Finally, smaller software developers tend to come and go and can leave your product unfinished. That means you have to start all over with another developer and lose a lot of time and money.

CONSIDER FILING A PATENT APPLICATION

At first, your product will continue to change as you think of new features. Then, once you settle on the core features of the product, you should consult with an attorney on how to protect your intellectual property in the product and other valuable company assets. This discussion should include:

- how to protect any trade secrets both for the product and other proprietary data such as customer lists, designs, and financial information on costs and prices;
- a discussion on trademarking your company's name and logo and the product line for your product(s); and
- what printed materials and software should be copyrighted.

If you think you might have invented something new, consult with an attorney about getting a patent. In the meantime, don't publicly disclose your "secret sauce" or other features of your invention before you file the application. If you do, then you only have one year from when the public disclosure was made in which to file for a patent or you will lose that opportunity.

Filing a patent application not only gives you exclusive rights to develop, sell, import, and export the product; it has other benefits. Investors will ask whether your product is patentable or if others would be able to produce the same thing. If you've applied for a patent, investors will feel more comfortable making an investment. It also helps with marketing when the product is "Patent Pending" (or "Pat. Pend."). That gives customers the sense that you're the market leader and have something that's unique.

Patent Search

As discussed in Chapter 3, consider conducting a patent search before filing your patent application. You'll find out if your invention has already been patented. If so, you can't be issued a patent. With a search you'll be able to fine tune your claims and avoid ones that are already in other patents. Finally, it will give you ideas that can lead to filing a better application.

> TIP: DO YOU HAVE AN INVENTION? TALK TO A LAWYER RIGHT AWAY—THE FIRST TO FILE WINS AND YOU DON'T WANT TO LOSE YOUR RIGHT TO PATENT BY DISCLOSING YOUR SECRET SAUCE.

Stay Under the Radar

When you file a provisional patent application, it's not published. And if you never file a non-provisional application, the provisional application simply will vanish, so your competition won't know what you're developing.

With a non-provisional application, the application will be published for comment by the U.S. Patent and Trademark Office promptly after eighteen months from when it was filed. That gives you an eighteen-month marketing advantage to develop your product under the radar without the competition knowing about it. Publication allows anyone to file a challenge to it before a patent is granted.[7]

You will need to talk publicly about your product to raise financing and market it. When possible, use a non-compete-non-disclosure agreement (NCNDA) to keep the proprietary information confidential. See Chapter 1 for details on that. You usually can disclose *what your product will do* without jeopardizing getting a patent. But don't talk about your "secret sauce," which is *how it does it* because that will be what's in your patent claims. And once those claims are out in the public they become "prior art" which means that your invention isn't "new" and has already been invented so you can't get a patent for it.

MARKETING AND SALES STRATEGY

Good marketing requires good planning. If you're not familiar with marketing, get some expert advice. You can hire someone for that or put a marketing person on your board of directors or board of advisors. Map out milestones for your marketing campaign. One of your key milestone results is to show "traction" for your product which makes it easier to get financing.

Traction

Investors want to see traction toward sales. Sometimes it doesn't make sense to try to raise money from investors if all you have is an idea and no traction. Investors don't like risk and you're in a very risky period. Ideally, to satisfy an investor you'd have successive quarters of growing profitability, but that's impossible if you're pre-revenue. So how else can you show traction?

At a minimum, you should have proof typically in the form of bench tests or field tests that prove the product works.

Get a couple of letters from potential customers that might say something like this, "If you can produce this product in this price range, and it works when I test it, then I'll buy x number of these over y period of time." Don't just give potential customers products to test. If possible, have them sign a commitment that, in return for your giving them a test model, they agree to buy some products if the testing is successful.

> **TIP: WHEN GIVING OUT TEST SAMPLES MAKE SURE THEY'RE TIED TO SALES OR YOU'LL END UP WITH NOTHING.**

And don't let a potential customer take advantage of you. One of my clients, I'll call them Zipco, had spent over $200,000 on a training program and offered a free trial to a large potential customer that liked it and wanted to have others in the company use it. The program was used again and again with various groups in the company. Finally, all the employees had been trained on it and still the company refused to pay anything. My client had created the impression that the product might be free and ended up walking away with nothing. To avoid this, when you're offering a demonstration be specific up front about what will be free and what must be paid—and get it in writing.

You might have to heavily discount the price to get that first sale. That's okay if you really need that first sale to show traction.

Once you know the price that a customer will pay, you can extrapolate income and expenses and calculate potential profits. See chapter 5 for more on how to calculate a company's value.

WHAT ARE YOU SELLING—A PRODUCT, SERVICE, OR BOTH?

Licensing

In addition to selling your product, you could license it to users as a service. That could include a flat fee for providing it or a subscription payment or both. Many cell phone apps are an example of this model.

Software as a Service (SaaS)

Consider a SaaS model for sales. This is a software distribution model, also called "cloud computing" in which a cloud provider hosts applications and the user accesses them over the internet. This allows a company and its employees to store data and have access to it anywhere. It can reduce costs by eliminating the need to purchase and maintain servers. Amazon Web Services (AWS) and Microsoft Azure are examples of cloud computing providers.

Product Lines

Think like a crude oil refiner. Their product can go into gasoline, diesel, and other fuels but there are so many more uses, like tires, wax, ink, pantyhose, shampoo, aspirin, and eyeglasses. What are your product's uses? Or is it just an end-use product that's always in the same form?

Grants and Loans

Even while you're selling products, you can get additional income from grants, and operating funds from low-cost government loans.

Franchise Your Product or Service

If your product and brand show growing sales, you could create a franchise to distribute it in other locations rather than open and run offices yourself. A franchise is a method of distributing products or services. A franchisor who owns the rights to them enters into a franchise agreement with the franchisee who sells them under the franchisor's brand name. The franchisor sets out standards of operation to maintain quality and protect the brand and may provide training, site identification, and other support to the franchisee that may pay an up-font cost for the franchise plus a periodic fee to the franchisor for those services. While this is usually a tactic for more mature companies, startups can also use it.

PUBLICITY

When you start your business, nobody is going to knock on your door to find out about it. So, how do you let people know what you are doing and why? Dennis Welch, president of Articulate PR and Communications, www.BeArticulate.com, offers some valuable publicity suggestions.

One way is to advertise to alert your audience to your new endeavor. The other way is a publicity campaign. I discussed this with Dennis, and here's what he told me:

Publicity creates awareness—with the media in particular—about who you are, what you do, and why you do it. A publicist has to answer three questions every day for the media:

- What's the message?
- Who's the messenger?
- Why should I care about it today?

That last question gets to urgency. The media have a lot of incoming matters and it usually deals with the most important issue in the shrinking news cycle. Some people in top media outlets get as many as a thousand pitches a day. If you plan to cut through that noise to get a hearing, you will have to know what you are doing or hire an expert. The best publicists know how to create "hooks" much like the best songwriters. What cuts your message out of the herd of messages they are receiving every day? Without a hook or two you are sure to be lost in the shuffle. And the most successful publicists are also relentless.[8]

You need to be prepared to do effective interviews. On TV you might get five minutes if you're lucky. Radio interviews can last longer. Think about what really matters and write down some talking points to stay on your message. Don't ramble. Success in the publicity campaign can help your marketing and salespeople when they reach out on your behalf. Suddenly, you aren't a stranger to their targets. It helps if you have some visibility, name recognition, and credibility. That opens the door for a dialogue about you and your mission and that's how sales are likely to happen. Publicity can make that happen.

But publicity alone won't move the needle for you. So, your marketing and sales people need to roll up their shirt sleeves and get busy piggybacking on any publicity traction you may be getting.

Dennis Welch, president of Articulate PR and Communications, offers some publicity tips:

- A great press kit can be the best conversation starter you have and may crack the door open for an appearance or interview of some kind.
- Don't call media people on the phone. Find their email address and reach out there. Attach your press kit to the first email you send. If you don't get any responses, then try again next week without the press kit attached. Some media people (especially the bigger outlets) have filters that screen out any message with an attachment.
- Write down your talking points in quick hitting bullets. Practice them. Get comfortable conversing about each.
- Be relentless without being a pest. Reaching out a few times on email is completely acceptable.

- Don't brag. Be humble. Make it about your mission. People are much more likely to engage with you if you are not on your high horse.
- Believe in yourself and your work. If you do, that will come through loud and clear. People like connecting to other people who are on a mission.[9]

SALES PROGRAMS, ADVERTISING, AND TACTICS
How Will You Sell Your Product? Here Are Some Choices
Door-to-Door Sales

Door-to-door sales used to be much more common with Fuller Brush, vacuum cleaner, insurance, and encyclopedia salespeople. The only door-to-door salespeople I've seen recently in our Northern Virginia area are tree trimmers (just happened while I was writing this), paving companies ("We're paving your neighbor's driveway and can give you a great deal"), and non-profits (that was last night at dinner time). It's still happening but extremely inefficient compared to social media and other sales channels.

> **TIP: WHEN YOUR POTENTIAL CUSTOMER SAYS "NO" AND GIVES YOU THE "BRUSH OFF," APPLY "FTB"—THE FULLER BRUSH TREATMENT!**

Internet Marketing

Social media is the other extreme—no people, no doors, just sales. With social media, electronic communication is used to connect to users for sales, marketing, and messaging, to create virtual communities, and other purposes over the internet. It's highly efficient, relatively inexpensive, and can micro-target messages to particular customers. Create a website (the "platform") for your product and sell from that. Use one-click button links to take the customer right to the order page. You also can place ads on other platforms such as Facebook, LinkedIn, Twitter, YouTube, TikTok, and Instagram or use content on those sites to drive customers to your site.

Gary Vaynerchuk's classic book *Crushing It!*[10] provides practical advice on how to use social media platforms and do whatever it takes to unleash their potential for your product. That's an excellent starting point for an understanding of this critical space.

Influencers

Get noticed by an influencer. Influencers are people on social media or elsewhere who have a reputation for their knowledge and expertise, or simply have popularity in a particular field who can influence followers in their purchasing and other decisions. They flood social media with blogs, posts, and pictures on Instagram to build their brand. If you can get an endorsement for your product on social media from an influencer, that can have great results.

Oprah Winfrey was a new kind of influencer. She didn't just endorse other products like books or perfume. She was the first black person to form a major production studio, Harpo Brands. Then she used that to create her *own* brands including *O Magazine* and other products. And, of course, her "favorite things" tend to sell out quickly. See if you can find an influencer to help sell your product.

E-mail Marketing

There are many e-mail mailing list companies on the web that will sell you curated mailing lists. These can be tailored by location, income levels, professional titles, type of business, and other attributes. One publisher I was talking to told me that when his author purchased a one-million-person e-mail mailing list and sent out an e-blast, the book soared to a brief top ten place on Amazon.

Advertising

You can place paid ads in any media, from social media to magazines, radio, and TV. You also could use printed flyers and distribute those, although social media is more efficient and can reach far more people.

One of my clients with a cell phone app gets income from companies using the product and from a ninety-nine cent a month fee to subscribers. In addition, the company runs ads that change as the user goes to various pages on the application. These multiple sources of ad revenues help to smooth out revenue flows from other product sales channels.

Content Marketing

Content marketing is a market strategy to create useful and consistent content for a clearly defined customer audience which drives customer action. With content marketing you're not directly pitching your product. You're providing information the customer finds useful or interesting. Within that, information about your product appears and the recipient then responds to your product. You can find companies to create content marketing on the internet, devise strategies, produce useful content for you, and distribute it via social media or mailings.

Sales Representatives (Reps) and Distributors

Some products such as more expensive machines, industrial products, and products sold to retailers like books sold to books stores, are sold via third party reps and distributors who regularly meet with customers and keep them supplied with products and help answer questions. For example, major book distributors have sales teams that meet with book publishers and learn about upcoming books many months in advance. The books go into their sales catalog. Then when they visit bookstores or have discussions with large online accounts, they can advise the stores and accounts about what books seem to be most popular and have the best reviews.

A "rep" or "sales representative" is a sales professional that carries a line of one or more products and engages the customer, answers questions, and helps the customer if there are post sales questions. A rep doesn't keep the products in inventory and doesn't sell the product. It arranges a sale that is completed by the company with the customer; and the rep is usually paid on a commission basis by the company.

A distributor, on the other hand, helps the company by providing warehousing and distribution of the products as well as closing the sale.

Contracting with Reps and Distributors
If you are using a rep or distributor, here are some legal and business considerations.

Specify the Term of the Contract

Until you know how the rep will perform, you want to be able to easily fire it. So, you might have a term of one year with an "evergreen provision" that says, "This Agreement is in effect until one year from its effective date and will automatically renew on successive one-year anniversaries unless either party provides thirty days' written notice of termination to the other."

Include Sales Goals

For example: "Unless rep achieves sales of $100,000 of the product on or before x date, this agreement will terminate."

Prevent Misstatements by the Rep

Language should specify that "the rep shall only provide prospective and current customers with product information, pricing, and terms approved by the company and shall not exaggerate or make any unsure performance or other claims regarding the product."

Prevent Bribes

"Rep shall not provide any monetary or other inducements to prospective and current customers." In international transactions language should be added to prevent violations of the Foreign Corrupt Practices Act (FCPA) which prohibits bribery of public officials for certain classes of people.[11]

Joint Ventures
In selling your product, your supplier or downstream customer could also help. For example, Home Depot sometimes finances its suppliers to ensure adequate product volumes. If your product is used in combination with other products, yours could be listed in their sales materials and vice versa.

Presentations to Trade Associations
There are trade associations for virtually any product or service. They often have many thousands of members who could be potential targets for your product. Get on their programs as a speaker or develop ready-to-go articles for their publications regarding your product. This way you can reach many customers at once.

Webinars
Provide content marketing through webinars. The audience that signs up will already have self-selected as being interested in your subject area. You could charge a fee for your webinar or become part of webinar series conducted by universities, university alumni programs, or others.

Sales Materials Should Match the Niche Market
When your product is sold to different markets, you should have focused spec sheets with performance and other data, brochures, and strategies for each different market segment. For example, if your product is sold to veteran groups, it could stress its value to those who have served.

Continuous Innovation and Cost Cutting

At some point in a product's history, the price becomes even more important to customers. For a while if you have an innovative product, with limited or no competition, you can charge a premium price. But eventually it will attract competition, be available from many others, and become more like a commodity. Then, a downward cycle of price warfare can happen. To keep ahead of the competition and price competition you need to continually innovate to keep your product better, faster, more efficient, etc. And you need to operate more efficiently to survive that cost cutting. John D. Rockefeller Sr. was an expert at cutting costs to increase profitability.

Rockefeller was relentless in ferreting out ways to cut costs. During an inspection tour of a Standard Oil plant in New York City, for instance, he observed a machine that soldered the lids on five-gallon cans of kerosene destined for export. Upon learning that each lid was sealed with forty drops of solder, he asked, "Have you ever tried thirty-eight?" It turned out that when thirty-eight drops were applied, a small percentage of the cans leaked. None leaked with thirty-nine, though. "That one drop of solder," said Rockefeller, "saved $2,500 the first year; but the export business kept on increasing after that and doubled, quadrupled—became immensely greater than it was then ... and has amounted since to many hundreds of thousands of dollars."[12] Over the course of his career at the helm of Standard Oil, Rockefeller cut the unit costs of refined oil almost in half.[13]

Rockefeller's extraordinary drive and attention to detail are legendary. "I shall never forget how hungry I was in those days," he later recalled. "I stayed out of doors day and night; I ran up and down the tops of freight cars when necessary."[14]

> **TIP: USE THE FREEDOM OF INFORMATION ACT (FOIA) TO GET COMPETITOR'S COST INFORMATION TO BEAT THEIR PRICE ON THE NEXT BID.**

FOIA and Pricing Your Bid

Whether it's a bid on a government or private contract, price is a key factor along with past performance and capability to perform. You want to have a bid that's low enough to win compared to the competition but high enough to reach your profit target. How can you find out what your competition will be bidding? You can use the Freedom of Information Act (FOIA)[15] at the federal level or the equivalent state FOIA laws in state contract bids. FOIA is a federal law that provides that any person has a right, enforceable in court, to obtain access to federal executive branch (and independent federal commission) "records." This excludes Congressional records. Only "records" can be requested, not general information.

FOIA allows you to see competitor's costs in past bids unless this information is not available or redacted because of FOIA's trade secret exemption.[16] From the competitors' cost and total contract price you can estimate what the competitor's profit and bid price might be. This works even better when you can do this with several bids from the same company to fine tune your results.

The FOIA Process

Each federal agency has its own FOIA procedures and you can make FOIA requests online or by mail with that agency. Before making a request, check to see if the information is public at the agency or on the internet. There is no required form for filing a FOIA request but there are general requirements which must be met. See Appendix 8 for an example of a FOIA written request.

Once the request is filed the agency will acknowledge it. Requests are processed in order of receipt. There is usually no charge for the first two hours of agency search time or for the first one hundred pages of records provided. You can request a limit on the amount you are willing to pay for the records search. If the amount is over twenty-five dollars, the agency will inform you of that. There are procedures for expedited handling such as when there are threats to a person's physical safety. You generally cannot obtain information about another person without their consent. See FOIA.gov for more information.

AVOIDING LEGAL LIABLITY

> **TIP: DON'T LET YOUR ADVERTISING CLAIM BECOME A LEGAL CLAIM AGAINST YOU!**

Avoid False Advertising

When you're marketing, you need to be careful not to exaggerate to the point of making misleading or false statements. There's usually no problem with broad claims or puffery such as "this is a great product." But when claims are misleading or false, you're inviting lawsuits by competitors and legal action by the Federal Trade Commission (FTC), with its consumer protection authority, and the Better Business Bureau. Customers will often see through exaggerated claims anyway.

Both the federal government and states have false advertising statutes. Under the Lanham Act, the FTC and private parties can file civil suits for false advertising, including a false or misleading description of fact or origin that misrepresents the nature, characteristics, and qualities of goods and services and is likely to cause confusion or deceive.[17] Some of the more common advertising mistakes that companies make include:

Exaggerated Claims

You should have sound backup for any specific facts that you advertise. Never claim performance statistics without proof. Independent studies of the claims can provide additional protection from lawsuits.

In 2018, the FTC and the Maine attorney general settled a lawsuit against Marketing Architects, an ad agency that created and disseminated radio ads for diet products pitched with a host of allegedly misleading radio ads. One product was touted as "so powerful, it even works while you sleep!" The ads also claimed, "With the metabolism-boosting benefits of AF Plus, you can keep eating your favorite foods and STILL lose pounds and inches—in fact, we guarantee it!"[18]

Illustrations Can Be Misleading

In the 1990s, US natural gas distributors were fighting advertising battles with the oil jobbers over market share in the Northeast United States. Some oil jobber ads featured houses destroyed by gas explosions. The gas companies responded by notifying the FTC and asked the Better Business Bureaus to investigate. When the claims weren't substantiated, many of the ads were stopped.

"Green" and "Organic"

Terms like "green" energy, "cleaner," and "organic" may invite challenges unless there is sound factual backup. Consumers are becoming more proactive in challenging such claims.

Deceptive Pricing

Going out of business claims when only a price reduction is happening would be deceptive pricing, along with price claims that don't include other fees that the customer would have to pay.

PRODUCT AND SERVICE PROMOTIONS
Promotion

A promotion is a time-limited campaign to encourage customers to buy products. It's different from advertising which seeks to reach a broader audience to introduce them to your product. Promotions include special pricing, two-for-one sales, coupons, jingles, contests, and free samples. As in any promotion or advertising campaign you should establish your goals for the campaign and measure the results.

Financing

Sometimes, customers want to buy your product but don't have the necessary funding in their capital budget. In that case you could provide a financing package. Financing allows you to sell and install your products with no capital or other upfront costs to the customer because the purchase could be paid from the customer's operating budget by a monthly or quarterly installment payment. In addition, financing could provide additional income to you. The bank providing the financing could pay you a finder's fee for each financing closed.

GOVERNMENT SALES—DON'T GIVE YOUR RIGHTS AWAY!

Selling to the government is more complex than private sector sales. Government agencies often live up to their moniker of being bureaucratic. When you're a government contractor, you automatically become subject to many regulations including the Federal Acquisition Regulations (FAR) which the General Services Administration (GSA) administers,[19] internal agency regulations, and employment and other federal laws. FAR is some two thousand pages long. That fact alone should give a startup and small business some pause about doing business with the federal government. If you sell to the Department of Defense (DoD), you will also be subject to the Defense Federal Acquisition Regulation Supplement (DFARS) to FAR which is administered by the DoD.[20]

The good news is that: Even as a startup you can do business with the federal government. It's not impossible. It just takes a lot of time and patience. While it is hard to learn how to sell to the government, once you understand the programs and have built a pipeline into an agency and can show successful past performance, it becomes much easier to get follow-on and other contracts.

The government issues huge contracts, sometimes in the billions of dollars to prime contractors. Startups don't have past performance or the resources to handle big contracts which government customers like to see, so they are more likely to be subcontractors or to get smaller contracts. Government contracts can be a good source of income to smooth out the volatility in the private sector economy. At times, however, the opposite happens. The government can have spending freezes caused by political machinations or otherwise, such as the budget sequestration in 2013 which cut federal spending by $85.4 billion.[21] Such actions can freeze federal programs and spending and if your contract is caught in the freeze it can do great damage to your company. As a result, you might want to consider selling to both the private sector and the government.

GSA and SBA provide lots of guidance, training, and other support for small businesses looking to do business with the government.[22] And SAM.gov provides searchable listings of federal contract opportunities.

> **TIP: GOVERNMENT BIDS ARE COMPLEX. THE FIRST TIME YOU ARE BIDDING ON A FEDERAL CONTRACT, CONSIDER HIRING A PROFESSIONAL PROPOSAL WRITER.**

Government Requests for Proposal (RFPs)

This section on responding to government requests for proposal (RFPs) focuses on the federal government. State and local governments have similar processes but have local variations.

Governments often require competitive bidding for major purchases. They publish an RFP and you submit a bid. The process can take months. If there's a bid protest by a losing bidder, it can take much longer. The good news is that once you've won a bid and done a good job you have a "past performance" rating. If you score well this helps you in another competition and follow-on bids. While it can be hard to win against many competitors, once you've established good relationships with the government contracting officers, you can gain information on upcoming opportunities more easily. The bad news is that it takes a lot of effort to submit a bid. They can be many pages long and require lots of financial and other information. Here are some tips for winning those bids.

Consider Hiring a Proposal Writer

You can outsource much of the bid writing to a proposal writer. If it's a medium size bid, you might pay between $10,000 and $20,000 for that service. An example of that would be a Small Business Innovative Research (SBIR) proposal to fund R&D to get you to commercialization.

GSA Schedule

The GSA Schedule, also called the Federal Supply Schedule and Multiple Award Schedule (MAS), is a long-term indefinite-delivery-indefinite-quantity contract (IDIQ) that provides a way for commercial companies to list millions of products as available to the government at set prices and terms. Your product becomes "listed." This makes it easier for companies to sell to the government and for the government to buy products. However, it can take several months to a year to get on the schedule. To qualify, companies must have been in business for at least two years, have past performance, the products must be commercially available, and the company must be financially stable. Products also must be manufactured or substantially altered within the United States or a "designated country" as defined by the Trade Agreements Act.[23] You could use a contractor to prepare your application for listing to GSA. That might cost five to ten thousand dollars depending on the complexity of the filing.

Sales Opportunity Services

Private companies such as Deltek's GovWin IQ help contractors uncover new government contracting opportunities before they are announced and provide teaming opportunities by listing your company as looking to support certain projects. While the cost of these services can run into many thousands of dollars per year, they can be very useful.

> **TIP: DON'T LOSE YOUR IP TO THE GOVERNMENT. DEVELOP IP WITH NON-GOVERNMENT FUNDS IF POSSIBLE BEFORE CONTRACTING WITH THE GOVERNMENT.**

Protect Your Intellectual Property When Contracting with the Government

When dealing with any party, civilian or government, it's important to protect your company's intellectual property which may be your company's most valuable asset. With a government contract, which party owns which IP rights is more complex because FAR and DEFARS regulations,[24] as well as regulations of the specific agency, are involved. Those rights also vary depending on whether the contract is civilian or military, the items involved are "commercial," and the specifics of each transaction. The following are some general concepts involved, but be sure to consult your attorney on any transaction because there are many exceptions to these general principles.

The Government's Default IP Rights Position

The default position for IP rights is that your company owns any intellectual property that it brings to the contract. In that case, the issue is what licensing rights the government can still get. In cases where the government is funding the development of the IP in whole or part, the government will generally want more rights.

There are three basic kinds of rights the government will seek: unlimited rights, government purpose rights, and limited/restricted rights.

Unlimited Rights

Unlimited rights give the government authority to use computer and technical data for any purpose. It can provide those to your competitors and the public. Such broad rights arise when the IP is developed only from a government contract or other government support.

Government Purpose Rights

When the IP is developed with both government and contractor funds, then the government often receives government purpose rights that allow the government or third parties to use that IP only for government purposes and the commercial rights are retained by the contractor.

Restricted Rights

If the IP is developed exclusively by the contractor, then the government only receives restricted rights to computer software, such as limiting the number of computers on which the software can be used, and limited rights to use of the technical data.

Some Key Definitions

Many IP issues in government contracting center around the party's rights to "Technical Data" and "Computer Software" and whether the item purchased is a "Commercial Item." Here are some definitions.

Technical Data

Per section 52.227-14 "Rights in Data-General" of FAR:

Technical data means recorded information (regardless of the form or method of the recording) of a scientific or technical nature (including computer databases and computer software documentation). This term does not include computer software or financial, administrative, cost or pricing, or management data or other information incidental to contract administration. The term includes recorded information of a scientific or technical nature that is included in computer databases (See 41 U.S.C. 116).[25]

Computer Software

Also per FAR:

Computer software (1) means

(i) Computer programs that comprise a series of instructions, rules, routines, or statements, regardless of the media in which recorded, that allow or cause a computer to perform a specific operation or series of operations; and

(ii) Recorded information comprising source code listings, design details, algorithms, processes, flow charts, formulas, and related material that would enable the computer program to be produced, created, or compiled. (2) Does not include computer databases or computer software documentation.[26]

Commercial Items

A "commercial item" is one that is sold, licensed, or leased to the general public.[27]

Tips for Dealing with These IP Issues

1. Get a commercial advantage. You will be able to retain more rights from the government if you can convince the government that you have a commercial item, called Commercial-Off-The-Shelf (COTS).

2. Develop IP before government contracting. Develop your IP with non-governmental funds as much as possible before contracting with the government for funding that will add to it.

3. File your patent and copyright applications. You could file patent and copyright applications to eliminate doubt about your having the rights involved. Filing the patent also captures the filing date which is important because the first to file a patent wins. Filing for a copyright with the US Copyright Office also qualifies you to enforce your rights against copyright infringers.

4. Be sure to list assertions of IP rights in the contract. The government contract requires that you list any IP property rights which you claim. Be sure to do that or you may lose those rights and end up with unlimited government rights to release your IP to the public.

5. Mark it or lose it. Be sure to comply with FAR and DEFARS item marking requirements. This involves putting certain restrictive and other language on the items provided. That's essential to restrict the government's use of your computer software and technical data.

Examples of Marketing Legal Issues

Scooter's client gets caught by the government for false advertising under the Lanham Act and learns how to deal with trademark infringement claims from competitors.

Cold Fingers was catching up. He was just a few cars behind now. Canal Road had reversible lanes. This time of day all three lanes were open going Scooter's direction heading out of DC. Scooter took a careening left turn at the light off Canal Road onto Chain Bridge. As soon as he passed the sensor he had planted on the left bridge rail, he hit a button on his dash and the traffic light on Canal Road behind him changed from green to red. All the cars right behind him screeched to a stop. The cars from Chain Bridge now saw a green light and came pouring around the corner and screeched to a stop right in front of those cars, creating a five-car pileup. He could see Cold Fingers' BMW sandwiched between cars from both directions. It would be a long time before Cold Fingers got out of that mess.

Scooter crossed Chain Bridge and headed up Glebe Road into Arlington toward home. Near the top of the hill on his right he chuckled as he passed the historical marker where Senator John Randolph and Secretary of State Henry Clay held a dual in 1876. He smiled. They both got away alive, just like Scooter and Cold Fingers.[28]

When Scooter got home, there was a black sedan parked outside. Two men were in it. He breathed a sigh of relief when he saw JW and Jason.

Jason rolled down his window. "Can we talk?"

"Not unless you've got something I want to hear."

"We do."

"Let's talk outside. Cold Fingers and his thug Crunch have been following me home."

They sat in the back yard with a view of the street.

"Could you call Sammy? I want him to hear this, too." Sammy had been watching from the window and came out the dog door.

"We checked with CIA's scientists. They think they can remotely deactivate the chip. They were working on a kill switch for it when it was installed but didn't have a chance to test it. They don't know if deactivation will work, but we can try it. In any event, the micro-battery will die in ninety days and the chip will be permanently inactive anyway. But before we turn it off, we'd like to keep it going a few days. And the scientists believe that funny feeling Sammy has will go away but they don't know how soon. Here are the details…"

Scooter and Sammy listened carefully. "Give me a minute with Sammy."

They moved away from the agents.

"Look, Sammy, do you feel better about the chip now?"

"Yes and no."

"Sounds like the worst case is that you'll still be able to talk. And the funny feeling should go away. This may be the best way out. What do you think? I'll keep on the CIA to help you, okay?

"Okay … Sammy try."

They rejoined the agents. Scooter signed the papers that Jason brought and Sammy put his paw print on them.

"Look," said JW, "now that's done, you should go somewhere else for a while. We can get one of our guys to protect you here, but it would be better if you disappeared for a while."

"Yeah, if you could stay around for a few minutes in case CF shows up, I'll pack up."

"Scooter, you need to get back to CF and try to meet him tomorrow," said JW. "Can you do that?"

"Yeah … okay." They discussed how to do that. Then Scooter sent Cold Fingers a text. "CF: you win, I've got the files for you. Let's meet tomorrow. 2:00 PM, parking lot at the Episcopal Church on Glebe Road, wide open, no cops."

Cold Fingers texted right back. "Okay." Scooter wished he had said more so he'd know what to expect. But one thing was clear, "He's probably madder than hell at me."

***

While Scooter was packing, JW got Dr. Johansson on his speaker phone for everyone to hear.

"Okay, guys. JW has to get a video of Cold Fingers admitting he's going to do something illegal. Scooter, you and Sammy need to get that on camera. Then JW will arrest CF and hold him somewhere outside the country until the CIA does its thing at a black site and gets the rest of what they need. Sammy, try to keep looking at CF so if the audio fails we can read his lips."

Johansson continued. "Scooter and Sammy, we still don't have a kill switch but we've got a temporary work-around. We've set up the nanochip so that it's off at first. You may feel a little different. That's so Cold Fingers won't be able to pick up any signal if he checks to see if Scooter's wired. Scooter, you need to pet Sammy on the left ear to activate the chip, but not until CF checks for a wire. Remember the left ear is the key."

"Got it? Any questions?"

Scooter and Sammy both said, "Yes" at the same time.

"My guys have been working around the clock to get the chip to work right. It's always been a little quirky. Try to stay out of direct sunlight. It seems to be temperature sensitive. Let's hope this all works. Good luck tomorrow."

JW and Jason left, followed by Scooter and Sammy. While driving to stay at a hotel in Annapolis, Scooter tried to stay focused on his work, but he was worried about the next day's meeting with Cold Fingers. What would happen? Cold Fingers was an angry killer and Crunch probably was too…

***

That night, Susan Glover, COO of Aeris Gloves, was on the line.

"Scooter, glad you're there. I'm in big trouble. The FDA just seized both of my glove warehouses and locked me out."

"Do you mean the FTC? They regulate false advertising."

"No, FDA."

"Good gosh, why?"

"They said I was selling medical devices. That's ridiculous; I'm just selling gloves."

"Tell me about the gloves."

"The same lines of gloves I've been selling for years. The Aeris Vibrotoner's."

"What did your ads say?"

"The Aeris Vibrotoner driving glove stimulates the blood flow in your fingers and makes you feel better."

"Give me a minute to pull up FDA's definition of a medical device." Scooter tapped on his iPhone.

"Okay, I'll read you the key part … Section 201(h) of the Food, Drug, and Cosmetic Act. Section 3 says a medical device is anything that 'affects the … function of the body of man.' 'Feeling better' probably wouldn't make it a medical device but you've combined that with 'stimulates blood flow' so they might have a point. Let me give the FDA a call. Looks like you need to tone down your advertising. Send me some different copy without the blood flow language, and I'll see if I can get the FDA to unlock the warehouses and get the new approved. You'll probably need to sign a consent order and agree not to do this again."

"Thanks, but there's more."

"What's that?"

"Another glove company is threatening to sue me for trademark infringement."

"What's their claim?"

"Their name is Eris Gloves and the name Aeris Gloves infringes on their name."

"Did they say whether they have a registered trademark?"

"They didn't say."

"Okay, here's the deal. Trademark infringement is the unauthorized use of a trademark in connection with goods or services that's likely to cause confusion, deception, or mistake about the source of the goods or services."

"But the two names are spelled differently!"

"That doesn't matter if they sound the same." And you're both in the same line of business so it would cause confusion. It's not like it's Eris Hardware and Aeris Gloves, which would be okay.

"Really? Wow! What should I do?"

"Send me the letter. Let's see what's really bugging them. If necessary, we can try to show that no one's confused. And maybe you were in business and using your name before they used theirs in which case, you'd have a possible infringement case against them to give you some leverage. Infringement litigation can get very expensive so they may back down. Send me their letter and let me check on some things, and I'll get back to you."

"Thanks, Scooter."

"We need to meet. I'd like to discuss something else with you."

"Sure, I'll get back to you with a date."

***

The Episcopal Church parking lot was a big open area surrounded by woods near Chain Bridge. Scooter and Sammy showed up first. Then Cold Fingers and Crunch drove in and got out. Crunch was even bigger up close. Scooter stayed as far away as he could from both of them and wrestled several boxes of files out of his car and put them on the ground as Cold Fingers and Crunch were scanning the nearby woods for any signs of cops.

***

At the same time, Dr. Johansson and his lab assistant were panicking. "I just ran the chip protocol again, now the chip is off and won't turn on at normal temperatures. I'm sorry, we just didn't have time to run all the tests we needed! We're screwed!" said Johansson.

***

Cold Fingers opened each of the boxes.

"That's every one of files I have in the Molly Bloom case," said Scooter, handing over the banker's boxes. "My private notes, everything."

Crunch came over with a scanner and scanned Scooter and the box for weapons and wires.

"Clear, boss."

"Why'd you bring the dog?" asked Cold Fingers. "I don't like dogs. I do like dog meat, though. Maybe I'll take this one with me!" He spit on the ground.

As Scooter moved toward Sammy to touch his ear and start the video, Sammy lost it and lunged at Cold Fingers. Cold Fingers grabbed at Sammy's head but it slipped through his fingers.

Scooter lurched forward to pull Sammy away from Cold Fingers.

"Sorry, Sammy's really touchy."

"Shut up, Magee. Keep that stupid dog off me. You did your thing. I've got your files. If it's not all here, I'll kill you."

"What are you going to do with these files?"

"The files will lead me to the money left over from Molly's Game. The rest is none of your business unless the files don't get me the money. Then I'll be back and you'll see what happens."

"What about the camera?"

"Maybe I can help you sell it."

"Forget that."

Cold Fingers and Crunch got in their car and left.

When they were out of sight, Scooter yelled, "Sammy! What the heck!? Why did you attack CF? You could have gotten us both killed, and I didn't get a chance to touch your ear to turn on the video!"

"Me sorry, me hate him, me hate him..."

Scooter and Sammy trudged silently back to the car.

Just then, Jason and JW pulled into the lot from their hiding place on the other side of the woods.

"Great work, guys, we got the video and Cold Fingers and Crunch are on the way to jail! You guys were great!"

"What? But we never started the video?"

"We just talked to Dr. Johansson. It turned out the video wouldn't have started the way we planned anyway because the chip was acting up. It only turned on when something colder than its surroundings touched the ear. It looks like when Cold Fingers grabbed Sammy by the head, his cold fingers did it. Way to go, Sammy! If you hadn't jumped on him, this never would have worked!"

Sammy smiled and did a little circle on his hind legs. Scooter yelled, "All right!!"

***

Later that night, Scooter called Megan.

"Megan, you'll never believe what happened today." Scooter told Megan all about it.

"So, I've made a lot of mistakes. Maybe we could start over. The lawsuit's over; the court has dismissed the case with prejudice."

"What does that mean?"

"It means that the case can't be reopened. It's done. Cold Fingers is under arrest, and the CIA's sending him to a black site in Thailand for interrogation. He'll be out of reach of the US courts, lawyers, and even the Red Cross. The FBI created that whole lawsuit just to put pressure on me. It wasn't my fault after all.

"And you won't have to worry about Scarlett anymore. Nothing ever happened with her anyway. She's disappeared, gone. Her phone is even disconnected. Probably went back to South America. Look, Megan, I'm sorry, no one could ever take your place, and I'm really sorry about all the mess I got you into."

"I'm sorry I attacked you about the lawsuit. And there were those other times when I…"

Scooter interrupted her. "Look, let's not go over that stuff, it's done. We need to be looking ahead."

"So … does all this mean we can get the house in France?"

"Ah … I haven't thought about it but maybe, yeah."

"Wow!"

They talked for a while.

"Let's talk again tomorrow; there's more we should discuss."

"Okay, bye."

Chapter 7

USE "MANAGEMENT ZEN" TO REDUCE STARTUP CHAOS

How should a man be capable of grooming his own horse, or of furbishing his own spear and helmet, if he allows himself to become unaccustomed to tending even his own person, which is his most treasured belonging?

—Alexander the Great

MANAGING YOURSELF—LIFE BALANCE AMID STARTUP CHAOS

There are over one thousand management books. They range from Peter Drucker's 1985 classic *Management, Tasks, Responsibilities, Practices*, with its broad overview of many managers' tools and techniques, to Stephen Denning's *Age of Agile*, which deals with today's unstoppable business revolution that connects everyone and everything all the time. There are so many management theories and practices. Which management tools are the most useful for entrepreneurs?

Fortunately, management is simpler for startups. A startup is as different from a mature company as a toddler is from an adult. As a startup you're not fine tuning anything. You're creating everything—finishing the wings while the plane is flying. You don't have to worry about multi-level management problems or rotating employees into different divisions. Your "team" may just be you—or a few people. You're in survival mode. You need to laser focus on just a few things.

That's minimum smart management (MSM). Get those things right and you're launched. If you don't, the company dies. At its core, MSM consists of just two pieces: managing yourself and managing your company.

> **TIP: YOU CAN'T MANAGE YOUR COMPANY WITHOUT FIRST MANAGING YOURSELF.**

Why do you need to manage yourself? Your startup is a reflection of you, the CEO. It starts out as your baby, bred from your culture and DNA. In fact, it's a lot like actually having a baby. It will dramatically change your life. You'll get less sleep, more chaos, and some screaming, but there's great hope for the future. Your team, investors, and customers want to know they can rely on you, and that you're focused and effective in implementing the company's goals. But if your head's not in the game with the right attitude, and you act frustrated, worried, and are always fighting fires, you'll lose everyone's trust and the company will fail.

To manage your company effectively you first need to manage yourself. You need to know what challenges you're facing, get the necessary tools to meet those challenges, and develop the right attitude—a calm, intuitive, and balanced approach. This is "Management Zen.™"

Let's begin by looking at what being an entrepreneur involves to see if it's really for you and, if so, how to handle its challenges.

BEING AN ENTREPRENEUR—THE GOOD, BAD, AND THE UGLY

Here's the good, bad, and the ugly about being an entrepreneur. Make sure you want to jump into this shark infested water because it will take you on a wild ride to a place that you can hope for but may never see.

First, the Good News
You're the Boss
Are you tired of working for someone else? Is your job boring? Now you can have an adventure; you're the boss. Being the boss is the

good news and the bad news. You're in charge, but now you're fully responsible, not just for your employees, but for your shareholders, vendors, customers, and everyone else who is counting on you to do what you said you could do. Are you okay with not having a clue how to solve a problem but still moving ahead through the fog? If so, that's good, because it happens a lot.

Remember That You're a Leader, Not Just a Manager

Kevin Cruse, a *Forbes* commentator, has defined leadership as "a process of social influence, which maximizes the efforts of others, towards the achievement of a goal."[1] He points out that it's not really about position, titles, or even management, although those things are often involved: "Managers need to plan, measure, monitor, coordinate, solve, hire, fire, and so many other things. Typically, managers manage things. Leaders lead people."

Sally Jenkins, sportswriter for the *Washington Post*, puts it this way, "The source of true power is buy in ... As Steve Kerr of the Golden States Warriors explains: 'A coach has to have the humility to ask for their [players'] input and the awareness that not every decision is going to pay off ... There are two angles to this: number one, the angle of how are my staff and I going to come up with a decision to a problem on an issue, and number two how are we going to include the team; How is the team going to accept it.'"[2]

You May Be Happier

Some research has shown that on the average entrepreneurs are happier than wage-earning employees. This is even though, on the average, they earn less money, work thirteen hours more per week, forfeit leisure time, and the work is very stressful. How is that possible? According to Boris Nikolaev, assistant professor of entrepreneurship at Baylor University, the "sense of autonomy and doing something important can outweigh stress."[3]

As professor Ute Stephan professor at Kings College London explains: What entrepreneurs "are doing is important to them, it's part of who they are, it's part of their identity, and that's why it has such a positive impact on well-being."[4]

Being an Entrepreneur Is Creative
It's like having a lot of empty white boards you fill in. You'll get a chance to (and must) think outside of the box because there is no box. This can be fun, stimulating, and rarely boring. At SkyBuilt Power, we painted a twenty-foot wall with white board dry-erase paint. In a team meeting when ideas were floating all over the place, we could throw ideas up there and it helped to pin things down and identify plans and the actions needed. Those sessions were creative and often fun, particularly when developing new products.

You Might Just Hit a Financial Jackpot
This is unlikely but certainly possible. The vast majority of startups fail in the first year either slowly or violently. Sometimes there's a financial mess to clean up afterwards. Some are even smoking holes in the ground surrounded by predatory lawyers. But anything is possible. And for some entrepreneurs, even the risks alone are exciting.

You might Do Something Really Good for Society that Has Lasting Value
That would be great!

Why Do You Want to Be an Entrepreneur?
Make money? Do something different? Leave a boring job? Make a difference? What's your exit strategy? Cash out quick or build a big company? If you're not sure about being an entrepreneur, then you could try it part time while you have a regular job. But don't get stuck for too long with one foot on the dock and one in the startup boat. You won't be able to do either job that well. Your startup can't be successful without your total dedication. There just are too many things that must be done all the time that have to work well together.

What Are You Giving Up Being an Entrepreneur?
You're giving up a lot of leisure time with friends and family and probably some quality sleep because you never really leave the office at night. There's also an impact on your friends and family. Can you and your family afford the loss of steady income for years, if necessary?

Your company may take off, or it might take ten years to get to profitability. In the meantime, you constantly may be raising money to survive. Along the way you need to solve hundreds of tough problems. Sometimes during product development, you solve one problem but it creates even more. One component is no longer available. The new one has different characteristics, lower performance, or it's too big and that affects every other component in the subsystem, and everything in that subsystem must be revised.

Do You Want to Leave Your Comfort Zone?
Suppose you work for a company and write computer code. That's mostly what you do, it's what you enjoy and you do it really well. Suddenly you decide to become the CEO of a tech company based on your code. That's a big change. Now you won't be able to do as much of what you really understand and like to do. You have much broader duties, marketing, legal, personnel, etc. This continues until you can build up a team and delegate the things you're not good at or don't want to do to them. And you need to put on and take off different hats. One day you're selling the company to investors, the next day you're meeting with your accountant on how to find the money to meet payroll.

Can You Handle the Volatility?
Being a CEO of a startup is like working triage in a hospital emergency room on a roller coaster. Some days I'd get a call about a big sale and was so happy. Then ten minutes later something had caught on fire. As an entrepreneur you're not a postal employee on a fixed route. Or maybe you are, but there's a growling dog chasing you on every block!

Is Your Product or Service Likely to Succeed?
Will your idea work and be cost competitive? How hard will it be to break into the market? Are the technical challenges difficult to solve? Do a reality check on your idea before you sink too much time, money, and emotional energy into it. Make sure you do your market research first. See chapter 6 on marketing for what makes a good product and how to conduct market research.

If you've gone through this list and still think being an entrepreneur is for you, the next question is what mindset do you need to deal with this chaos and what tools might be useful?

MANAGEMENT ZEN™

When managing yourself, your goal is to keep a sense of inner calm, acceptance, and life balance, while executing the business amid the chaos. This is the Zen of Self-Management or Management Zen. Of course, there are speed bumps—it's life—but keep on going. Don't look back except to learn. Self-Management is difficult. It's a goal, not a daily victory. Your startup experience is like raising a real child. Sometimes the best you can do is all you can do and it's not enough. And the farthest you can see is one day at a time. Accept all that. It's not always okay. But that's okay. Keep practicing the goal.

Robert T. Kiyosaki, in his all-time bestseller *Rich Dad Poor Dad*, said it well: "Life pushes us all around. Some give up and others fight. A few learn the lesson and move on. They welcome life pushing them around. To those people, it means they need and want to learn something. They learn and move on. Most quit, and a few like you fight."[5]

Once I was with Nathan Keen, CEO of Kform, a specialized manufacturing firm in Virginia. He had a hundred urgent balls in the air. National security customers urgently needed equipment for the war in Iraq. People were busy in all directions. I asked him how things were going. "Crazy," he said. Then he smiled and wiped his hand across the top of his head. "But I just let it all flow right over me." Nathan was getting it all done. But he wouldn't let it take too much out of him. He was in the flow. He was in the Zen of Self-Management amid all the chaos. Here are a few things to help you be a better manager.

Be Humble and Understand Your Strengths and Weaknesses

You're probably pretty good at some things, maybe very good at one or two. But just because you can play the cymbals better than anyone you know doesn't mean you can lead the orchestra. You need to identify your strengths and weaknesses. Here are some ways to do that on a continuous basis.

Use Your Own Feedback Analysis

As Peter Drucker points out,

> There is only one way to find out [his weaknesses]: Whenever one makes a key decision ... one writes down what one expects will happen. And nine months or twelve months later, one then feeds back from results to expectations. I've been doing this for some fifteen to twenty years now. And every time I do it, I am surprised.[6]

Institute a 360-Degree Review

Another way to get feedback is to have a 360-degree review process for yourself and every employee. This works better in larger organizations where the feedback can be anonymous, so you may need to wait on that—or use an outside party to make any survey responses less identifiable.

Get a Mentor on Your Board of Directors

Meet regularly with some board members individually and ask them to tell you candidly how you're doing. They can be very helpful. Listen carefully because they may only hint at things you need to improve and don't want to be unkind. At SkyBuilt, my good friends Bob Hahne, formerly with Deloitte, was very helpful with financial analysis; Ken Schweers, former president of ICG Kaiser, advised on complex business matters; and S. Kinney Smith, brilliant lawyer and former chairman and general counsel of CMS Energy was invaluable in helping with legal matters.

Take Some Courses on Things You Need to Know

For example, if you've never dealt with accounting, you could take an online accounting course. Or get a book on it. One of the most useful accounting books I found for accounting basics is *How to Read a Financial Report*.[7]

Build Your Emotional Well-Being Skills

Nataly Kogan, entrepreneur and author of the book *The Awesome Human Project*, reminds us that happiness while you work is not an elusive state of mind but a set of tangible skills. These skills can make you happier which also makes you and those on your team more productive as well. Per a profile of Kogan in the *Wall Street Journal*:

> Being 'actively kind' to others and gentler toward herself, and feeing more attuned to even the smallest sources of pleasure or uplift—her morning coffee in her favorite mug; a luminous sunset on her commute—made her more at ease in her life. When she stopped trying to run away from her negative emotions she found she could reckon with feelings of frustration or fatigue better. "Awareness gives us choices," she explains.[8]

Finally, stay positive and believe in yourself. You can do this. It will be hard, and it will take more time, energy, and effort than you planned, but persevere. Some days your attitude is "Bring me another alligator while I drain the swamp." But the reality is that one day you're the pigeon and the next day you're the statue. Keep in mind your competitors are going through the same things. Sometimes just surviving is winning!

MANAGING WITH MINIMUM SMART MANAGEMENT™ (MSM)

TIP: KEEP IT SIMPLE. STAY FOCUSED WITH THE "FIVE CORE STARTUP ACTIVITIES."

Once you're managing yourself, you can more effectively manage your company. To manage your startup you need laser-like focus on the Five Core Startup Activities. That's minimum smart management™ (MSM)—the least amount of management to get the job done without burdening your staff. Get this right and you're launched. Miss it and the company dies.

THE FIVE CORE STARTUP ACTIVITIES
The Five Core Activities you need to focus on are:
1. Create a business entity—usually an LLC or a corporation.
2. Build a good management team.

3. Raise enough money to develop a product for commercialization before you run out of money.
4. Focus, focus, focus—just do it!
5. Maintain total situational awareness (TSA) and don't drop any important balls.

Those five core activities are simple to write and hard to do. I know it sounds strange to think that management can be this focused and simple. Of course, you need to do lots of other things like engage a lawyer and accountant, get insurance, and open a bank account. But they are details. The reason you need to focus on the Five Core Activities is they are essential to launching the company. The minute you start working on your company full time you'll be drinking from a firehose. You'll get pulled into product design, engineering, development issues, legal questions about patent and copyrights, accounting questions, personnel matters, financial issues, and marketing. Your phone will constantly be ringing. You're doing triage. If it isn't a cost overrun, it's a personnel issue. Someone will sound interested in your product but it's only the competition trying to steal your ideas. There's only one answer to this. You have to say no to things that distract you from your Five Core Activities until you can build up enough support staff to handle all the other issues.

Let's examine the Five Core Activities.

Create a Business Entity

If you're conducting business before you create a separate business entity, you're a "sole proprietorship"—an unincorporated business entity. With a sole proprietorship, there is no distinction between you and the business; your debts, assets, and income are comingled. Whether you create a business entity or not, you still need to file for a business license and comply with other business requirements.

Why do you need to form a business entity? Most importantly, creating a business entity protects you from personal liability. When you're a sole proprietorship, your personal income and assets are in your name. If you're sued and lose, a judgment could be issued against you personally, your personal assets could be seized, and your income could be garnisheed (a court-ordered payment from your income) until the debt is paid. On the other hand, when you create a company such as a corporation or LLC, if the entity is sued the entity is responsible for the debt, not you personally. In the worst case you can dissolve the company and start over. Of course, you might be sued too, but courts are reluctant to "pierce the corporate veil" and hold individuals in the company responsible unless there is misconduct such as intermingling personal and company assets, you're using a company for personal purposes, or there is fraud. See chapter 1 for details.

You also have more credibility in the business world if you have a company. You need to look like you're ready to do business and this isn't just a personal hobby. It's easier to get funding from investors because they can purchase shares in your company. Your key personnel can get options, stock, or other incentives from the company. That provides an alternative to paying them as much when operating cash is limited. You might not be able to get insurance for certain business activities unless you form a separate entity. Your homeowner's insurance usually won't cover business activities although there may be exceptions for personal rental properties.

Build a Good Team

I'm not the smartest fellow in the world, but I can sure pick smart colleagues.

—Franklin D. Roosevelt

Your investors and customers will want to see a strong, experienced team that knows how to execute. This includes your management team and a board of directors. You need a management team as a force multiplier because one person can't do a good job with all the things that need to be done. There should be a balanced team for support in areas where you don't have experience, such as marketing, legal, financial, and technology. It takes a village of expertise to be commercially successful. Keep your startup management team

small, maybe five people. If you need more support, use independent contractors for special projects that need additional expertise
and focus.

Thomas Edison was an amazing entrepreneur. Despite an insatiable demand for his products and developing an entire electric utility system to support them, Edison never built an effective management team. He was a one man show. That's fine for a cymbal player
but not for the orchestra leader. As a result, many of his companies
failed when they got to mid-size and he had to be bailed out and
replaced by professional management.[9]

A board of directors can be very useful. It sends a signal to your
investors and customers that you're a real company that is ready for
business and provides you with valuable advice and contacts. Keep
the board small. You as CEO and one other person on your management team should be on it, along with experienced persons with
marketing, financial, and other skills. Then add a couple of people
who can open doors to your target markets. Your attorney doesn't
need to be on the board but should attend board meetings. That's
because attorneys are good at spotting and avoiding potential problems before they hatch and the egg gets scrambled all the way to
Startup Suicide.

As Guy Kawasaki puts it in *The Art of the Start*:

It's much easier to do things right from the start than to fix them
later. At least at this stage, you are forming the DNA of your
startup, and this genetic code is permanent. By paying attention
to a few important issues, you can build the right foundation
and free yourself to concentrate on the big challenges.[10]

Raise Enough Money to Get Your Product or Service to Commercialization

Money is the fuel for your startup. It's hard to raise financing. You
need to start early and never stop, to keep enough money to develop
an MVP that can generate revenue. Some products take a lot of capital to develop and have a long sales cycle after that so they need a
long financial runway—even years. Some don't. But a good bet is
that it will always take longer to raise money than you want and

you'll need more than you think. For detailed steps on raising money see chapter 6.

Focus, Focus, Focus. Just Do It

My formula for success is rise early, work late and strike oil.

—J. Paul Getty

You can't just work a little on a startup and expect to succeed. It takes too much focus and effort. It's not a hobby. You need to be one hundred percent committed and focus, focus, focus. Many investors will require that you have one hundred percent of your skin in the game and are working full time at the company before they'll provide funding.

This intense focus has a positive and interesting effect. Psychologist Mihaly Csikszentmihalyi coined the term "flow" to "describe the sense of creativity that emerges from an intense absorption in a challenging activity, whether in the arts, sports, business or a hobby."[11] He found that when you focus so intensely your self disappears along with a sense of time, your goals and feedback become clearer, and a feeling of effortless arises: "Every action, movement, and thought follows inevitably from the previous one, like playing jazz. Your whole being is involved, and you're using your skills to the utmost."[12] In other words, when you focus intently, your mind takes you to a different place—a place that's designed to help you succeed at the task. That's the "flow."

What to focus on is set by the business plan and its milestones. Consider picking three key goals per quarter and focusing on them. Do those well and they will be stairs to the next goals. Learn to say no to "shiny object goblins"—interesting but distracting interruptions that take you away from your Five Core Activities.

Simultaneously, Maintain Total Situational Awareness (TSA)

Situational awareness is the perception of environmental elements and events with respect to time or space, the comprehension of their meaning, and the projection of their future status."[13] In simple terms you need to know what's happening around you, understand what it means, what's going to happen because of it, and take timely, appropriate actions.

A common type of Startup Suicide is the entrepreneur who's a software wizard writing code for a new cell phone app. We all prefer to work on what we know and enjoy doing. That's just human nature. While developing the software, this wizard is unaware that his staff is unhappy. And he doesn't have time for awkward and testy personnel issues. One day there's not enough money to pay the team what they think they're worth. Without using TSA, he misses the opportunity to nip the problem in the bud and people start quitting.

You must be able to focus while also knowing what's going on around you that might explode. But how can you do this when they're contradictory goals? There are ways and you need to build this into your company's DNA by adopting the right processes. Here are some suggestions:

Schedule Weekly Meetings with All Hands on Deck
Keep that meeting time sacred. First thing every Monday morning might be a good time to set up things for the week. Ask the team for agenda items on Friday so meetings are focused. Keep them as short as possible. Put time limits on the topics to be discussed. Don't allow more than a few minutes on routine matters. Listen carefully in these meetings about what's going on.

Your Management Dashboard
Create a chart of the tasks in the business plan. What is the task, who's responsible, and what is the due date? Use that as a dashboard to keep tasks on schedule.

Water Cooler Management
Schedule a little time, if only ten minutes a day, to walk around and talk individually to your employees. This is water cooler management.™ They will tell you things they wouldn't when others are around. Thomas Edison spent a lot of time walking around his

factories, randomly talking to his staff. He'd ask what they were working on and how it was going and would offer suggestions. That built a trust and loyalty and kept ideas flowing faster.

Corporate Rhythm

Get staff comfortable with what and how they should perform and turn that into a rhythm that's predictable and provides a structure for their performance. That helps everyone to stay on the same page and row in the same direction.

Quarterly Performance Reviews

To keep the team on task, schedule quarterly reviews with each team member. That lets them know that they can't put off scheduled actions for too long and you can have a deeper discussion on what they need to do in their job and what you need to do to support them.

Quick Recognition for Outstanding Performance

Employees need support and recognition. When an employee does something well, promptly send them an e-mail or personally tell them you appreciate it. That does wonders for motivation. Most employees will give you 50 to 70 percent effort routinely. You need to get that to 80 percent and more and this is a good way to do it, along with unscheduled bonuses, good pay, and good working conditions. When they're happy, they're more likely to trust you and share more with you about what needs to be done and that increases productivity.

Schedule Regular Feedback from Board Members, Investors, Suppliers, and Others

Lisa Jacobson, president of the Business Council for Sustainable Energy, is an excellent executive who knows how to stay close to her stakeholders. She regularly schedules calls with board and association members to get feedback. She also has developed a detailed performance review process for herself and staff. This includes a self-evaluation rating on ten management duties, such as job knowledge and teamwork, a report on the past year's results, and the upcoming year's goals and objectives. This is evaluated by the executive committee of the board. A score of at least 80 percent on the performance rating is necessary to be considered for a bonus (See a sample performance review form in Appendix 9).

Get an Outsider's Perspective
Management and the board can get used to plodding along in the same direction which is easier than thinking about new directions. You're breathing your own fumes. Have an annual planning session with outside experts to question your assumptions and see if they still hold up with changing conditions.

LEADERSHIP

Your leadership role in a startup is both easier and harder than in later stage companies. It's easier because you have fewer people to lead. It's harder if your startup is using part-time people with other interests. They may be wondering if your startup is going to succeed, so they might not be fully committed to your company. In their book *First Break All the Rules*, Marcus Buckingham and Curt Coffman highlight the importance of being a good frontline manger to attracting and retaining talented employees. They argue that being a good manager is more important to your employees than benefits, promotions, and training. As the CEO of a small startup you are both the leader and frontline manager. Your role is to be a catalyst, "speeding up the reaction between the employee's talents and the company's goals, and between the employee's talents and the customer's needs.[14] To do that you need to focus on four key catalyst activities: Select a person, set expectations, motivate the person and develop the person,"[15] building on the person's unique strengths rather than trying to fix the person's weaknesses.

What Are Some Typical Management Failures that Cause Startup Failure?
Here are a few:
- The leader hasn't had experience in how to lead and build a team.
- The leader doesn't even have anyone with leadership experience on the team. Few startups have human relations professionals.

- Often leaders don't pay enough attention to personnel matters. They're too focused on the product or service they need to develop along with everything else; and they don't have enough time to think about their leadership style.
- Personnel matters are sometimes awkward and it's more comfortable to push them off rather than tackle them.
- Startup CEOs often are hard charging, focused, Type A personalities. They tend to think they know what's best and may have trouble listening or delegating. And they find it hard to trust employees and let them make mistakes.

What Should You Do to Improve Your Management Skills?

- Your goal is to get the greatest buy-in from your staff with the least amount of effort and expense. Most employees will give you 60 percent or more of their effort, if only to keep their job. Your job is to get them to put in more effort while helping them feel fulfilled and willing to do it as part of the team.
- It takes a lot of time and money to find good people and keep them. Hire carefully, and if an employee is doing well, keep that employee happy and motivated. The flip side to this is that if an employee is simply not performing or responding to your encouragement and/or probation, don't keep hoping things will change. Set a time by which the employee stays or goes. My experience is that bad employees seldom get better.
- Hire a consultant or take a course on leadership. You could spend a few hours with a consultant to get up to speed quickly on some leadership basics. You're not born to be a great leader; you need to learn how to do it, like any other skill.
- Make sure you're listening. This is one of the best ways to build team buy-in. Listen to what your staff, customers, and others are telling you. They are your perimeter early warning system for issues that might flare up. If you've built up trust, then they'll let you know what's not working and you'll need their buy-in to fix it.

MANAGING LAWYERS—GETTING HIGH QUALITY SERVICES AT REASONABLE PRICES

Now, let's shift to a different area—managing lawyers. Lawyers aren't just another senior staff member. They often play a unique and vital role for startups. They help structure the company, provide personnel agreements, and negotiate with investors, vendors, and customers. Because they know the law, they help management avoid mistakes. One of the biggest risks for startups is not knowing what's illegal, like hiring someone who's not a licensed broker-dealer to raise funds for you (a violation of SEC rules); running a background check without written permission from the job applicant (civil and criminal penalties); or violating FTC rules with exaggerated marketing claims. Here are some tips on dealing with lawyers.

How Can You Find a Good Startup Lawyer?

Ask around. See if other startups or startup groups like angel groups or incubators have recommendations. You also can go online to search for "startup lawyers" on sites like Avvo.com and martindale.com. You need a lawyer who is familiar with startups and with whom you feel comfortable. Ask about the lawyer's experience. Has the lawyer worked with other startups? Is the lawyer on your creative and fast-paced wavelength?

> TIP: IF YOU HAVE A HEADACHE, YOU CAN TAKE AN ASPIRIN. YOU DON'T NEED THE MAYO CLINIC. AND YOU DON'T NEEED A BIG FIRM EXPENSIVE LAWYER FOR ROUTINE LEGAL TASKS.

Cutting Legal Expenses

Lawyers are expensive. As the joke goes, "You need a lawyer to protect you from your lawyer!" Legal fees are one of the major expenses for startups. You need a lawyer to draft basic legal documents, prepare offering agreements for investors, and non-disclosure, personnel, and other agreements.

You Don't Always Need a Lawyer

To keep expenses down, have a discussion with your lawyer about what you can do yourself. For example, it's not hard to file a copyright application with the US Copyright Office. You can do that. But a lawyer should file your trademark and patent applications. Ask your lawyer to prepare documents in a standard form that can be used for similar transactions so you don't need legal review each time.

Plead Poverty and Get Discounted Legal Services

After all you're a startup with no revenue. Ask up front about fees and whether there are deferred payment plans and discounts. Most lawyers will be willing to help. In addition, larger firms often have pro bono attorneys particularly for socially conscious startups and you may be able to get free services. Also, firms may offer fixed fees to prepare basic startup documents, such as articles of incorporation and an offering memorandum.

Sometimes law firms offer good up-front deals but then once those are over, those $300–$500 per hour fees start coming. Ask for a fixed price on whatever your lawyer does. Sometimes that doesn't work, such as with open ended litigation that's too hard to predict, but it should work with document preparation.

Unbundle Your Lawyers

Don't use partners when they're not necessary. Ask if paralegals can handle routine items. Larger firms can be very expensive. They must be because of the big overheads from their marble palaces, art collections, and overseas offices. One law firm I hired wouldn't allow their lawyers to send a quick fax. They required that an assistant handle faxing which created another billable item. Another time I was working with a partner at an international firm in DC. It has thousands of lawyers worldwide. She asked me if I wanted some coffee. We went to their coffee bar which looked like it came from Balthazar Restaurant in New York. The elaborate coffee, espresso, and whatever else machine was a gigantic complex of shiny pipes, brass fittings, and valves. She never could get it to work and we went to Starbucks around the corner. Do you really want to pay for that stuff?

One of the patent lawyers I was using left a major international patent firm because his billing rate was over $800 per hour and he couldn't justify it to clients. "For that price," he said, "they'd expect a Supreme Court Justice!" He opened his own firm and now charges 30 percent less. So, look for lawyers from the best firms that now are practicing on their own. Same expertise, lower rates. It's the lawyer that matters, not the firm. There are exceptions such as in big corporate cases when you want to intimidate the opposition with a big-name firm packed with junk yard velociraptors. You could also save money by using lawyers from big national firms in the Midwest who charge less than lawyers from the same firm at the firm's East and West coast offices.

Law firms want all your legal business. That's natural. There is an argument that one-stop law firms keep things better coordinated. But consider using more than one firm to keep your costs more competitive and compare the quality of the services you receive.

Some Other Tips for Working with Lawyers

Both you and your lawyer want a successful, long-term relationship. These tips may help to make it mutually beneficial.

- Don't be intimidated. Lawyers can be imposing and some throw in a few Latin terms as well. They may know Latin but you know English, which is a lot more useful.
- Make sure your lawyer understands your business and goals. Then you'll get better, more focused advice.
- Tell your lawyer exactly what you want done and not done and get the price. Be very clear on this. For example, "I don't want a legal memo on anything. No footnotes or law review articles. Just send me an e-mail with an answer, yes, no, maybe and a few sentences as to why."
- Lawyers multiply like coat hangers. Don't let your lawyer engage any more lawyers without your permission. Associates are under pressure from their partners to "develop their client" which means increasing your billings. You might ask for a simple contract from your lawyer and end up with a bill for that plus relevant tax or antitrust advice from another lawyer

in the firm you never met. If you get a bill you don't like or see another lawyer's name on it that you don't recognize, talk to your lawyer. It's common practice for partners to sign off on bills to clients. In one case I got a bill signed by the partner charging for his review of the bill. I knew he never signed that and was at his ranch out West. He never did that again. You need to establish expectations on billings.

- Your lawyer shouldn't waffle on legal advice. "Well on the one hand … and on the other hand" is not the answer you deserve. Lawyers often provide conservative advice when they are in a partnership because if one lawyer makes a big mistake there's potential liability for all the others. You're paying for your lawyer's best judgment. Nothing is 100 percent predictable but at least your lawyer should be able to tell you what the odds are (30 percent or 60 percent) of an event happening or not based on experience.

- Tell your lawyer, "Tell me what I need to hear, not what I want to hear. Give it to me straight. Give me your best judgment—that's what I'm buying. If wanted a waffle I'd go to Waffle House."

> **TIP: ALWAYS USE "METHICS"™—MANAGEMENT ETHICS.
> IT'S GOOD FOR YOU AND YOUR BUSINESS.**

"METHICS"™—MANAGEMENT ETHICS

There are hundreds of business books at your local bookstore and just a couple with "ethics" in the title. But ethics isn't just a personal matter. It's a critical part of business. You will be tempted to cut corners on ethics. Don't do it. The word will get out and hurt you and your business. You need your team, board, and stakeholders to know that you'll play fair. If you don't, people won't want to deal with you and your team won't give 100 percent. In addition, you'll prevent disputes that can lead to lawsuits. At a startup even one small lawsuit or regulatory investigation can scare investors and customers away.

Examples of Using Management Zen to Reduce Startup Chaos

*Scooter emerges from chaos, gets a handle on life balance,
and finds the Zen of management ... until...*

Six Months Later

Things had settled down for Scooter. He'd finally gotten his finances under control. When he met with Susan Glover, she explained that the CEO had forced her into using the more aggressive language to market the gloves. This was just one of the problems with the CEO. He needed to go. Scooter and Susan discussed how to pull this off with the board of directors. That worked well. Susan took over as CEO and brought Scooter in as a board member. Along with the $100,000 annual director's stipend, Scooter was eligible to participate in Aeris' IPO, which took off. After the ninety-day restriction on selling Aeris stock, Scooter sold over one million dollars' worth of stock—more than enough to purchase Megan's dream house in France. And he still had two million dollars left.

Also Six Months Later

Scooter and Megan were on their way to France on the Queen Mary 2. They were having a drink at the Pavilion Pool and Bar on deck twelve. The understated elegance was soothing. The ebony bar, the pale blue lighting on the marble wall, and the ocean views had a way of slowing time. Sammy was with them alternating between snoozing and keeping one eye on a couple drinking Piña Coladas at the bar.

Scooter finally was leaving the chaos behind and getting his life balance back. If he could maintain that, then he was entering "Management Zen," that mental state where you were in the zone and could calmly deal with business challenges as they came and accept the inevitable failures without losing your focus.

He was taking another sip of his Vesper Martini, the one that James Bond enjoyed in *Casino Royale*, when the waiter came over with their lunch, two salads, a filet, and some newspapers on the tray.

"Who had the filet?"

Sammy's paw went up. The waiter tried not to laugh.

"I'll take the *New York Times*," said Scooter. He took a quick glance through the *Times* but stopped suddenly when he saw the brief story on page 16:

Uruguay suddenly has withdrawn from the extradition treaty with the United States. President Hidalgo called it, "a necessary step to protect our citizens from creeping US interference in the legal rights of our citizens." According to sources, some influential businesses, including fashion conglomerate Zapata, have been behind this surprising change in policy. The President also denies rumors about his relationship with socialite Scarlett Montevideo, who has recently been seen with him several times at his seaside villa.

Scooter was still trying to process this when he was interrupted by a well-dressed man who approached their table. "Pardon me, are you Professor Magee?"

"Yes..."

"Hello. I'm H. Bosley Jenkins, III; call me Bos. I saw that article in *Forbes* about you. I wonder if I might have a minute of your time."

"Oh ... okay."

Megan tuned out while Jenkins described some investment opportunity.

Later, Scooter and Megan strolled through the curved Atlantic Room, with its green felt covered tables, and onto the forward Observation Deck for a final view as the 1,100-foot ship was pulling onto the dock at the Damen Shipyard at Brest. This wasn't the ship's usual stop but it worked great for the Magees who were going to their new house in France.

Megan asked Scooter about Jenkins. "He wants me to go in with him as an investor and paid consultant on his high efficiency solar panel company. Could be very profitable," said Scooter.

Megan rolled her eyes. "Scooter J. Magee, not again! We just got things back to normal with your business. We don't even have any idea who this guy really is..."

"Don't worry, I'll do all the due diligence..."

Sammy spoke up. "Let's flip a coin to do or not."

They laughed. "Okay, but just for fun."

Scooter fumbled in his pocket for a quarter.

"You call it in the air, Megan."

Scooter threw it up, Megan called "heads," and as it was coming down, Sammy jumped up high in the air and knocked it away with his paw.

They laughed. "Well, I guess we know how Sammy feels about this!"

"Megan," Scooter said. "I've got a surprise for you. I actually told Bos I wasn't interested in his investment. I've finally learned my lesson."

Meghan looked at him and laughing, she said, "You ... you ... rascal!"

Scooter walked Sammy one last time around the "poop deck" complete with a lamppost from London and a fire Hydrant from New York City, and then dropped Sammy off at one of the twenty-four kennels. He checked back an hour later. He looked in room after room. Finally, he found him. Sammy was lying on his back on a massage table with his head on a silk pillow, humming Sinatra's "I Did It My Way" while getting a belly rub and pedicure. In the dog dish under the table was a virgin Piña Colada covered with floating cherries and topped with a chocolate umbrella.

"Okay, Sammy, party's over; time to go."

"It's great to finally arrive in France!" Megan said. "I can't wait to get to our new house." The house thing was starting to worry Scooter. It wasn't really the house; it was that Megan seemed to care more about money and the house than him. He felt a little used. Then he thought again. People need to feel loved in different ways. Maybe having that house was the reassurance or security she needed but in a way he didn't understand.

An hour later, they were in line waiting to go down the gangplank. Sammy looked through the railing at the crowd on the dock. Some nice cars. Next to a silver Maserati was a well-dressed woman, maybe thirty-five. Then the sun reflected off the diamond on her boot strap. She looked up and saw Sammy. He froze for a second and then barked, "It's Scarlett!"

Megan and Scooter turned to look. Their expressions showed how surprised they were. Scooter looked too, but if you had seen his face, he wasn't surprised at all.

***

A few weeks earlier...
Scooter was cleaning up the back yard, raking and mulching. He was finishing up around the rosebushes. *What's happened to the dirt around this bush?* thought Scooter. *Looks like the squirrels have been tearing things up for nuts. No ... it's too big a mess, must have been a dog or something.* He was raking the area back into shape when he hit something. *What's this?* He saw the corner of an envelope, pulled it out, and banged it against a tree to get the dirt off. "How'd that get here?" he said out loud, brushing off the rest of the dirt. He finally got the plastic envelope open and started reading.

"Oh my gosh!" he said out loud, "Oh my gosh, She..." and sat down on the grass. "What am I going to do now?"

***

Who knows what will happen next? Is Scarlett back in Scooter's life? What will happen with Scooter and Megan? Is the CIA telling the truth about ending their control of Sammy? Who was Cold Fingers working for? What happened to the camera the CIA was after?

Now, Scooter and Sammy are ready for the next big adventure!

THE END

CONCLUSION:

CALL TO ACTION FOR A NATIONAL ECO-SYSTEM TO SUPPORT STARTUPS (NESS)

THE PROBLEM: THOUSANDS OF SILOS

If the government can pay farmers *not* to grow something, it should be able to support entrepreneurs *to grow* businesses. In this book, we've described the tools to help you succeed as an entrepreneur. Being an entrepreneur can be a lonely job, sitting around the kitchen table trying to figure everything out. It takes a village of support to get from an idea to a commercial success. An entrepreneur with a day job may need years and $100,000 just to develop the prototype of a product or service. But that's only the beginning. Getting to a commercial product requires hiring lawyers, forming a business, developing a business plan, finding investors, marketing to customers, and more.

THE STARTUP GRAND CANYON

Entrepreneurs create valuable new products and services that help grow the economy and keep America competitive during these times of greater international competition. One example of that competition is that China has overtaken America on the patent front—an indicator of innovation activity.

China was the biggest source of applications for international patents in the world in 2020 for the second consecutive year and extended its lead over No. 2 filer the United States...China filed 68,720 applications in 2020 while the United States filed 59,230.[1]

Often, entrepreneurs are lone inventors. Some have little business experience and are afraid of having their idea stolen. Most startups run out of time and money in a year or two, and the inventions fail to cross the "Startup Grand Canyon"—the huge chasm between an idea and a profitable product.

Obviously, the system isn't efficient. But it's worse than that. There's no system at all. What can be done to create an eco-system to support and to help the thousands of scattered startups to succeed?

THREE STEPS TO BAKE THE STARTUP CAKE

To cross the Startup Grand Canyon, three problems need to be addressed. Let's use baking a cake as an analogy. To bake a cake you need three things—all the ingredients in one place, an oven to bake them, and getting it done on time.

The Necessary Ingredients Are Scattered

While there are a lot of resources to help startups, such as innovation programs at universities, workspaces and accelerators, these are siloed and disconnected. Suppose you have an idea for a new widget and need to link up with others across the country interested in it. You'll need a patent attorney, business plan, marketing support, and help finding government grants and investors. There's no central clearing house for all of those. *Everything's there somewhere, but somewhere equals nowhere.* Government agencies may be willing to fund inventions and innovative enterprises, and private companies may want them. But how can all of the essential stakeholders connect?

Step One: Bring All the Ingredients Together in One Place. Create the Sbay—A Startup eBay

Let's create an online, one-stop, virtual information meeting place for all parties interested in specific products or services, enabling buyers, sellers, inventors, grantors, venture capital firms, government agencies, and patent lawyers to meet in a virtual marketplace for any subject area, such as "faster battery charging systems."

The U.S. Department of Energy has taken helpful steps by assembling scientists in its Energy Innovation Hubs. And there are online services that have tried to bring the pieces together. Yet these efforts don't include *all* of the necessary stakeholders.

Let's use proven Business to Business (B2B) internet techniques to speed up information exchange and connect the dots with all the stakeholders. Visionaries like Bill Gates, investment banking firms, or others such as DARPA or IBM could easily fund this new Sbay web platform and profit from it.

Step Two: Even Worse, There's No Oven to Bake the Startup Cake. Let's Create Local Startup Centers (LSCs)

There also is no *physical* meeting place for the diverse parties. An inventor alone at home needs to find business partners and lawyers, investors, money, etc. And a prototype may need to be fabricated and tested in a facility at a reasonable price with advice from experts. But all these players and essential ingredients scattered and trying to connect is inefficient.

Let's create Local Startup Centers (LSCs) in each state, perhaps a hundred of them nationally—where inventors, business firms, law firms, investors, government representatives, and engineers all could meet. Startup federal funding could be provided to each state in connection with state universities, with guidelines for the center's operation and flexibility for the states to create different approaches, so that best-of-breed systems could be replicated.

These LSCs would be like an entrepreneur's bazaar. They would have meeting rooms, secretarial support, and engineering software. Entrepreneurs could get advice on patents and business matters from law firms, consultants, and venture capital firms, and meet with research institutions. Federal and state agencies could help inventors find government funding. There would be facilities for rapidly fabricating prototypes. It would be buzzing with activity and synergies, with all the players finally working together. Retired executives, engineers, and others could be added as a "Startup Volunteer Corps"—or be paid with equity in the company. Cross fertilization and deals would happen on the spot around the water cooler. Everything could happen faster.

Step Three: The Cook Takes Too Long to Bake the Cake. Let's Have a Startup Moon Shot and Aim to Launch New Companies in Ninety Days

Third, let's speed up and cut the costs of launching a new business. LSCs could grant or advance winning startups $100,000 ten days after walking in the door, plus provide hands-on guidance. At the LSCs, entrepreneurs would present their ideas and simple business plans to a panel of experts. In ten days, a decision would be made on whether to fund it. Winners would receive a grant or long-term, below market-rate loan of up to $100,000 to spend at any LSC for anything—legal support, engineering advice, prototyping, help with a business plan, etc. The goal would be a startup moonshot—to launch companies in only ninety days. A chart showing how this LSC process would work is on the following page.

In addition, it costs too much and takes too long to get a patent—often many years and tens of thousands of dollars. Let's create a faster patenting system. The U.S. Patent and Trademark Office has an accelerated examination option, but this is still a costly process for small startup companies. If more inventions could get to market faster, companies would grow faster. The earlier tax revenues could help pay for the additional patent examiners and staff to speed up the process and everyone would win.

These Steps Can Pay for Themselves, Plus Generate Tax Revenues and Profits

The LSC process would include a clear outline of the project and a timetable. Government seed money could start up the centers. Next, the entrepreneur could sell a small percentage of the company's equity to the LSC to participate.

- If the new company becomes profitable, the LSC can sell its equity share in the company to support its operations and the inventor would be able to pay back the funds received plus interest.
- If the new company fails and can't pay back the LSC, the LSC could cover that loss by creating a reserve fund for such an event.

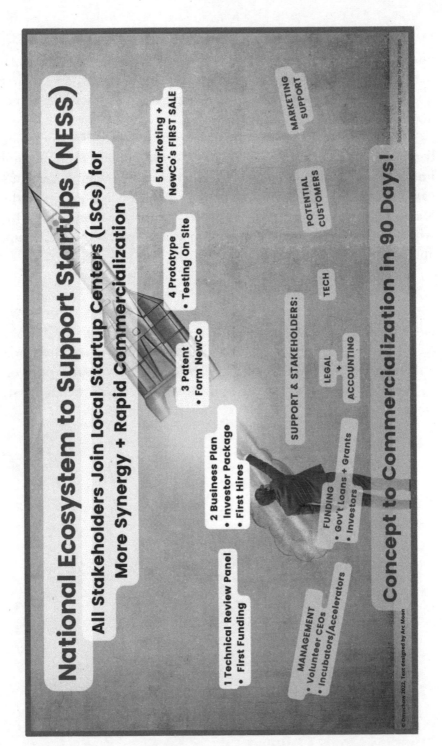

Or a private investment group could raise private funds to co-invest with the government to start up the LSCs or handle the whole investment itself. That investment fund would benefit by getting the first up-close look at thousands of promising inventions, monetize some, and earn a fair profit in return.[2]

These are just some ideas to start the discussion. There may be better and other ways to solve these problems. But let's think big and finally bring all the ingredients together to bake the entrepreneur's cake. Create Sbays, LSCs, speed up the patent process, and solve the Startup Grand Canyon problem with a Startup Moon Shot! This will help entrepreneurs, maintain America's innovation leadership, and create more jobs faster.

***

Dear reader, welcome to the startup world and congratulations on taking the leap! I hope that the information in this book will help you to be successful. I'd be pleased to hear from you so feel free to contact me at dmuchow@muchowlaw.com. Best, Dave Muchow.

APPENDICES

IMPORTANT LEGAL NOTICE: THE DOCUMENTS AND OTHER MATERIALS IN THIS APPENDIX ARE SAMPLES ONLY AND ARE ABRIDGED. LAWS CHANGE FREQUENTLY SO DO NOT USE ANY OF THIS LEGAL LANGUAGE WITHOUT FIRST CHECKING WITH YOUR ATTORNEY.

1 Sample Bylaws Provisions

BYLAWS
OF
XYZ CONSULTING SERVICES, INC.

ARTICLE I

Offices

1.1   **Principal Office.** The principal office of **XYZ Consulting Services, Inc.** (hereinafter called the "Corporation") is at _____, or such other places as may be designated from time to time.

1.2   **Registered Office.** The registered office of the Corporation is at _____.

1.3   **Other Offices.** The Corporation may also have other offices at such places as the Board of Director may from time to time designate or the business of the Corporation may require.

1.4   **Change of Location.** The Board of Directors or the Registered Agent may change the address of the Corporation's registered office and the Board of Directors may make, revoke, or change the designation of the registered agent.

ARTICLE II

Meetings of Stockholders

2.1   **Annual Meeting.** The annual meeting of the stockholders of the Corporation for the election of directors and for the transaction of such other business as may properly come before the meeting shall be held at the registered office of the Corporation, or at such other place within or without [State] as the Board of Directors may designate, on the date specified in the notice of such annual meeting.

2.2   **Special Meetings.** Special meetings of stockholders, unless otherwise prescribed by law or the Corporation's Certificate of Incorporation (as amended or restated, the "Certificate of Incorporation"), may be called at any time by the President, by order of the Board of Directors, or at the request of stockholders owning a majority of the shares of stock. Special meetings of stockholders shall be held at such place within or without [State] as shall be designated in the notice of such special meeting.

2.3   **List of Stockholders Entitled To Vote.** The officer who has charge of the stock ledger of the Corporation shall prepare and make, at least ten (10) days before every meeting of stockholders, a complete list, based upon the record date for such meeting determined pursuant to Section 5.4, of the stockholders entitled to vote at the meeting [etc.].

2.4   **Notice of Meeting.** Whenever stockholders are required or permitted to take any action at a meeting, a written notice of the meeting shall be given to all stockholders entitled to vote at such meeting, which notice shall state the place, date, and hour of the meeting and, in the case of a special meeting, the purpose or purposes for which the meeting is called [etc.].

2.5   **Adjourned Meetings and Notice Thereof.** Any meeting of stockholders may be adjourned to another time or place, and the Corporation may transact at any adjourned meeting any business that might have been transacted at the original meeting [etc.].

2.6   **Quorum.** At any meeting of stockholders, except as otherwise expressly required by law, the holders of record of at least a majority of the outstanding shares of capital stock entitled to vote or act at such meeting shall be present or represented by proxy in order to constitute a quorum for the transaction of any business. Less than a quorum shall have power to adjourn any meeting until a quorum shall be present. When a quorum is once present to organize a meeting, the quorum cannot be destroyed by the subsequent withdrawal or revocation of the proxy of any stockholder.

2.7   **Voting.** At any meeting of stockholders, each stockholder entitled to vote at such meeting shall have one (1) vote for each share of stock held by such stockholder [etc.].

2.8　Action by Consent of Stockholders. Unless otherwise provided in the Certificate of Incorporation, any action required or permitted by law, the Certificate of Incorporation, or these Bylaws to be taken at any annual or special meeting of the stockholders of the Corporation may be taken without a meeting, without prior notice and without a vote, if a consent or consents in writing, setting forth the action so taken, shall be executed by the holders of a sufficient number of outstanding shares of stock.

ARTICLE III

Board of Directors

3.1　General Powers. The property, business, and affairs of the Corporation shall be managed by the Board of Directors. The Board of Directors may exercise all such powers of the Corporation and have such authority and do all such lawful acts and things as are permitted by law, the Certificate of Incorporation, or these Bylaws.

3.2　Number of Directors. The Board shall consist of no more than eight (8) members.

3.3　Qualification. Directors need not be residents of [State] or stockholders of the Corporation.

3.4　Election. Except as otherwise provided by law, the Certificate of Incorporation, these Bylaws, or any Investor Rights Agreement, after the initial meeting of the directors of the Corporation, directors of the Corporation shall be elected at an annual meeting of stockholders, or at a special meeting in lieu of the annual meeting called for such purpose, by the vote of a majority of the shares of stock cast at such meeting. Notwithstanding any other provisions in these Bylaws the following persons shall constitute the initial Board of Directors until successors are elected:

3.5　Term. Each director shall hold office until his or her successor is elected and qualified, except in the event of the earlier termination of his or her term of office by reason of death, resignation, removal, or other reason.

3.6　Resignation and Removal. Any director may resign at any time upon written notice to the Board of Directors, the President, and the Secretary. The resignation of any director shall take effect upon receipt of notice thereof or at such later time as shall be specified in such notice [etc.].

3.7   **Vacancies.** Except as otherwise provided in the Certificate of Incorporation or any Investor Rights Agreement, any vacancy in the Board of Directors, whether arising from death, resignation, removal (with or without cause), an increase in the number of directors, or any other cause, may be filled by the vote of a majority of the directors then in office, though less than a quorum, or by the sole remaining director, or by the stockholders entitled to vote at the next annual meeting thereof, or at a special meeting thereof [etc.].

3.8   **Quorum and Voting.** A majority of the total number of directors shall constitute a quorum for the transaction of business [etc.].

3.9   **Special Voting.** Except as otherwise provided in the Certificate of Incorporation, and without limiting anything in any Investor Rights Agreement, the affirmative vote of three quarters of the directors constituting the whole Board of Directors shall be necessary for the Corporation, in the name of the Board of Directors, to:

> (i)   propose or adopt any plan to partially liquidate, dissolve, reorganize, consolidate, merge, or recapitalize the Corporation, or transfer all or substantially all of its assets, or amend its Certificate of Incorporation in connection with any of the foregoing;
>
> (ii)   issue or sell any shares of capital stock of the Corporation or any options or rights to purchase any shares of capital stock of the Corporation, whether or not such shares have been previously authorized or issued; or
>
> (iii)   purchase, retire, or retain any shares of capital stock of the Corporation, or set aside any funds for such purpose.

3.10   **Rules and Regulations.** The Board of Directors may adopt such rules and regulations for the conduct of the business and management of the Corporation, not inconsistent with law or the Investor Rights Agreement or the Certificate of Incorporation or these Bylaws, as the Board of Directors may deem proper [etc.].

3.11   **Annual Meeting of Board of Directors.** An annual meeting of the Board of Directors may be called and held for the purpose of organization, election of officers, and transaction of any other business [etc.].

3.12   **Regular Meetings.** Regular meetings of the Board of Directors shall be held at the time and place, within or without [State], as shall from time to time be determined by the Board of Directors. Except as otherwise provided by law, any business may be transacted at any regular meeting.

3.13   **Special Meetings.** Special meetings of the Board of Directors may be called from time to time by the President and shall be called by the President or the Secretary upon written request of a majority of the entire Board of Directors directed to the President or Secretary [etc.].

3.14   **Notice of Meetings; Waiver of Notice.** Except as provided in this section and in Section 3.11, notice of any meeting of the Board of Directors must be given to all directors [etc.].

3.15   **Compensation of Directors.** The Board of Directors may from time to time, in its discretion, fix the amounts which shall be payable to directors and to members of any committee of the Board of Directors for attendance at the meetings of the Board of Directors or of such committee and for services rendered to the Corporation.

3.16   **Action Without Meeting.** Any action required or permitted to be taken at any meeting of the Board of Directors or of any committee thereof may be taken without a meeting if all members of the board or committee thereof, as the case may be, consent thereto in writing [etc.].

3.17   **Telephonic Meeting.** Unless restricted by the Certificate of Incorporation, any one or more members of the Board of Directors or any committee thereof may participate in a meeting of the Board of Directors or such committee by means of a conference telephone or other communications equipment by means of which all persons participating in the meeting are able to hear each other. Participation by such means shall constitute presence in person at a meeting.

ARTICLE IV

Officers

4.1   **Principal Officers.** The principal officers of the Corporation shall be elected by the Board of Directors and may include a Chairman, President and CEO, a Secretary, and a Treasurer; and may, at the discretion of the Board of Directors, also include one or more Vice Presidents or other officers. One person may hold the offices and perform the duties of any two (2) or more of said principal offices [subject to state law]. None of the principal officers need be directors of the Corporation.

4.2   **Election of Principal Officers; Term of Office.** The officers of the Corporation shall hold office until their successors are chosen and qualified. Any officer elected or appointed by the Board of Directors may be removed at any time by the affirmative vote of two thirds of the Board of Directors. Any vacancy occurring in any office of the Corporation shall be filled by the Board of Directors.

4.3   **Subordinate Officers, Agents and Employees.** In addition to the principal officers, the Corporation may have one or more Assistant Treasurers, Assistant Secretaries and such other subordinate officers, agents and employees as the Board of Directors may deem advisable [etc.].

4.4   **Duties.** The powers and duties of the several officers shall be as provided from time to time by resolution or other directive of the Board. In the absence of such provisions, the respective officers shall have the powers and shall discharge the duties customarily and usually held and performed by like officers of corporations similar in organization and business purposes to the Corporation.

4.5   **Compensation.** Officers may be paid such reasonable compensation as the Board may from time to time authorize and direct.

4.6   **Resignation.** Any officer may resign at any time by giving written notice of resignation to the Board of Directors, to the President or to the Secretary. Any such resignation shall take effect upon receipt of such notice or at any later time specified therein. Unless otherwise specified in the notice, the acceptance of a resignation shall not be necessary to make the resignation effective.

ARTICLE V

Capital Stock

5.1   **Stock Certificates.** Certificates representing shares of the Corporation shall be in such form (consistent with applicable law) as shall be determined by the Board [etc.].

5.2   **Stock Ledger.** A record of all certificates for capital stock issued by the Corporation shall be kept by the Secretary or any other officer, employee, or agent designated by the Board of Directors. Such record shall show the name and address of the person, firm, or corporation in which certificates for capital stock are registered, the number and series of shares represented by each such certificate, the date of each such certificate and, in the case of certificates that have been cancelled, the dates of cancellation thereof [etc.].

5.3   **Regulations Relating to Transfer.** The Board of Directors may make such rules and regulations as it may deem expedient, not inconsistent with law, the Certificate of Incorporation, any Investor Rights Agreement, or these Bylaws, concerning issuance, transfer, and registration of certificates for shares of capital stock of the Corporation. The Board of Directors may appoint, or authorize any principal officer to appoint, one or more transfer clerks or one or more transfer agents and one or more registrars and may require all certificates for capital stock to bear the signature or signatures of any of them.

5.4   **Fixing of Record Dates.** The Board of Directors may fix, in advance, a record date, which shall not be more than sixty (60) nor less than ten (10) days before the date of any meeting [etc.].

5.5   **Restrictions on Transfer.** During the term of any Investor Rights Agreement (as of the date of such agreement) containing restrictions on transfers of shares of capital stock in this Corporation and other stockholder action, no stockholder of the Corporation shall transfer [etc.].

ARTICLE VI

Indemnification

6.1   **Indemnification.** Each person who was or is made a party or is threatened to be made a party to or is otherwise involved in any action, suit, or proceeding, whether civil, criminal, administrative, or investigative (hereinafter a "proceeding") [etc.].

6.2   **Indemnification Insurance.** The Corporation may maintain insurance, at its expense, to protect itself and any director, trustee, officer, employee, or agent of the Corporation or another enterprise (as defined in paragraph (1) of Section 6.1) against any expense, liability, or loss, whether or not the Corporation would have the power to indemnify such person against such expense, liability, or loss under the laws of [state].

ARTICLE VII

Miscellaneous Provisions

7.1   **Corporate Seal.** The seal of the Corporation shall be in such form as shall be approved by the Board of Directors.

7.2   **Fiscal Year.** The fiscal year of the Corporation shall be the calendar year.

7.3   **Waiver of Notice.** Whenever any notice is required to be given under any provision of law, the Certificate of Incorporation or these Bylaws, a written waiver thereof, signed by the person or persons entitled to such notice, whether before or after the time stated therein, shall be deemed equivalent to notice [etc.].

7.4   **Execution of Instruments and Contracts.** All checks, drafts, bills of exchange, notes, loans, or other obligations or orders for the payment of money shall be signed, endorsed, or accepted in the name of the Corporation by such officer or officers or person or persons as the Board of Directors may from time to time designate [etc.].

7.5   **Voting of Securities in Other Entities.** Unless otherwise provided by resolution of the Board of Directors, the President, from time to time, may (or may appoint one or more attorneys or agents to) cast the votes that the Corporation may be entitled to cast as a stockholder [etc.].

ARTICLE VIII

Amendments

8.1   **By Board of Directors or Stockholders.** Subject to any provisions to the contrary provided in the Certificate of Incorporation or any Investor Rights Agreement, these Bylaws may be amended or repealed.

ARTICLE IX

Conflict of Terms

Notwithstanding the foregoing, in the event of any conflict between the terms of these Bylaws and the terms of the Agreements, the terms of the Agreements shall govern and control.

CERTIFICATE

The undersigned, being the duly elected and authorized President, CEO, and Secretary of the Corporation, does hereby certify that the foregoing copy of the Bylaws of the Corporation, as amended, is true and correct in all respects and has been duly adopted and approved by the Corporation.

IN WITNESS WHEREOF, the undersigned has executed this Certificate which is made effective as of _____.

_____

Signed

2 Organizational Action in Writing Sample

ACTION BY UNANIMOUS WRITTEN CONSENT
IN LIEU OF THE ORGANIZATIONAL MEETING
OF
NEWCO, INC.

The undersigned, constituting all of the shareholders of the **NEWCO, INC**, a [State] Corporation (the "**Company**"), hereby adopts the following resolutions by unanimous written consent:

APPOINTMENT OF DIRECTORS; PRIOR ACTS AUTHORIZED

RESOLVED, that a Board of Directors may become effective at any time when all of the Shareholders consent to such action; and the authorized number of directors shall be initially set at no more than five (5); and that all other prior acts of the Manager, directors and officers, and organizing counsel are ratified and approved. The original shareholder of the Board of Directors is [Name] who shall take office immediately and serve until the earlier of that person's resignation, replacement, or incapacity to serve.

CERTIFICATE OF INCORPORATION

RESOLVED, that the Articles of Incorporation of the Company filed with {State] on [Date] be, and hereby is, ratified and affirmed.

ELECTION OF OFFICERS

RESOLVED, that the following persons be, and they hereby are, elected as officers of the Company, to serve until the next annual meeting or until their successors are duly elected and have qualified: President, CEO, Secretary, and Treasurer: _____

EMPLOYER TAX IDENTIFICATION NUMBER

RESOLVED, that each of the appropriate officers of the Company is authorized to apply to the IRS for an employer's identification number.

TAXES

RESOLVED, that the Treasurer be, and she/he is hereby authorized and directed to consult with the bookkeeper [etc.].

DESIGNATION OF DEPOSITORY

RESOLVED, that the President and the Treasurer of the Company be, and each of them hereby is, authorized to designate one or more banks or similar financial institutions as depositories of the funds of the Company [etc.].

FISCAL YEAR

RESOLVED, that the fiscal year of the Company shall end on the 31st day of the month of December of each year.

PRINCIPAL OFFICE

RESOLVED, that the first principal executive office of the Company shall be at [Address] or at such other places as may be directed.

ISSUANCE OF STOCK

RESOLVED, that the Company, which has _____ shares of authorized [Type of Stock, Common, Series A, etc.] Stock, hereby issues _____ shares of Common Stock to [Name]. The Company hereby determines, after consideration of all relevant factors, that the fair market value of the stock is $_____per share.

MANAGEMENT'S POWERS

RESOLVED, that the officers of the Company be, and each of them hereby is, authorized to sign and execute in the name and on behalf of the Company all applications, contracts, leases, and other deeds and documents [etc.].

ORGANIZATIONAL EXPENSES

RESOLVED, that the officers of the Company be, and each of them hereby is, authorized and directed to pay the expenses of the organization of the Company.

ADDITIONAL FILINGS

RESOLVED, that the appropriate officers and attorneys of the Company be, and each of them hereby is, authorized and directed, for and on behalf of the Company, to make such filings, applications and corrections [etc.].

This Action by Unanimous Written Consent may be signed in one or more counterparts, each of which shall be deemed an original, and all of which shall constitute one instrument. This Action by Unanimous Written Consent shall be filed with the minutes of the proceedings of the Company.

IN WITNESS WHEREOF, this Action by Unanimous Written Consent of the Shareholders is made effective as of _____,

_____
     Signature

3 Non-Compete Non-Disclosure Agreement (NCNDA)

NON-COMPETE NON-DISCLOSURE AGREEMENT (NCNDA)

Whereas: [*Company Name*] (**Company**) and the undersigned (**Undersigned** herein) are interested in sharing information related to [*various business ventures*]; and

Whereas: the Company and the Undersigned are referred to individually as "**Party**" and collectively as **Parties** herein;

Agreement

Now therefore, the Parties, in consideration of the mutual promises made herein and for other valuable consideration, the receipt of which is mutually acknowledged, hereby enter into this non-compete non-disclosure agreement (**Agreement**) effective as of _____ (the **Effective Date**), with the following terms:

1. **Maintaining Confidentiality.** Each Party agrees to maintain in confidence all **Confidential Information** defined below, previously disclosed or to be disclosed to it by the other Party and agrees that the receiving Party shall not make use of it for its own advantage, or to compete with the other, or disclose it to any third person or party without the express prior written consent of the disclosing Party, except as it exclusively may be used to carry out the purposes in this Agreement.

2. **Use of Confidential Information.** The Parties acknowledge that the Confidential Information of the disclosing Party is confidential, trade secret property, and that the Confidential Information disclosed will be used solely for the purpose

of evaluating their possible collaboration and whatever business relationships they may agree to undertake together. No Party shall use such Confidential Information for any other purposes.

3. **Warranty and Title.** Each Party warrants that it has the right to make unrestricted disclosures (**Disclosures**) of Confidential Information to the other Party under this Agreement. Title to the Confidential Information shall remain solely in the disclosing Party. No Party acquires any license or other intellectual property rights of the other Party pursuant to this Agreement, except that recipient acquires a limited, royalty free right to use, in confidence, the discloser's Confidential Information for the purposes of this Agreement. No Party is required to disclose Confidential Information or to purchase any service or product from the other Party. No agency or partnership or other relationship is or shall be created by this Agreement.

4. **Recipient's Obligations.** The recipient shall:

   a. protect the discloser's Confidential Information by using at least the same degree of care, which shall in no event be less than reasonable care, to prevent unauthorized use and/or dissemination and/or publication of discloser's Confidential Information as recipient uses to protect recipient's own information of like nature;

   b. disclose such Confidential Information only to recipient's employees and/or representatives and agents who have a need to receive it;

   c. limit such disclosure to only so much of the Confidential Information as is necessary for the particular employee or agent to perform the desired work and/or evaluation;

   d. inform these employees and/or representatives of the nature and the obligation of this Agreement;

e. In the event that a recipient is required by judicial, administrative, or other official process to disclose the other Party's Confidential Information, the recipient may disclose Confidential Information pursuant to any governmental, judicial, or administrative order, subpoena, discovery request, regulatory request, or similar action, provided that the recipient promptly notifies, to the extent practicable, the disclosing Party in writing of such demand for disclosure so that the disclosing Party, at its sole expense, may seek to make such disclosure subject to a protective order or other appropriate remedy to preserve the confidentiality of the Confidential Information. In the case of a broad regulatory request with respect to the receiving Party's business (not targeted at disclosing the Party), the receiving Party may promptly comply with such request provided the receiving Party gives the disclosing Party prompt notice of such disclosure. The receiving Party agrees that it shall not oppose and shall cooperate with efforts by, to the extent practicable, the disclosing Party with respect to any such request for a protective order or other relief. Notwithstanding the foregoing, if the disclosing Party is unable to obtain or does not seek a protective order and the receiving Party is legally requested or required to disclose such Confidential Information, disclosure of such Confidential Information may be made without incurring liability from the other Party.

5. **Markings.** Information or products considered confidential or proprietary to discloser does not need to be marked "Confidential" or "Proprietary" to be Confidential Information for purposes of this Agreement; provided, however, that such information is in some reasonable manner identified or obvious by its content or otherwise to the recipient as Confidential or Proprietary of the discloser.

6. **Non-Circumvention and Non-Compete.** Recipient shall not reverse engineer or disassemble any products or intellectual property disclosed; and shall not use the Confidential Information to compete with discloser or use it for its own purposes or to enter into any dealings or discussions or actions with other parties that might involve or attempt to do those things or to attempt to bypass any products or services that the discloser currently offers or may offer in the future.

7. **Intellectual Property.** No intellectual property is transferred by either Party to the other by this Agreement.

8. **Term.** This Agreement may be terminated at any time by a writing signed by both Parties. Each Party agrees to hold any disclosed Confidential Information it has received from any other Party under this Agreement in confidence and not to use it in any way, except for the purposes of this Agreement, for a period of three (3) years following the date the Agreement is terminated. However, this three (3) year confidentiality term shall not apply to any Information that meets the definition of a trade secret under applicable law (**Trade Secrets**). The obligations set forth herein with respect to Trade Secrets shall survive the expiration or termination of this Agreement and will continue to be in effect so long as that information remains a Trade Secret under applicable law.

9. **Definition of Confidential Information.** "Confidential Information" shall mean (1) any and all information relating to the business opportunities that are created, developed, or discovered by that Party from or through the other Party not being generally known to the public or to other persons, (2) each Party's patents, ideas, products, copyrighted matter, and trade secrets ("**Intellectual Property**"), and (3) other information that is non-public, confidential, or proprietary in nature including all designs, analyses, compilations, data,

studies, or other documents based in whole or in part on any such furnished information or reflecting any Party's review of, or interest in, such activities.

Confidential Information shall not apply to:

a. Information that is known to recipient prior to the time such information is acquired from the discloser;

b. Information that becomes generally known to the public as a result of an intentional disclosure by the owning Party, or its authorized representatives;

c. Is independently developed by recipient, provided said independent development is by employees and/or representatives thereof to whom discloser's Confidential Information has not been disclosed;

d. Is disclosed by recipient with discloser's prior written approval;

e. Information that is acquired, at any time, by any Party in the ordinary course of business in good faith, from a third Party not under an obligation of confidentiality; or information that is required to be disclosed pursuant to a subpoena, court order, or other legal or administrative process.

10. **Return of Confidential Information.** Upon the disclosing Party's request, the receiving Party shall immediately return and redeliver to the discloser all tangible material embodying the Confidential Information provided hereunder and all notes, summaries, memoranda, drawings, manuals, records, excerpts, or derivative information deriving there from, and all other documents or materials (**"Notes"**) (and all copies of any of the foregoing, including "copies" that have been converted to computerized media in the form of image, data, or word processing files either manually or by image capture) based on or including any Confidential Information, in whatever form of storage or retrieval, upon the earlier of (i)

the completion or termination of the dealings between the parties contemplated hereunder; or (ii) the termination of this Agreement; provided however that the receiving Party may retain such of its documents as is necessary to enable it to comply with its document retention policies.

11. **Notice of Breach.** The receiving Party shall notify the disclosing Party immediately upon its discovery of any unauthorized use or disclosure of Confidential Information by receiving Party or its representatives or agents, or any other breach of this Agreement by receiving Party or its agents and will cooperate with efforts by the disclosing Party to help the disclosing Party regain possession of Confidential Information and prevent its further unauthorized use.

12. **Warranty.** NO WARRANTIES WHATSOEVER ARE MADE BY EITHER PARTY UNDER THIS AGREEMENT. The Parties understand that no representation or warranty as to the accuracy or completeness of the Confidential Information is being made by either Party. Further, neither Party is under any obligation under this Agreement to disclose any Confidential Information it chooses not to disclose. Neither Party hereto shall have any liability to the other Party or to the other Party's agents resulting from any use of the Confidential Information except with respect to disclosure of such Confidential Information in violation of this Agreement.

13. **Other.**
    (a) This Agreement constitutes the entire understanding between the parties and supersedes any and all prior or contemporaneous understandings and agreements, whether oral or written, between the parties, with respect to the subject matter hereof. This Agreement can only be modified by a written amendment signed by the Party against whom enforcement of such modification is sought.

(b) The validity, construction, and performance of this Agreement shall be governed and construed in accordance with the laws of [state] applicable to contracts made and to be wholly performed within such state, without giving effect to any conflict of laws provisions thereof. The courts located in [state] shall have sole and exclusive jurisdiction over any disputes arising under the terms of this Agreement.

(c) Any failure by either Party to enforce the other Party's strict performance of any provision of this Agreement will not constitute a waiver of its right to subsequently enforce such provision or any other provision of this Agreement.

(d) Although the restrictions contained in this Agreement are considered by the parties to be reasonable for the purpose of protecting the Confidential Information, if any such restriction is found by a court of competent jurisdiction to be unenforceable, such provision will be modified, rewritten or interpreted to include as much of its nature and scope as will render it enforceable. If it cannot be so modified, rewritten, or interpreted to be enforceable in any respect, it will not be given effect, and the remainder of the Agreement will be enforced as if such provision was not included.

(e) Any notices or communications required or permitted to be given hereunder may be delivered by hand, deposited with a nationally recognized overnight carrier, electronic mail, or mailed by certified mail, return receipt requested, postage prepaid, in each case, to the address of the other Party first indicated above (or such other addressee as may be furnished by a Party in accordance with this paragraph). All such notices or communications shall be deemed to have been given and received (i) in the case of personal delivery or electronic mail, on the date of such delivery, (ii) in the case of delivery by a nationally recognized overnight carrier, on the third business day following dispatch, and (iii) in the case of mailing, on the seventh business day following such mailing.

(f) This Agreement is personal in nature, and neither Party may directly or indirectly assign or transfer it by operation of law or otherwise without the prior written consent of the other Party, which consent will not be unreasonably withheld. All obligations contained in this Agreement shall extend to and be binding upon the parties to this Agreement and their respective successors, assigns, and designees.

14. **Definition of Parties.** The term Parties herein, includes their officers, directors, employees, agents, consultants, attorneys, and affiliates; and the definitions apply both in the singular and plural.

15. **Disputes.** The Parties shall attempt to settle any claim or controversy arising out of this Agreement through consultation and negotiation in good faith and spirit of mutual cooperation. Any dispute between/among the Parties relating to this Agreement will first be submitted in writing to a senior executive of both Parties, who will promptly meet and confer in an effort to resolve such dispute. Each Party's executive will be identified by notice to the other Party. Any agreed decision of the executives is final and binding on the Parties. In the event the executives are unable to resolve any dispute within thirty (30) days after submission to them, either Party may then take other appropriate legal actions. Any such actions shall be held in [*venue*] using [*state*] procedural and substantive law without reference to conflict of laws doctrines; and the Parties agree to waive a jury trial. Nothing in this section will prevent either Party from resorting to seeking an injunction if interim relief from a court is necessary to prevent serious and irreparable injury to that Party or to others. Performance by the Parties under this Agreement shall not be suspended during the pendency of any dispute unless the Parties otherwise agree.

16. **Entire Agreement.** This Agreement contains the entire agreement of the Parties and supersedes any prior oral or written understandings related to the subject matter hereof and may be amended only in writing signed by both Parties.

Accordingly, the undersigned Parties hereby warrant that they are authorized to execute this Agreement, and that which does not conflict with any other agreements or obligations and hereby agree to its terms.

Undersigned Name:	Company Name
Name (Print):	Name (Print):
Signature:	Signature:
Title:	Title:
Address:	Address:
Type of Company (LLC, Corp., etc.) and Country and State:	
Phone:	Phone:
Fax:	Fax:
Date:	Date:

4 Employment Agreement Sample

Example of Typical Provisions in an Employment Agreement

This employment agreement (**Agreement**) is entered into as of [date] between [Company name] (**Company**), located at [address]; and [employee's name] (**Employee** or **You**) located at [address]. It is effective as of [date] (**Effective Date**). The Company and Employee also are referred to individually as **Party** and together as **Parties**.

The Company and Employee, for good and valuable consideration, the receipt of which is acknowledged, hereby agree as follows:

1. <u>Duties and Scope of Employment.</u>
   (a) Position. You are employed as _____ in the Company. You will report to _____. The Position Description for this position is attached at Schedule A.
   (b) Term. Your employment begins on _____ (**Start Date**) or such other date as may be agreed to by the Parties and will continue until terminated in accordance with Section 7, Termination (below).
   (c) Obligations to the Company. You agree not to engage in any other employment, consulting, or other business activity except with the prior written consent of the Company. While You render services to the Company, You will comply with the Company's policies and procedures in any current or future employee handbook, Job Description, or other Company documents (**the Documents**). If there is a conflict between provisions in this Agreement and the Documents, this Agreement will supersede them and prevail.
   (d) No Conflicting Obligations. You warrant that you are under no obligations or commitments, inconsistent with your obligations under this Agreement. You shall not compete against the Company or solicit its employees for the term of this Agreement and for two years thereafter, etc.

(e) Duties and Responsibilities. You will faithfully perform the Duties specified in Attachment A. All Attachments are incorporated into this document by reference and are a part of it.

2. <u>Compensation</u>. The Company shall compensate You as provided in Schedule B attached. Any change in compensation shall be in writing.

3. Expenses. The Company shall pay or reimburse You for reasonable expenses approved by Company and incurred by You in performing your duties.

4. Goals and Objectives. Periodically, at the option of the President, You shall meet to establish goals and objectives. These goals and objectives shall be established in writing and be among the criteria by which You are evaluated for performance [*and any Bonus*].

Except as described in Section 7.b) below, if the President (**"President"** includes President's designee) determines that your performance is unsatisfactory the President shall describe in reasonable written detail, the unsatisfactory performance. The evaluation may include recommendations for improvement. You will receive a copy of the written evaluation. You shall have the right to make a written response which will be placed in Your personnel file. The President may meet with You as necessary to discuss the evaluation report in detail.

5. <u>Hold Harmless</u>. You shall assist as requested in defending the Company against all claims, suits, actions, and legal proceedings (**"Claims"**) brought against the Company. If You should fail to follow the Company's required directions, or Your actions or inactions result in any Claims or your actions or inactions were illegal, willful, or grossly negligent, you shall hold the Company harmless and indemnify it, etc.

6. <u>Professional Conduct and Gifts</u>. You shall notify the President of any gifts offered by anyone wanting to do business with the Company and shall not accept any without prior permission except those with a value of under $25.00 and business meals.

7. <u>Termination.</u> If Your performance is acceptable in the sole determination of the President, this Employment Agreement shall be in effect for one year from the Effective Date. Thereafter it shall be renewed for successive one-year periods unless:

    a) You or the President notifies the other in writing at least thirty (30) days prior to the termination date that either wishes to terminate the Agreement; or
    b) You commit a felony, are grossly negligent, or fail to follow direct orders, etc. or
    c) Unless the President, determines that the financial or other condition of the Company requires modification or termination of the Agreement; or
    d) You fail to follow the rules in the Documents or other lawful requests of the Company.

Failure of the Company to take immediate action after any violations of this Agreement shall not constitute a waiver of the Company's rights under this Agreement.

8. <u>Confidential Information:</u> You agree that the information, observations, and data available to You during employment with the Company (**Confidential Information**) concerning the business of the Company are the property of the Company and an office-provided computer, software or data are the Company's property.

You agree, during the employment period and for three (3) years following the termination of your employment, not to disclose any Confidential Information obtained while employed by the Company without the Company's prior written consent, unless such matters become public other than as a result of your actions, etc. Upon your termination you will immediately return to the Company all Confidential Information and Company property. Failure to do so will be considered a breach of this Agreement and can lead to disciplinary action up to and including termination.

9. <u>Inventions and Works of Authorship and Assignment.</u>

   a) You hereby assign to Company all rights that You own or acquire in any **Invention** or **Work of Authorship** made during your employment and for five (5) years after the employment ends, if they are derived from Confidential Information, etc.

   b) You agree to disclose to Company all activities and all tangible work products produced relating to the Company's activities. You hereby warrant that work is your own, etc.

   c) You agree to execute such documents and take such other actions as the Company requires necessary to obtain and enforce intellectual property rights relating to such Inventions and/or Works of Authorship, etc.

   d) "Inventions" and "Works of Authorship" mean without limitation, all discoveries, etc.

10. <u>General Provisions.</u>

   (a) Severability. If any provision of this Agreement is held to be invalid such invalidity will not affect any other provision, etc.

   (b) Complete Agreement, Modifications. This Agreement and the documents referred to herein are the complete Agreement between the Parties and supersede any prior agreements between the Parties written or oral, related to the subject matter herein. Agreement may be amended or modified only by written agreement by the Parties.

   (c) Counterparts. This Agreement may be executed in separate counterparts, each of which is deemed to be an original and all of which taken together constitute the same Agreement.

   (d) Disputes. In the event of any disputes, the Parties agree to seek to resolve such disputes in good faith. After ten (10) days if the dispute still exists, any legal action that may be sought shall be in the State of [State]; and the Parties agree to waive jury trial, etc.

   e) Choice of Law. This Agreement shall be construed under the laws of the State of [State] without regard to any conflict of laws provisions.

    f) Successors and Assigns. This Agreement is not assignable by You without prior written permission but may be assigned by the Company, etc.

    g) Descriptive Headings, Interpretation. The headings are inserted for convenience only, etc.

IN WITNESS, WHEREOF, the Parties hereto have executed this Agreement.

Company

_____   Date: _____

Employee

_____   Date: _____

Attachments:

Schedule A, Position Description
Schedule B, Compensation

5 Employee Handbook Table of Contents

Employee Handbook Table of Contents

6 Business Plan Table of Contents and Balance Sheet

Table of Contents, Business Plan

[Balance Sheet Example Follows]

Pro Forma Balance Sheet as of Jan. 1, 20XX			
Assets		**Liabilities & Equity**	
Current Assets		Current Liabilities	
Cash	$ 31,865	Accounts Payable	20,361
Billed	$ 60,386	Accrued Wages	550,000
Unbilled Receivables	$ 35,232		
Total	$ 127,483	Accrued Payroll Tax	-
		Accrued Vacation	2,963
Fixed Assets		Other Accrued Expenses	50,000
Equipment	$ 8,932	Line of Credit	
Web Page Design	$ 13,036	Total	623,327
Software	$ 8,357		
Leasehold Improvements	$ 157	Long Term Notes Payable	40,000
	$ 30,482		
Less Depreciation & Amortize.	$ (22,825)		
Net	$ 7,657		
Other Assets		Stockholders' Equity	
Patents & Trademarks	$ 43,358	Common Stock	1,627
Syndication	$ 56,622	Class A Stock	530,491
	$ 99,980	Preferred Stock	196
Less Depreciation & Amortiz.	$ (20,400)	Additional Paid in Capital	583,001
Net	$ 79,580	Current Year Retained Earnings	(297,522)
Claims Receivable	$ 63,000	Accumulated Prior Year Loss	(1,203,397)
Total Other Assets	$ 142,580	Total Stockholders' Equity	(385,604)
Total Assets	$ 277,721	Total Liabilities & Equity	277,721

7 Return on Investment Calculation

RETURN ON INVESTMENT (ROI)		
To Calculate Return on Investment (ROI)		Usually Stated as a % so You can Compare This to Other Investments
Dollars this Shareholder Invested	$5,000	
Total Dollars Invested by all Shareholders	$100,000	
Thus, This Shareholder's % of Equity in the Co.	5%	$5,000/$100,000
If Company Paid out all Net Profits ("Dividends") for the Year	$7,500	Usually Co. Wouldn't pay out all Profits - It would Invest for Growth
$ Paid to Shareholder	$375	5% of $7,500
If Company has 100,000 Shares Issued	100,000	
Then, the No. of Shareholder's Shares is 5% of the Total 100,000 shares	5,000	5% x 100,000 Shares
Income/Share	$ 0.08	$375 Dividend/5,000 Shares Owned
ROI - Return on Investment	8%	$0.08x5,000 Shares = $400. $400 in Dividends/$5,000 Invested = 8%
ROI = Income from Investment/Cost of Investment. Note that ROI must refer to some time period. To adjust for that you could use Rate of Return (ROR), Net Present Value (NPV), or Internal Rate of Return (IRR) calculations. https://www.investopedia.com/terms/r/returnoninvestment.asp		

8 Freedom of Info. Act (FOIA) Request Form

TO FEDERAL TRADE COMMISSION (FTC)

Freedom of Information Act Request
Office of General Counsel
Federal Trade Commission
600 Pennsylvania Avenue, NW
Washington, DC 20580

Dear Sir/Madam:

This is a request under the Freedom of Information Act. I request that a copy of the following document(s) be provided to me: [*identify the documents as specifically as possible. i.e., all investigative records concerning ABC company, located at 555 Main Street, City, State, in the years 1997-1999. This company is offering franchises to sell widgets.*]

In order to help determine fees, you should know that I am a [*insert description of requester. i.e., individual, attorney, company, news organization*] [*Optional*].

I am willing to pay fees up to $_____. If you expect the fees will exceed this, please contact me before proceeding.

[*Optional*]

I request a waiver of all fees for this request. Disclosure of the requested information to me is in the public interest because it is likely to contribute significantly to public understanding of the operations or activities of the government and is not primarily in my commercial interest. [*Include a specific explanation.*]

If you need to discuss this request, I can be reached at [*daytime phone number*]. Thank you for your consideration of my request. Sincerely,

Name
Address
City, State, Zip
Telephone Number

9 Performance Review Form

NEWCO

CEO'S PERFORMANCE APPRAISAL

Employee Name		Position/Title	Hire Date
Evaluation Date	Date of Last Evaluation	Evaluator	
Reason for Evaluation (Annual or Other)			

I   **KEY RESPONSIBILITIES:** List major responsibilities, primary duties, or important functions of this Employee or attach Position Description. You may use attachments to supplement any of these questions.

II   **KEY PERFORMANCE FACTORS:** Employee will self-rate and then employer will also rate employee's performance in each Performance Area listed below and note where the employee excels and where improvement is necessary.

Rating Scale:

1   **Does Not Meet Expectations:** Does not meet the minimum requirements of the position or only occasionally acceptable.
2   **Needs Improvement:** Performance is inconsistent; meets some job requirements but not consistently.
3   **Meets Expectations:** Consistently meets the requirements of the position in all aspects.
4   **Exceeds Expectations:** Consistently exceeds the requirements in all respects.
5   **Outstanding:** Unique and exceptional accomplishments – very rarely given – for example: a major breakthrough or accomplishment far beyond Exceeds Expectations.

Bonus Plan – Employees whose average total Performance Score is a 4 or 5 may be eligible to participate in the Annual Bonus Program. NEWCO reserves the right to modify or cancel this Bonus Program at any time depending on its financial situation and other factors.

III. Ranking of Current Performance (1-5, 5 is highest)			
Employee: Self-rate your score. (1-5, 5 is highest) and Reviewer will also provide a rating. **Employer:** Describe how the employee's performance compares to stated expectations and objectives communicated at last appraisal and throughout the rating period. Identify areas where you see improvement is necessary.			
KEY PERFORMANCE AREAS	**EMPLOYER'S COMMENTS**	**E/e's Score**	**NEWCO Score**
Management of NEWCO: Successful management of staff, programs, and budget, building membership, and working with the Board of Directors			
Job Knowledge: Individual's efforts to learn new skills and maintain up-to-date job related information. Applies technical and procedural know-how to get the job done			
Communication: Effectively conveys and receives ideas, information, and directions; listens effectively; demonstrates good verbal and written communication			

Teamwork/Collaboration: Successfully works with others to achieve desired results; contributes to team projects; helps prevent, resolve conflicts; develops positive working relationships; is flexible, open-minded			
Problem Solving: Anticipates and prevents problems; defines problems, identifies solutions; overcomes obstacles; helps team solve problems			
Initiative: Pursues goals with commitment and takes initiative eagerly; results-oriented; desires to excel on the job; works steadily and actively			
Customer Orientation: Listens, identifies, and responds quickly and effectively to internal and external customers' needs and sets work activities accordingly; goes beyond what is expected and follows up to ensure customer satisfaction			
Total Performance Score			

PAST YEAR'S PERFORMANCE of OBJECTIVES: Number and list the major objectives from your last review and describe your accomplishments and performance of them. Self-rate your performance under each Objective on a scale of 1-5 (5 is highest). Use additional pages if necessary.

Objectives 1, 2, etc.

IV. NEW GOALS AND OBJECTIVES: the employee should initially establish Goals and Objectives, and then finalize in consultation between the employee and the supervisor.
NOTE: The number of objectives set is discretionary. Complete as many as needed and use additional sheet if necessary.

Following are suggested guidelines for establishing Goals and Objectives:
1. Objectives should be related to principal areas of job responsibility and may be assignment or skill-oriented.
2. They should be specific.
3. They should be objectively measurable.
4. They should be realistic and attainable yet contain some "stretch."
5. They should be modified during the year as appropriate.

EMPLOYEE'S COMMENTS: Enter below any comments you wish to make about your appraisal.

V.   CAREER DEVELOPMENT: List desired growth directions over mid- to long-term.
VI.   OBJECTIVES: List for the upcoming year.

Employee's Signature _____ Date _____

(Your signature does not necessarily signify your agreement with the appraisal; it simply means that the appraisal has been discussed with you.)

Reviewer's Signature _____Date _____

Ver. No. _____

NOTES

CHAPTER 1

1   Rick Wartzman, "Six Drucker Questions that Simplify a Complex Age," Nov. 6, 2013, https://hbr.org/2013/11/six-drucker-questions-that-simplify-a-complex-age.

2   Small Business Administration, "Choose a Business Structure," https://www.sba.gov/business-guide/launch/choose-business-structure-types-chart\, Feb. 18, 2018.

3   Ibid.

4   Virginia State Corp. Commission, "Annual Corporation Requirements," March 2008, https://scc.virginia.gov/getattachment/ed800451-1222-41e4-9e4e-0da15bc81566/an_fee.pdf.

5   Small Business Administration, "Choose a Business Structure." https://www.collective.com/blog/business-setup/llc-vs-s-corp-which-is-the-best-for-freelancers/.

6   Wikipedia, "Benefit Corporation," Jan. 6, 2022, https://en.wikipedia.org/wiki/Benefit_corporation.

7   Ibid.

8   International Cooperative Alliance, "Statement on the Cooperative Identity," Nov. 27, 2020, at the Wayback Machine.

9   Regulation (EU) 2016/679 of the European Parliament and of the Council of 27 April 2016 on the protection of natural persons with regard to the processing of personal data and on the free movement of such data and repealing Directive 95/46/EC (General Data Protection Regulation).

10   California State Legislature, California Legislative Information, AB-375, Chau. Privacy: personal information: business, Nov. 19, 2018. https://leginfo.legislature.ca.gov/faces/codes_displayText.xhtml ?division=3.&part=4.&lawCode=CIV&title=1.81.5

11   World Intellectual Property Organization, "What is Intellectual Property?" https://www.wipo.int/about-ip/en/.

12   There is a one-year period after the first public disclosure or offer for sale of an invention by an inventor during which a patent application must be filed. This "statutory bar" is unforgiving, which means that an inventor who does not file for patent protection on her invention within this one-year grace period after disclosure will lose all right to obtain patent protection on the invention. This one-year clock may start by something as innocuous as showing the invention to friends without any obligation of confidentiality. See 35 U.S.C. 101 and the US Patent and Trademark's Office Manual of Patent Examining Procedure (MPEP). Bitlaw, https://www.bitlaw.com/patent/requirements.html#:~:text=There%20is%20an%20exception%20to%20these%20requirements%20for,during%20which%20a%20patent%20application%20must%20be%20filed. Section 2153.01(a).

13   An "accredited investor" is defined by SEC Rule 501 of Regulation D as a person with an annual income exceeding $200,000 ($300,000 for joint income) for the last two years with the expectation of earning the same or a higher income in the current year; or a person with a net worth exceeding $1 million, either individually or jointly with their spouse. The SEC also considers a person to be an accredited investor if they are a general partner, executive officer, or director for the company that is issuing the unregistered securities.

14   The "83(b) election" allows a startup founder or an employee to pay taxes on the total market value of restricted stock at the time it is granted. This reduces your taxes if the earlier grant of stock has a lower price than a subsequent grant. However, if the value of the stock declines, then you would have overpaid your taxes.

15 The Fair Labor Standards Act (FLSA) 29 U.S.C 8, establishes minimum wage, overtime pay, recordkeeping, and youth employment standards affecting employees in the private sector and in federal, state, and local governments. Covered nonexempt workers are entitled to a minimum wage of not less than $7.25 per hour effective July 24, 2009. Overtime pay at a rate not less than one and one-half times the regular rate of pay is required after forty hours of work in a workweek.

- FLSA Overtime: Covered nonexempt employees must receive overtime pay for hours worked over forty per workweek (any fixed and regularly recurring period of 168 hours—seven consecutive twenty-four-hour periods) at a rate not less than one and one-half times the regular rate of pay. There is no limit on the number of hours employees sixteen years or older may work in any workweek. The FLSA does not require overtime pay for work on weekends, holidays, or regular days of rest, unless overtime is worked on such days.

- Hours Worked: Hours worked ordinarily include all the time during which an employee is required to be on the employer's premises, on duty, or at a prescribed workplace.

- Recordkeeping: Employers must display an official poster outlining the requirements of the FLSA. Employers must also keep employee time and pay records.

- Child Labor: These provisions are designed to protect the educational opportunities of minors and prohibit their employment in jobs and under conditions detrimental to their health or well-being. See https://www.dol.gov/agencies/whd/flsa.

16 E. Ries, *The Lean Startup* (New York: Random House, 2011), p.96, etc.

17 Jefferson O. Imgbi, "Thomas Edison, Too Stupid to Learn," The SureWord.org, Feb. 20, 2015, https://www.thesureword.org.uk/component/acymailing/archive/view/listid-1-daily-devotion/mailid-472-thomas-edison-too-stupid-to-learn/tmpl-component.

18 Henry Petroski, "The Investor's Dilemma," *The Wall St. Jl.*, Sept. 4, 2021, C7.

19 This sign actually was in a café in North Conway, New Hampshire.

CHAPTER 2

1 https://www.wisesayings.com/risk-management-quotes/.
2 International Organization for Standardization, *"ISO/IEC Guide 73:2009 (2009). Risk management — Vocabulary,"* https://Wikipedia.org/wikiRisk_management.
3 *Turping v. United States,* 913 F.3d 1060, 1065 (Fed. Cir. 2019); *Hanlin* 316 F. 3d at 1328; *City of Cincinnati,* 153 F.3d at 1377.
4 Wikipedia, "Molly's Game," https://en.wikipedia.org/wiki/Molly%27s_Game.

CHAPTER 3

1 *Aquazzura Italia, SRL v. Ivanka Trump, IT Collection LLC, et al.,* Case 1:16-cv-04782-KBF (S.D.N.Y. 2016), complaint, p. 10.
2 Ibid, p. 1.
3 Ibid, p. 3.
4 Ibid, p. 1.
5 Margaret Sutherlin, "Ivanka Trump, Marc Fisher Make Counterclaim Against Aquazzura," *Yahoo Finance,* Aug. 23, 2016, https://finance.yahoo.com/news/ivanka-trump-marc-fisher-counterclaim-205127022.html.
6 *Christian Louboutin S.A. v. Yves Saint Laurent Am. Holding, Inc.,* No. 11-3303 (2d Cir. 2013).
7 Katie Abel, "Aquazzura's Legal Battle With Ivanka Trump is Over," *Footware News,* Nov. 17, 2017, https://footwearnews.com/2017/fashion/designers/aquazzura-ivanka-trump-trademark-lawsuit-settlement-457481/.
8 Jim Zarroli, "Kellyanne Conway Tells Americans to Buy Ivanka Trump's Products," *NPR Org., The Two Way,* Feb. 9, 2017, https://www.npr.org/sections/thetwo-way/2017/02/09/514317345/kellyanne-conway-tells-americans-to-buy-ivanka-trumps-products.
9 *Modern Appealing Clothing vs Ivanka Trump Marks, LLC,* Sup. Ct. of Cal., No. CGC-17-557575 (Mar.15, 2017).
10 Cassidy Mantor, "Ivanka Trump brand settles trademark lawsuit over copied fabric," *Fashion Network,* Oct. 18, 2017, https://ww.fashionnetwork.com/news/ivanka-trump-brand-settles-trademark-lawsuit-over-copied-fabric,881786.html.

11 M. Barrett, *"Intellectual Property – Patents, Trademarks &
    Copyrights,* " Berkeley, CA, Emanuel (2000), C-1.

12 The need to have a successful copyright registration filed
    before an American can file an infringement case was decided
    in a unanimous U.S. Supreme Court case, *Fourth Estate
    Public Benefit Corp. v. Wall-Street.com LLC,* et al. 139 S. Ct.
    881(2019).

13 Mary Bellis, "The History of Coca-Cola," *ThoughtCo,* July 29,
    2019, https://www.thoughtco.com/history-of-coca-cola-1991 477;
    "John Doc Pemberton and his Amazing Medicine," Museum of
    Arts and Sciences, Jan. 28, 2017; Nikita Cochhar, "Only two
    people in the world know Coca-Cola's recipe, and they aren't
    allowed to travel on the same plane," *Logically,* Oct. 8. 2021.

14 Pub.L. 114–153, 130 Stat. 376, enacted May 11, 2016, 18
    U.S.C. § 1836, et seq., is a United States federal law that allows
    an owner of a trade secret to sue in federal court when its trade
    secrets have been misappropriated.
    https://fairuse.stanford.edu/overview/fair-use/cases/#:~:text=
    Not%20a%20fair%20use.%20A%20television%20news%20
    program,film.%20%28Roy%20Export%20Co.%20Estab.%
    20of%20Vaduz%20v.

15 *Waymo v. Uber Technologies,* cv-00939-WHA (N.D. Cal. May
    15, 2017).

16 United States Copyright Office, "Works not Protected by
    Copyright," https://www.copyright.gov/circs/circ33.pdf.

17 Roy Export Co. Estab. of Vaduz v. Columbia Broadcasting Sys.,
    Inc., 672 F.2d 1095, 1100 (2d Cir. 1982).

18 *Kelly v. Arriba Soft Corp.* 336 F.3d. 811 (9th. Cir. 2003),
    https://www.copyright.gov/fair-use/summaries/kelly-arriba-
    9thcir2003.pdf.

19 Ibid.

20 17 U.S.C Sec.101 et seq. (1976).

21 Bitlaw Guidance, "When Should a Patent be Filed?" https://
    www.bitlaw.com/guidance/patent/when-to-file-a-patent-
    application.html; Application of Foster, 343. F.2d 980 (1965),
    cert. denied, 383 U.S. 966 (1966) re Sec. 102(b) of the U.S.
    Patent Act (35 U.S.C. Sec. 101 et seq.).

22　Ibid. Christian Louboutin case.

23　Remand at *Kelley-Brown v. Winfrey*, 717 F.3d 295, 313 (2d Cir.2013); *Brown v. Winfrey*, Summary Order, No. 15-697-cv, 9 (2d Cir. 2016), affirming Defendant's motion for summary judgment. Cert. Den., *Kelly-Brown v. Winfrey*, 137 S. Ct. 1098, 197 L. Ed. 2d 183, 2017 U.S. LEXIS 1291, 85 U.S.L.W. 3390.

24　Ibid.

25　35 U.S.C. 101-103.

26　United States Patent and Trademark Office, USPTO Prioritized Patent Examination Program, https://www.uspto.gov/patents/initiatives/usptos-prioritized-patent-examination-program.

27　A. Petri, "You try to wake up. But you are living in the suburban Lifestyle Dream," *Wash. Post.* A. 21., Aug. 1. 2020.

28　Title of Episode 6, "Inventing Anna," Netflix (2022).

CHAPTER 4

1　ZipRecruiter.com

2　Heather Long and Eli Rosenberg, "Hiring falters over shifting priorities," *Wash. Post*, Nov. 9, 2021, A22.

3　15 U.S.C. 1681b.(b), https://www.consumer.ftc.gov/articles/0157-background-checks.

4　15. U.S.C. 1681o and 1681n.

5　D.C. Code 2-1402.66.

6　D.C. Code 21-256.

7　Nolo.com, "What are ban the box laws?" https://www.nolo.com/search?query=ban+the+box/.

8　U.S. Equal Employment Opportunity Commission, "Employers," https://www.eeoc.gov/employers. Pub. L. 88-352, Title VII, as amended, 42 U.S.C, 2000e et seq. Title VII prohibits employment discrimination based on race, color, religion, sex, and national origin. The Civil Rights Act of 1991, Pub. L. 102-166, (CRA) and the Lily Ledbetter Fair Pay Act of 2009, Pub. L. 111-2, amended several sections of Title VII. In addition, section 102 of the CRA amends the Revised Statutes by adding a new section following section 1977, 42 U.S.C. 1981, to provide for the recovery of compensatory and punitive damages in cases of intentional violations of Title VII, the Americans with Disabilities Act of 1990, and section 501 of the Rehabilitation Act of 1973, https://www.eeoc.gov/statutes/title-vii-civil-rights-act-1964.

9 https://www.eeoc.gov/prohibited-employment-policiespractices.

10 Ibid.

11 Ibid.

12 Ibid.

13 Ibid.

14 Age Discrimination in Employment Act of 1967, Pub. L. 90-202, (ADEA), as amended, 29 U.S.C. 621 et seq. The ADEA prohibits employment discrimination against persons forty years of age or older and other age-related discrimination.

15 U.S. Equal Employment Opportunity Commission, "What You Can Expect After a Charge is Filed," https://www.eeoc.gov/employers/what-you-can-expect-after-charge-filed.

16 Ibid. "Remedies for Employment Discrimination."

17 15 U.S.C. Sec. 1125(a).

18 Sebastien Roblin, "Secret is Out: Russia Weaponized and Trained Dolphins and Whales," *The National Interest*, Jan. 9, 2021; https://nationalinterest.org/blog/reboot/secret-out-russia-weaponized-and-trained-dolphins-and-whales-176151.

19 American Psychological Association, "Smarter Than You Think: Renowned Canine Researcher Puts Dogs' Intelligence on Par with 2-Year-Old Human," https://www.apa.org/news/press/releases/2009/08/dogs-think.

20 As you probably suspect, dear reader, none of this is true.

CHAPTER 5

1 Scale Finance, "Non Qualified" vs. "Qualified Stock Options," https://scalefinance.com/nonqualified-versus-qualified-stock-options/.

U.S. Securities and Exchange Commission, "Accredited Investors – Updated Investor Bulletin," (April 14, 2021); https://www.investor.gov/introduction-investing/general-resources/news-alerts/alerts-bulletins/investor-bulletins/updated-3.

2   Ibid. "Investor Alerts Bulletin, Crowdfunding for Investors, (April 14, 2021)," https://www.sec.gov/oiea/investor-alerts-bulletins/ib_crowdfunding-.html.

3   Go to irs.gov and download Form 1024, Application for Recognition of Exemption Under Section 501(a).

4   Small Business Administration, "SBIR-STTR," https://www.sbir.gov/about.

5   Ibid. "Program Basics," https://www.sbir.gov/tutorials/program-basics/tutorial-3.

6   Euny Hong, "How Does Bitcoin Mining Work?" *Investopedia*, March 14, 2022; https://www.investopedia.com/tech/how-does-bitcoin-mining-work/.

7   Ibid. Jake Frankenfield, "Bitcoin Mining," March 14, 2022; https://www.investopedia.com/terms/b/bitcoin-mining.asp.

8   In 2019 the SEC ordered a blockchain company to pay a $24 million penalty for an unregistered initial coin offering (ICO). U.S. Securities and Exchange Commission, "SEC Orders Blockchain company to Pay $24 Million Penalty for Unregistered ICO," https://www.sec.gov/news/press-release/2019-2022.

9   Ofir Beigel, "Who Accepts Bitcoin as Payment," Bitcoins (Jan. 1, 1922), https://99bitcoins.com/bitcoin/who-accepts/.

10 Ibid, Frankenfield, "What is an Initial Coin Offering (ICO)? Investopedia," Jan. 3, 2022, https://www.investopedia.com/terms/i/initial-coin-offering-ico.asp.

11 John Huang, Claire O'Neill and Hiroko Tabuchi, "Bitcoin Requires More Electricity Than Many Countries. How is That Possible? *The New York Times*," Sept. 3, 2021; https://www.nytimes.com/interactive/2021/09/03/climate/bitcoin-carbon-footprint-electricity.htm.

12 Executive Order on Ensuring Responsible Development of Digital Assets. The White House, March 9, 2022. https://www.whitehouse.gov/briefing-room/presidential-actions/2022/03/09/executive-order-on-ensuring-responsible-development-of-digital-assets/.

13 Ibid.

14 Sebastian Smee, "What's an NFT in the art world?," *The Wash. Post*, Dec. 19, 2021, Sec. E.1.

15 Ibid, E.7.

16 "Convertible preferred" shares allow shares to be converted into common shares at the "exercise price" set by the company. "Cumulative preferred" shares pay shareholders all dividends, even those omitted previously. "Non-cumulative preferred" shares don't pay dividends in arrears. "Participating preferred" stock provides extra dividends.

17 15 U.S. Code CHAPTER 2A—SECURITIES AND TRUST INDENTURES, Subchapter I – Domestic Securities.

18 U.S. Securities and Exchange Commission, Investor.gov, "The Laws That Govern the Securities Industry," https://www.investor.gov/introduction-investing/investing-basics/role-sec/laws-govern-securities-industry.

19 Ibid.

20 Jumpstart Our Business Startups Act, Pub. L. No. 112-106 (April 5, 2012).

21 Securities and Exchange Commission, Investor.gov, Regulation D Offerings. https://www.investor.gov/introduction-investing/investing-basics/glossary/regulation-d-offerings.

22 See the definition of "accredited investors" earlier in this chapter.

23 Troy Segal, "Blue Sky Laws," "The term 'blue sky law' is said to have originated in the early 1900s gaining widespread use when a Kansas Supreme Court justice declared his desire to protect investors from speculative ventures that had "no more basis than so many feet of 'blue sky.'" *Investopedia*, Nov. 30, 2020. https://www.investopedia.com/terms/b/blueskylaws.asp.

24 U.S. Dept. of Justice, GPO, "*Asset Forfeiture Policy Manual,* (2021)," https://www.justice.gov/criminal-afmls/file/839521/download.

25 Section 3(a)(4) of the Securities Exchange Act. Brokers and dealers must be registered under Section 15(a)(1) of the Act.

26 Ibid, Section (3)(a)(5).

27 For example, In *SEC v. Kramer*, No.8:09-cv-455-T-23TBM (M.D. Fla. Apr. 1, 2011) the court found there was no SEC violation when Kramer had earned a fee from arranging a meeting and encouraging parties to invest in his client's company. The court

moved away from relying as heavily on SEC's test of whether there was "transaction-based compensation." Instead, it chose a six-factor test to determine whether registration as a broker-dealer is required: (A) person (1) works as an employee of the issuer, (2) receives a commission rather than a salary, (3) sells or earlier sold the securities of another issuer, (4) participates in negotiations between the issuer and an investor, (5) provides either advice or a valuation as to the merit of an investment, and (6) actively (rather than passively) finds investors.

28   SEC, Notice of Proposed Exemptive Order Granting Conditional Exemption from the Broker Registration Requirements of Section 15(a) of the Securities Exchange Act of 1934 for Certain Activities of Finders (Oct. 7, 2020), available at https://www.sec.gov/rules/exorders/2020/34-90112.pdf.

29   David J. Muchow, Chairman, Richard L. Thornburg, Asst. A.G., DOJ, "The Report of the Federal Advisory Comm. on False Identification," U.S. Dept. of Justice, GPO, Nov. 1976.

CHAPTER 6

1   Robert Izquierdo, "What are the Four Principles of Marketing?" *the blueprint*, Jan. 6, 2021, https://www.fool.com/the-ascent/small-business/email-marketing/articles/principles-of-marketing/.

2   See Thomas J. Law, "The Beginner's Guide to 7 Types of Internet Marketing," *Oberlo*, https://www.oberlo.com/blog/beginners-guide-7-types-internet-marketing.

3   Don Casarella, "What is the Difference Between Sales and Marketing and Why You Need to Know," U.S. Chamber of Commerce, https://www.uschamber.com/co/grow/sales/sales-vs-marketing.

4   "The Fuller Brush Man Gets His Foot in the Door," New England Historical Society, https://www.newenglandhistoricalsociety.com/the-fuller-brush-man-gets-his-foot-in-the-door.

5   The pet rock was simply a smooth stone from Mexico, sold like a pet in a small wooden box with breathing holes and straw. Over one million were sold for four dollars each for a six-month fad by advertising executive Gary Dahl in 1975-6. "Pet Rock," Wikipedia, https://en.wikipedia.org/wiki/Pet_Rock.

6   "The Observation-Deck-Amenities War is Over the Top," Oct. 28, 2011, www.curbed.com.

7   35 U.S.C. Sec. 122, (b) (1) (A).

8   Dennis Welch, President of Articulate PR and Communications, interview with David J. Muchow, Feb. 12, 2002, www. BeArticulate.com.

9   Ibid.

10 Gary Vaynerchuk, *Crushing It!*, New York, HarperCollins (2018).

11 "The Foreign Corrupt Practices Act of 1977, as amended, 15 U.S.C. §§ 78dd-1, et seq. ("FCPA"), was enacted for the purpose of making it unlawful for certain classes of persons and entities to make payments to foreign government officials to assist in obtaining or retaining business." *"Foreign Corrupt Practices Act,"* United States Department of Justice https://www.justice. gov/criminal-fraud/foreign-corrupt-practices-act.

12 R. Chernow *Titan: The Life of John D. Rockefeller, Sr.,* New York, Vintage Books (1998) p. 180-181.

13 Id., p. 150.

14 Daniel Gross, *Forbes Greatest Business Stories of All Time,* John Wiley & Sons, Inc., New York (1996) p.45.

15 5 U.S.C. 552. For general information on FOIA, see FOIA.gov, the U.S. government's central website for FOIA.

16 There are nine exemptions such as classified national defense, foreign relations information, and trade secrets. For a list of those, see https://www.justice.gov/sites/default/files/oip/ legacy/2014/07/23/foia-exemptions.pdf. To see if the information you are requesting is under the trade secret exemption, see the U.S. Department of Justice ("DOJ") *Step-by-Step Guide for Determining if Commercial or Financial Information Obtained from a Person is Confidential Under Exemption 4 of the FOIA.*

17 15 U.S.C. Sec. 1125(a).

18 "Advertising Firm Barred from Assisting in the Marketing and Sale of Weight-Loss Supplements Deceptively Priced to Consumers," Federal Trade Commission, https://www.ftc.gov/news-events/ press-releases/2018/02/advertising-firm-barred-assisting- marketing-sale-weight-loss.

19   Federal Acquisition Regulations (FAR), U.S. General Services Administration (GSA), https://www.gsa.gov/policy-regulations/regulations/federal-acquisition-regulation-far.

20   *Defense Federal Acquisition Regulation Supplement (DFARS),* https://www.acquisition.gov/dfars.

21   Dylan Matthews, "The Sequester: Absolutely everything you could possibly need to know, in one FAQ," *The Washington Post,* https://www.washingtonpost.com/news/wonk/wp/2013/02/20/the-sequester-absolutely-everything-you-could-possibly-need-to-know-in-one-faq/.

22   Ibid, GSA, "How to Sell to the Government," https://www.gsa.gov/buying-selling/new-to-gsa-acquisitions/how-to-sell-to-the-government.

23   Ibid, GSA, "About GSA Schedule," https://www.gsa.gov/buying-selling/purchasing-programs/gsa-schedule/about-gsa-schedule.

24   For DFARS see 48 CFR 252.227-7013 and 252.227-7014.

25   Ibid, GSA, "Access the Federal Acquisition Regulation," Acquisition.gov, https://www.acquisition.gov/far/52.227-14.

26   Ibid.

27   Ibid, GSA, "52227-14 Rights in Data-General," https://www.acquisition.gov/far/52.227-14.

28   It was illegal to duel in Virginia in 1826, but when Sen. John Randolph of Virginia insulted Secretary of State Henry Clay in a speech on the Senate floor, calling him a "blackleg" (cattle diseased), Clay challenged Randolph to a duel. "Randolph simply shot into the air, clearly signaling that he wasn't participating...When Henry Clay saw Randolph's intent, he halted the duel and purportedly said 'I trust in God, my dear sir, you are untouched; after what has occurred, I would not have harmed you for a thousand words.' Randolph replied simply, 'You owe me a coat, Mr. Clay,' as one of the bullets had grazed his overcoat." https://boundarystones.weta.org/2013/09/04/guys-trying-get-themselves-killed-john-randolph-and-henry-clay.
"Henry Clay," *Wikipedia,* (https://en.wikipedia.org/wiki/Henry_Clay https://en.wikipedia.org/wiki/HenryClay.

CHAPTER 7

1 Kevin Cruse, https://www.forbes.com/sites/kevinkruse/2013/04/09/what-is-leadership/?sh=665a00985b90.

2 Sally Jenkins, "Real Leaders hear voices other than their own. The Wash. Post," Dec. 26, 2021, p. D3.

3 Andrew Blackman, "Are Entrepreneurs Happier Than Other People?" *Wall St. Jl.* Nov. 4, 2021, p. R1.

4 Ibid., p. 4.

5 Robert T. Kiyosaki, *Rich Dad Poor Dad*, Scottsdale, AZ, Plata Publishing (2017).

6 Ibid. P. 166.

7 John A. Tracy, Ph.D., CPA, *How to Read a Financial Report*, New York, John Wiley & Sons (1999).

8 Emily Bobrow, "Nataly Kogan, An entrepreneur discovered that emotional well-being is key to success," *Wall St. Jl.*, Feb.5-6, 2022, C6.

9 Peter F. Drucker, *The Essential Drucker*, New York, Routledge (2007) p. 207.

10 Guy Kawasaki, *The Art of the Start*, New York, Portfolio/Penguin (2015) p.5.

11 Matt Schudel, "Psychologist described 'flow' of human creativity," The Wash. Post, Nov. 3, 2021, p.B6.

12 Ibid.

13 Endsley, Micah; Jones, Debra. *Designing for Situation Awareness* (Second ed.). CRC Press. (2016-04-19) p. 13. ISBN 978-1-4200-6358-5.

14 M. Buckingham & Curt Coffman, *First Break All the Rules*, New York, Simon & Schuster (1999), p.59.

15 Ibid. p.61.

CONCLUSION

1 Emma Farge, "China Extends Lead Over U.S. in Global Patents Filings, U.N. Says," *U.S. News* quoting *Reuters*. Mar. 2, 2021. https://www.usnews.com/news/world/articles/2021-03-02/china-extends-lead-over-us-in-global-patents-filings-un-says. It is not clear if these raw number allow for disallowed filings.

2 For further details on this concept see U.S. Patent and
   Trademark Office, United States Patent Application Pub. No.:
   US 2011/0264590 A1, Muchow, David J., US 20110264590A1,
   Pub. Date: Oct. 27, 2011, METHOD FOR INCREASING
   THE RATE OF TECHNOLOGICAL INNOVATION.

INDEX